The Inner Stream

Torah Insights on The Parsha of The Week

From the Flowing Brook of Wisdom of Rabbi Nachman of Breslov

"The Inner Stream" is a collection of inspiring and encouraging essays by Mohorosh Shlit"a on the weekly Parsha all based on the timeless teachings of Rabbi Nachman of Breslov, striking a chord in the heart of every reader and crystallizing the application and relevance of each Parsha to our daily lives.

- The Inner Stream -

To obtain this and other Breslov publications write:

Breslov International

1129 42th St. Brooklyn N.Y. 11219

Tel. (718) 436-5062 Fax. (718) 437-0068

or

Heichel Hakodesh Breslov Williamsburg

651 Bedford Ave.

Tel. (347) 834-1126

Heichel Hakodesh Breslov Monroe

8 Hayes ct.

Tel. (845) 662-2548

Heichel Hakodesh Breslov Monsey

32 Dolson rd.

Tel. (845) 425-1481

In Eretz Yisroel:

Breslov City, P.O.B. 421, Yavne'el

Tel. 06-6708058

Or visit us on the web at:

www.mohorosh.org

Kindly send your tax deductible contribution to:

Mesfta Heichel Hakodesh Chasidei Breslov

1129 - 42nd St. Brooklyn, N.Y 11219

Seuda Shlishis, Parshas Braishis, 5766

At the third Shabbos meal, Mohorosh *Shlit"a* spoke inspiring words about "one's place in the world", based on *Lekutei Mohoran*, Part II, Lesson 56.

Rebbe Nachman says: "When a person has a pure heart, then [physical] 'place' is totally irrelevant to him. In fact, the heart is the place of the world, for G-dliness is in the heart, as it is written (*Tehillim*, Ch. 73): 'The Rock of my heart [is G-d]' and as Hashem says in the verse (*Shemos*, Ch. 33): 'Behold, a place is with Me" – for He is considered the place of the entire world rather than the world being His place. Therefore, he who has a Jewish heart, i.e. a heart that perceives G-dliness, it is inappropriate for him to say that the place where he finds himself is not good, for the concept of 'place' is totally irrelevant to him. For, due to his pure heart, *he* is the place of the world rather than the world being *his* place." (These are the words of Rebbe Nachman.)

Mohorosh explained that in this lesson Rebbe Nachman reveals to us that when a person is bound to Hashem, then there is no place where Hashem's G-dliness is hidden from him, for his attachment to Hashem actually goes with him everywhere. And every place he comes to, he finds Hashem's G-dliness there, for there is no absolute existence besides Hashem at all. And it is for this reason that Hashem is called *HaMakom* (The Place), for He is the place of the world rather than the world being His place.

Therefore, we find that Hashem Himself is, so to speak, the "place" a person is at, no matter where he may be. And he who has a Jewish heart, i.e. a heart that perceives G-dliness, and is bound to Hashem in truth will find Hashem everywhere. Therefore, we find in the *Mishnah* (*Pirkei Avos*, Ch. 5): "Ten miracles were performed in the Holy Temple...and no man said to his fellow, 'The place is too tight for me here to lodge in Jerusalem' ", and this was due to the great revelation of G-dliness in Jerusalem. For as soon as a person feels Hashem's G-dliness, all of the tightness and narrowness of the place is nullified and replaced by a feeling of relief and expansiveness.

Therefore, it is explained in the writings of the Ariz"l that the numerical value of Hashem's four-letter name *Yud-Kay-Vav-Kay* in a "rebounding" calculation i.e. – *Yud*(10) times *Yud*(10) + *Hay*(5) times *Hay*(5) + *Vav*(6) times *Vav*(6) + *Hay*(5) times *Hay*(5) has the same *gematria* as the word *Makom*(=186). This teaches us that if a person is bound to Hashem, then every place (*makom*) he turns he will see Hashem's four-letter name in a "rebounding" manner: his eyes emanate a light searching for Hashem and Hashem's light reflects back towards him; and there is no place that will hide Hashem's G-dliness from him.

And this is what *Dovid HaMelech* says (*Tehillim*, Ch. 30): "Hashem, with Your will, you have stood up for me as bold mountains" – Master of the Universe, when I was bound to Your will and Your G-dliness was revealed to me, then even when mountains of obstacles and hindrances encountered me, I jumped and skipped over all of them with holy boldness and I stood strong in all of them; but as soon as "You hid Your presence, I was terrified (the continuation of the verse)" – as soon as You became concealed and I no longer merited to feel the light of Your Providence, then I was confused and terrified from everything that passed over me.

Everything depends on being bound to Hashem. When a person is truly bound to Him, there is no place or occurrence that can distance him from Hashem. But when he falls into a state of concealment from His presence, G-d forbid, and afterwards much hardship passes over him, then he will not be able to find his place at all. Therefore, happy is the one who merits to purify his heart and bind himself to Hashem, for then, he will merit to find Hashem's G-dliness in every place and nothing will be able to conceal Hashem's light from him. And he will get a taste of the World to Come in his lifetime. Happy is he and fortunate is his lot.

Mohorosh connected these ideas to our parsha in the following way. It is written (*Bereishis*, Ch. 4): "Behold, You have driven me out today from the face of the earth, and from Your presence shall I be hidden. I shall be a fugitive and a wanderer in the land and it will come to pass that all that finds me will kill me." We need to understand the connection between Cain's words – "Behold, You have driven me out today from the face of the earth and from Your presence shall I be hidden" and the words – "I shall be a fugitive and a wanderer in the land" and finally – "all that finds me will kill me". According to the words of Rebbe Nachman we can understand the connection very well.

2

How was Cain punished? It was through the fulfillment of the words: "Behold, You have driven me out today from the face of the earth", which means that he was sent into exile. And how was he exiled? – "From Your presence shall I be hidden", in other words, he fell into a state of being concealed from the Presence of Hashem, as in the verse (*Tehillim*, Ch. 30): "You hid Your presence, I was terrified." For as soon as he was no longer able to feel Hashem's G-dliness it became impossible for him to find satisfaction and contentment in any place, as if he had been completely banished from every square inch of the earth, which is exactly what he continued to say – "I shall be a fugitive and a wanderer in the land", for he was going into a very deep exile and would not find contentment in any place at all. And finally "it will come to pass that all that finds me will kill me" – every occurrence that will find him will "kill" him, for as soon as a person falls under the control of Nature and *Mazal*, and Hashem's divine Providence becomes hidden from him, then any trouble that passes over him "kills" him in the sense that he feels a taste of death in it. Therefore, there is no other advice for a person than to bind himself to Hashem in truth, and then there will be no place that will hide Hashem's G-dliness from him and he will go out from his personal exile completely. May Hashem help us attach ourselves to Him in truth and we will not fear or be afraid of anything at all, until we merit to ascend and be included in Him completely, for now and evermore. *Amen v'amen.*

Seuda Shlishis, Parshas Noach, 5765

At the third Shabbos meal, Mohorosh *Shlit"a* spoke inspiring words about the great importance of the attribute of "Shalom" (peace), based on *Lekutei Mohoran*, Part I, Lesson 27.

Rebbe Nachman says: "In order to draw the entire world to His service, to serve Him with one consent, and all people will throw away their idols of silver and gold and pray to Hashem alone – this matter can be accomplished in each and every generation in accordance with the level of "Shalom" that exists in the generation. For by virtue of "Shalom" that exists between human beings, they will be able to work together to investigate and explain the truth to each other. And in this way, everyone will throw away their false gods of silver and gold and bring themselves close to the truth." (These are the words of Rebbe Nachman.)

Mohorosh explained that the main goal of creation is that all people should merit to recognize Hashem, pray to Him and serve Him with one consent, as it is written (*Zaphania*, Ch. 3): "For then, I will transform the nations to a pure language so they will all call upon the name of Hashem, to serve Him with one consent", and then everyone will throw away their idols of silver and gold and recognize that these things possess no intrinsic importance at all. And they will realize that the main thing is to serve Hashem alone and to turn to Him for all of their needs, for all of the silver and gold in the world are in His hand alone, as it is written (*Haggai*, Ch. 2): "Mine is the silver and mine is the gold, says Hashem, Master of Legions."

But as long as people have not yet merited to recognize Hashem, they will end up making silver and gold into independent entities and into ends unto themselves. And they will then begin to covet and infringe upon the money and property of their fellow man, because it seems to them that money is the main goal of life. But stealing totally prevents a person from reaching the real goal which is accomplished only by virtue of "Shalom" that exists in the generation; "Shalom" makes it possible for everyone to speak with everyone else, and work together to investigate and explain the true goal to each other, and thereby they will come to recognize Hashem.

But when there is strife between people, and especially when people are stealing from each other, then it is impossible for them to get together and explain the goal to each other, for everyone wants to swallow his fellow alive. And as soon as a person permits himself to steal from another, he thus makes himself fit to commit every sin, and there is no way to turn him back from his evil path (*Sefer HaMiddos*, Ch. Stealing #1). Likewise, Rebbe Nachman taught us that it is possible to extract a person from all types of lusts except for the lust for money (Rebbe Nachman's Stories, Story #12, The Master of Prayer).

When a person lusts for money and also permits himself to steal from his friend, it is almost impossible to pull him out of his error, let alone speak to him about the real goal of life. And this lust for money is a clear indication that he is a man who is badly blemished, because it is impossible for one to touch another's money unless one is badly blemished by the lust for sexual immorality. And this is what seduces him to covet the money of his fellow. Therefore, happy is the one who is involved in making "Shalom" among the people of his generation and who teaches them about the enormous blemish that comes from stealing another person's money. If there would be unity and Shalom in the generation, then people would be able to explain the truth to one another, and in the end they would come to serve Hashem with one consent, which is the ultimate goal in life.

Mohorosh connected these ideas to our parsha in the following way. We find in our parsha the tremendous blemish of the Generation of the Flood and how they corrupted their way upon the earth, as it is written (*Bereishis*, Ch. 6): "And the earth became corrupted before G-d, and the earth was filled with robbery." And Rashi explains that the word "*va'tishacheis* [ותשחת]" (became corrupted)" refers to sexual immorality and idolatry (*Talmud Sanhedrin* 56b). Afterward it is written: "G-d said to Noah, the end of all flesh has come before Me, for the earth is filled with robbery because of them." Rashi explains that their verdict was sealed only because of robbery and stealing.

We need to understand the reason why their verdict was sealed due to robbery and not because of sexual immorality and idolatry. We know that the punishment for the types of sexual sins the Generation of the Flood committed and for idolatry is more severe than the punishment for stealing and robbery. Immorality and idolatry are among the prohibitions for which we are commanded to give up our lives rather than transgress. But we are not commanded to give up our lives rather than transgress in regard to stealing, as stealing is a strict prohibition but not one of the three cardinal sins. Let's try to answer this question according to the words of Rebbe Nachman.

As long as there is no robbery and stealing in the world, even though there may be immorality and idolatry, it is still possible to communicate with people and to explain to them the true purpose of life, to bring them out from their errors and return them to the truth. But as soon as the blemish of robbery and stealing are found in the world and there is no "Shalom" among people, it becomes impossible for people to get together and explain to each other the true purpose of life and turn each other back from their errors. Therefore, the verdict of the Generation of the Flood was sealed because of robbery and stealing, since it had become impossible to remove them from their errors.

And this is what the Torah says about the Generation of Separation (*Bereishis*, Ch. 11:1): "And the entire earth was of one language and of one purpose." But in the end it is written (verse 9): "And from there Hashem scattered them all over the face of the earth." And Rashi asks on this verse: Which is worse, the sin of the Generation of the Flood or that of the Generation of Separation? The Generation of the Flood did not attempt to wage war against the belief in Hashem as the Generation of Separation did. But the Generation of the Flood were washed away whereas the Generation of Separation were not destroyed from the world. This is because the Generation of the Flood were thieves and there was strife among them, and this ultimately caused them to be destroyed. But the Generation of Separation treated each other with love and friendship, as it says: 'One language and one consent' and that is what saved them. This teaches us that strife is detested and that Shalom is great and this is exactly what Rebbe Nachman is saying here.

The main blemish of the Generation of the Flood was due to the strife between them, for in such a state, it is impossible to reach the true goal. With regard to the Generation of Separation, however, who had one language and one goal and among whom Shalom rested, it was still possible to bring them to the truth. Therefore, they were not punished like the Generation of the Flood. But when Hashem saw that the unity among them caused a rebellion against Him - because there was no one who could explain the true goal of life to them - they were punished measure for measure and their Shalom was taken away as the verse says: "And Hashem dispersed them from there upon the face of the entire earth", and in this way they were unable to bring their evil plan to fruition. May Hashem grant us a wondrous universal Shalom and may we grasp the desired goal of life, until we merit to see the rectification of the world, perfected under the Kingdom of Hashem, speedily in our days. *Amen v'amen.*

Friday Night, Parshas Lech Lecha, 5765

Friday night, at the first Shabbos meal, Mohorosh *Shlit"a* spoke inspiring words about the great importance of the character trait of *Shalom* (peace), based on *Lekutei Mohoran*, Part I, Lesson 33.

Rebbe Nachman says: "The general principle is that one should always seek *Shalom* – that there should be Shalom among the people of Israel; and there should be *Shalom* in each person within himself, that is to say, one should not be divided in his character traits irregardless of what happens to him in life. Rather, there should be no difference to him whether things are good or bad for him, for he will always find Hashem in it and praise Him for it. As King David says (*Tehillim*, Ch. 56): 'With Hashem I will praise the matter, with *Elokim* I will praise the matter.' Even in the face of the attribute of judgment (*Elokim*) I will praise Him." (These are the words of Rebbe Nachman.)

Mohorosh explained that the character trait of *Shalom* is greater than any other attribute a person could have, as our holy Sages have said (end of *Mishnayot Uktzin*): "Hashem found no vessel to hold blessing for Israel other than *Shalom*". *Shalom* is the main vessel within which all blessings are stored, for *Shalom* is one of Hashem's names (*Talmud Shabbos* 10b). And the more a person is bound to the trait of *Shalom*, the more he is bound to Hashem, and being bound to Hashem is the ultimate perfection a person can attain in life.

The attribute of *Shalom* includes two main categories: 1) *Shalom* between people – between man and his fellow and between husband and wife, and 2) *Shalom* between a person and himself – between his different traits and dispositions, for with *all* of one's traits and with *all* of one's life circumstances one can serve Hashem. And the main service of every person in this world is to acquire the trait of *Shalom* in every matter. This is a divine service of huge proportions and one should toil all the days of one's life to acquire it more and more. Attaining the trait of peace with all people, and in one's home with one's spouse is such a great divine service precisely because it is the nature of a person to be drawn after controversy and strife; and to mix into arguments that are not his own, which is in truth a great folly, for what will he get from these arguments besides anguish, pain and sorrow. And no profit will come from it, especially when the argument concerns the community where one group is arguing with another and they are brought to a state of hatred, jealousy and even murder, may G-d save us. There is nothing more contemptible than this.

The main reason for the length of the exile is that the souls of Israel cannot unite with one another and thus at every moment they transgress the Torah prohibition of "you shall not hate your brother in your heart". In this respect this prohibition is more severe than any other in the Torah, for with regard to the other prohibitions one only transgresses them for a moment and not non-stop all day long. But with the prohibition of "you shall not hate", one transgresses it whenever he still has hate in his heart for his fellow. Therefore, a person needs to do everything possible to be at peace with his fellow man. And even though he is not obligated to believe as they do or to agree with their opinions, it is forbidden to hate them and to pursue them for "strife is hateful to G-d and great is peace (*Bereishis Rabbah*, Ch. 38)". One needs to always be willing to sacrifice oneself for the trait of *Shalom*.

And this is the difference between a dispute for the sake of heaven and one that is not: a dispute for the sake of heaven is a dispute in *halacha* or *hashkafa*, as in the dispute between *Shammai* and *Hillel* – each one held in accordance with his own knowledge and understanding of the holy Torah and they did not budge from their views at all. But in their personal relationship with each other they showed only love, brotherhood, peace and friendship, as our holy Sages have said (*Talmud Yevamos* 13b): "The houses of *Shammai* and *Hillel* did not refrain from marrying into each other's families, and they acted with truth and peace towards each other", as the verse says "(*Zecharia*, Ch. 8) You shall love truth and peace".

And precisely *this* is the sign that a dispute is for the sake of heaven: when there is no personal hatred between the disputants. This is not true of a dispute that is not for the sake of heaven. This type of dispute is one of hatred and jealousy, in which one person wishes to uproot the other from the world and is completely unable to tolerate him. This was the dispute of *Korach* and his assembly "(*Bemidbar*, Ch. 17)". They were jealous of the greatness of *Moshe* and *Aharon* and wanted the glory for themselves. Our holy Sages were precise in the wording of the *mishnah* (*Pirkei Avos*, Ch. 5): "What type of dispute is for the sake of heaven? – The dispute of *Hillel* and *Shammai*. And what type was not for the sake of heaven? The dispute of *Korach* and his entire assembly." The Sages did not write, "The dispute of *Korach* and *Moshe*" as they wrote in reference to "the dispute of *Hillel* and *Shammai*",

2

because *Moshe* had a dispute with no one. On the contrary, he was at peace with everybody, for *Moshe Rebbeinu's* trait of *Shalom* was whole and complete. It was *Korach* who contended with *Moshe* and he seduced his entire assembly to also contend with him. And because they were all far from the trait of *Shalom*, therefore, even among themselves strife was rampant and this is why our Sages labeled it "the dispute of *Korach* and his entire assembly". Although, on a superficial level, they were able to unite against Moshe *Rebbeinu*. The Tzaddikim themselves have no disputes with anyone, as David *Hamelech* said (*Tehillim*, Ch. 120): "I am *Shalom*, but when I speak *they* are for war." "I am *Shalom*" – by this David *Hamelech* was saying, "I am at peace with all human beings. But when I want to speak *they* all come out to war against me, for they simply cannot tolerate me. But as for me, I have no dispute with them at all." And this is the way of the Tzaddikim. With them rests the trait of complete *Shalom* and they cling to the Supreme G-d whose name is *Shalom* and Who always desires to bless His people Israel with *Shalom*.

Just as one needs to increase *Shalom* in the world between people, one also needs to work on the attribute of *Shalom* within himself, by making *Shalom* between all character traits and everything one goes through in life. A person's sins cause strife and war within him, as it is written (*Tehillim*, Ch. 38): "There is no peace in my bones, because of my sin." And the *yetzer hara* confuses a person's mind with cynical questions and doubts on the way Hashem runs the world because it is difficult for him to understand why he must go through what he has to go through in life. It is also hard for him to understand why the other person has it good while for him everything is upside down. And this causes his heart to contend with Hashem, G-d forbid, and from this come all troubles, as it is written (*Hoshea*, Ch. 10): "Their heart is divided, now shall they bear their guilt." For as soon as one's heart is divided, sin begins. Wholeness or *shleimus* (from the word *Shalom*), however, means that one is not divided in his traits in the face of different situations he encounters in life; rather, whether in good times or the opposite, he will always find Hashem there, as David *Hamelech* said (*Tehillim*, Ch. 56): "With Hashem I will praise the matter, with *Elokim* I will praise the matter." – Whether it is G-d's attribute of loving kindness (Hashem) that I perceive or whether His attribute of strict justice (*Elokim*), in both of them I will praise and exalt His blessed name, for I know that it is all from Him alone for the sake of my eternal benefit. And this very realization itself is a taste of the World to Come (*Lekutei Mohoran*, Part I, Lesson 4) as well as the essence of cleaving to Hashem Whose name is *Shalom*. For as soon as I know that

3

everything is with Divine Providence, I have *Shalom* with all of my traits, and there is no strife in my heart at all.

All of the peace that a person has with others flows from the peace that he has with Hashem, for as soon as he is at peace with Hashem and he knows that all that happens to him – including things dealt to him by others – is through Supernal Supervision, then he has peace with everyone and it is totally irrelevant for him to be bothered by them at all. However, when one is angry, hateful and argumentative with others, this is a sign that he is not at peace with Hashem. In truth, one type of *Shalom* depends on the other.

The work of Moshiach will be to bring the most wondrous *Shalom* into the world. Therefore, before the arrival of Moshiach, *Eliyahu HaNavi* will come, as our holy Sages have said (*Talmud Aydius*, Ch. 8): "Eliyahu comes neither to push away nor to bring close...but only to make *Shalom* in the world." For through his making peace in the world, people will come together in unity and they will explain the truth to each other, and everyone will come to recognize Hashem, which is the true goal (*Lekutei Mohoran*, Part I, Lesson 27). Therefore, happy is the one who merits to acquire the trait of *Shalom* – *Shalom* in his entire being and among all of his character traits. This will cause him to be at peace with Hashem and with all of G-d's creatures. And then he will have a good and sweet life in this world and get a taste of the World to Come in his lifetime. Happy is he and fortunate is his lot.

Mohorosh connected the above ideas to our parsha in the following way. We find in our parsha the very first war in the Torah, as it is written (*Bereishis, Ch. 14*): "They waged war against *Bera*, king of Sedom, *Birsha*, king of Amorah, *Shinav*, king of Admah, *Shemeiver*, king of Tzevoyim, and the king of Bela, which is Tzoar." And Rashi explains as follows: "*Bera* (*be'ra* - 'with evil') means that he was evil to heaven and evil to mankind; *Birsha* (*b'resha* – 'with wickedness') – means that he rose to power through wickedness; *Shinav* (a combination of two words 'sonei [to hate]' and 'av [father]'– means that he hated his Father in heaven; *Shemeiver* ('he set his wing') – means that he flew and leaped against Hashem in rebellion." Perhaps we can say that the holy Torah is hinting here to the above teachings of Rebbe Nachman, namely, what is the source and cause of the trait of war and strife and how we can guard ourselves against it?

The first war in the Torah was waged by *Bera*, King of Sedom, who was evil to heaven and evil to mankind, that is, he was angry with and had arguments

4

13

against Hashem, and automatically he was also angry with all of Hashem's creatures. So too, *Birsha* who rose to power through his wickedness and *Shinav* who hated his Father in heaven and *Shemever* who rebelled against Hashem – it all began because their hearts, i.e. their character traits, were divided towards Hashem, and this caused them to make war and commit wickedness against all mankind. The way to save ourselves from the trait of strife is only by drawing close to the Tzaddikim who are called "*Bris Shalom* (a covenant of peace)" (Bamidbar 25:12), which is an aspect of *Avraham Avinu* who was the head of all those who would ever be circumcised and the first to teach the knowledge of Hashem throughout the world. For the Tzaddikim bring the trait of *Shalom* to the world so that all people can have *Shalom* with Hashem, and automatically they will also have *Shalom* with one another. May Hashem help us to acquire the trait of *Shalom* in truth, and may we merit to see the revelation of Eliyahu *HaNavi* and the coming of our righteous Moshiach swiftly in our days. *Amen v'amen.*

5

Friday Night, Parshas Vayera, 5767

Friday night at the first Shabbos meal, Mohorosh *Shlit"a* spoke inspiring words about the purpose of creation, based on *Lekutei Mohoran*, Part II, Lesson 39.

Rebbe Nachman says: "That which our Sages of blessed memory have said (*Talmud Eiruvin* 13b): 'It is better for a person not to have been created than to have been created' and likewise what is written (*Koheles*, Ch. 4): '[So I praised the dead that are already dead more than the living that are yet alive;] but better than both of them is he who has not yet been, [who has not seen the evil work that is done under the sun.]' – this matter is astonishing, for if it is so, then for what purpose was man created? But it is certain that these words were only said regarding this world; that according to the troubles of this world and the afflictions that people suffer in this world, certainly it would have been better had man not been created at all. However, with regard to the world to come, it is surely better that he was created, for it is precisely by going through this world that he will arrive at his goal and so have our Sages said (Avos Ch. 4) "more beautiful is one hour of *teshuvah* and good deeds in this world, than all of the life of the world to come.'" (These are the words of Rebbe Nachman.)

Mohorosh explained that the main goal of life is that a person should strive towards cleaving to Hashem to the point that he sees nothing before his eyes but the truth of Hashem's existence in every detail of creation. And then, the tremendous beauty and splendor of all of creation will be revealed to him. Who can fathom the greatness of Hashem that exists in the creatures of this world and all the more so in the other worlds which contain myriads of exceedingly awesome and wondrous things? And they were all created only for the sake of Israel, that they would recognize the truth of Hashem's existence through each and every detail of creation and thereby bring themselves and the entire world to the true goal.

Therefore, the way man comes to perfection is precisely by passing through this world. And from all of the details of creation he should meditate on the great acts of the Creator and thereby be inspired to serve Him. But in the life of this world people go through various troubles and afflictions and therefore, man is in great danger of having his heart become completely broken and of giving up hope of ever reaching his goal. Moreover, mighty obstacles and impediments are placed before him – obstacles which are actually filled with Hashem's Glory. But it is all done for the sake of giving man free choice and to test him: What will he do in a time of trouble – will he run *away* from Hashem, G-d forbid, because of his troubles or will he do the opposite and run *to* Him because of his troubles and thereby convert all of them into a powerful attachment to Hashem when he understands well that Hashem is calling to him from within everything he is going through. And he continuously comes to Hashem with prayers and supplications that He should have compassion on him and bring him close to serving Him truly and sincerely. And then he will merit to see Hashem's salvation and how all of the troubles and afflictions came only to purify him, to cause his spiritual essence to overpower his physicality and to attach his soul to Him. And then he will bless and praise His blessed Name for all of it, as it is written (*Tehillim*, Ch.118): "I will thank You because you have afflicted me and it became a salvation for me." And he will merit to truly arrive at his goal.

Therefore, that which our holy Sages have said (*Talmud Eiruvin* 13b): "It is better for a person not to have been created than to have been created", was only said in regard to the physicality and materiality of this world, i.e. with respect to the troubles and afflictions that people suffer in this world it would have been better if man would not have been created at all; but in relation to the life of the world to come – the life of the spirit – the cleaving to the Creator that one merits precisely through being in this world and through overcoming all of the obstacles and all of the troubles and afflictions – for this, it is certainly better that he was created, for it is only in this way that we come to the goal and merit all of the goodness of all the worlds. And Reb Nosson explains (*Lekutei Halachos, Kibud Av v'Em, halacha* 5) that precisely this is the foundation of the mitzvah of *Kibud Av v'Em* (honoring one's father and mother).

At first glance it is difficult to understand if it is better for a person not to have been created, then why must he honor his father and mother who brought him into this world – a place which is simply not worth coming to? But since our Sages said this only with respect to the life of this world, but with respect to the life of the world to come it is certainly better that we were created (as it is only through this world that we can reach the goal of life in the world to come), therefore, we certainly need to honor our parents who

2

brought us to this world which is the place where we merit to reach the life of the world to come. Therefore, happy is the one who merits to strengthen himself greatly in whatever he goes through in life and to fix his sights only on the ultimate goal – on cleaving to the blessed Creator. And in this way, he will merit to live the life of the world to come in this world. Happy is he and fortunate is his lot.

Mohorosh connected the above ideas to our parsha in the following way. We find in our parsha the episode of *Akeidas Yitzchak* (the Binding of Yitzchak), and how our father Yitzchak was ready to be sacrificed for the sanctification of Hashem's Name. We need to understand why the *Akeida* is always called by the name of Yitzchak – *Akeidas Yitzchak* – and never by the name of Avraham Avinu – *Akeidas Avraham*? Certainly, Avraham Avinu's test was exceedingly great and awesome, no less than the test of Yitzchak Avinu. In his love for Hashem, Avraham Avinu went to sacrifice his only son who was given to him after 100 years of life. So why do we always refer to the *Akeida* by the name of Yitzchak?

If we look deeply into the matter, we will see that Yitzchak Avinu's test in the *Akeida* with regard to the mitzvah of *Kibud Av v'Em* was extremely awesome and terrifying. His father was very old - a man of 137 - and he was just 37. It would have been very easy to escape and run away from his father rather than give himself over to be slaughtered. Not only did he not do this, but he even asked his father to tie him up very tightly so that he shouldn't be able to move and invalidate himself as an offering. So we see that Yitzchak's *Kibud Av'v'Em* was truly mind-blowing – he nullified himself before his father to the utmost degree and had perfect faith in his father's words that Hashem told him to sacrifice his son. Therefore, the *Akeida* is certainly called by his name, for Yitzchak attained a very lofty and awesome level in the mitzvah of *Kibud Av v'Em*.

And so it is brought in the Zohar (*Vayeira* 103a): "What is the [ultimate] case of a son who honors his father? - This is Yitzchak and Avraham. And when was this? - When he bound him upon the altar and wanted to bring him as an offering. Yitzchak was 37 and Avraham was very old. And if he would have kicked him with one foot, [Avraham] would have been unable to stand before him. But he honored his father and was bound before him like a lone sheep. It was all in order to do the will of his father [Avraham]." So we see that Yitzchak Avinu fulfilled the mitzvah of *Kibud Av v'Em* to the utmost degree, for he understood the purpose of the life of this world - that it is all for the

3

sake of the life of the world to come. And his merit endures for all the souls of Israel for all generations. Yitzchak *Avinu's* self-sacrifice at the *Akeida* and his total devotion to fulfilling the mitzvah of *Kibud Av v'Em* will stand up for all the souls of Israel to atone for their misdeeds and to redeem them from all of their troubles. May Hashem help us to fulfill the mitzvah of *Kibud Av v'Em* in the proper way and to reach a clear recognition of the goal so that we will be attached to Him forever. *Amen v'amen.*

Seudas Bris Milah, Parshas Vayera, 5767

On Thursday of Parshas *Vayera* 5767, there was a *Bris Mila* in the *Beis Medrash* of Mohorosh, may his light shine. At the meal celebrating the *Bris*, Mohorosh *Shlit"a* spoke inspiring words on matters pertaining to *Bris Mila*.

We say in the liturgical poem sung at a *Bris Mila* "*Yom L'Yabasha*", which was composed by Rabbi Yehuda Halevi, one the greatest of all religious poets, in the days of *Mahari Ibn Migash*, the teacher of the Rambam, and these words were surely said with *ruach hakodesh*: "Those who come with You with the covenant of Your seal and from the womb they are circumcised for Your name. Show their sign to all who see them, and on the corners of their garments they will make fringes." We need to understand the connection between the words "Those who come with You with the covenant of Your seal" – which is speaking about *Bris Mila* and the words "And on the corners of their garments they will make fringes" – which refers to the mitzvah of *tzitzis*.

According to the words of Rebbe Nachman (*Lekutei Mohoran*, Part I, Lesson 7), *tzitzis* are a protection against sexual immorality. And it is explained in the *Tikunim (Tikun 18)* on the verse (*Bereishis,* Ch. 9) "And Shem and Yafes took the garment –- and they placed it on both their shoulders" that this garment alludes to the garment of *tzitzis*. The *Tikun* continues: "'And the nakedness of their father they did not see' – for *tzitzis* covers nakedness." So too, our holy Sages have said (see Rashi on *Breishis* 9:23) that in the merit of Shem taking the initiative in covering his father's nakedness with the garment, Shem's children merited a *tallis* of *tzitzis*. And we also find in the Talmud (Tractate *Menachos* 44a) that the mitzvah of *tzitzis* saves a person from sin as it occurred to someone who was about to commit an act of

4

immorality that his tzitzis came and "slapped" him in the face. In this way he is prevented from committing a sin, for the power of the mitzvah of *tzitzis* shines the light of Hashem's G-dliness upon a person as it is written (*Bamidbar*, Ch.15) regarding *tzitzis*: "You shall see it." And our holy Sages have explained (Talmud *Yerushalmi* Brachos 7b) that the word "it" in this verse refers to the *Shechinah*. And as soon as a person draws the light of the *Shechinah* upon himself, he is saved from the lust of sexual immorality and protected from sin. And a revelation of the *Shechinah* is a sign of *Shmiras HaBris* (Guarding of the Bris). The holiness of the *Bris* is truly the root of a Jew's cleaving to Hashem.

According to the above explanation, we can now understand the connection between the words of the poem. "Those who come with You with the covenant of Your seal". Who are those that come with You and are attached to You in truth? These are the ones who come with the covenant of Your seal, i.e. those who fulfill the mitzvah of *Bris Mila* and guard the *Bris* truly and sincerely.

The people of Israel are so holy that they rejoice and yearn to fulfill the mitzvah of *Bris Mila* to the extent that "from the womb they are circumcised for Your name" – even when the child is still in his mother's womb the parents are already yearning and longing to fulfill the mitzvah of *Bris Mila* with the son who will be born to them. And how can we know that we are holding by the sanctity of the *Bris* in truth? On this the poet answers: "Show their sign to all who see them" – That is, what is the sign that we can show to the world that we are truly Guarding the *Bris* and that we yearn to be holy and pure with the true sanctity of the *Bris*? – The sign is: "And on the corners of their garments they will make fringes" – We fulfill the mitzvah of *tzitzis* with great joy and openly walk with *tzitzis* for all to see. In this way, everybody sees the Jew's longing and desire to merit the holiness of the *Bris*, for "the *tzitzis* cover nakedness", as mentioned before. And especially when we also merit to actually take part in a *Bris Mila* and to enjoy the festive meal that takes place afterwards. Our holy Sages have said (*Midrash*, See *Sefer Bnai Yissaschar: Tishrei* 4:7) that Hashem promised Eliyahu *HaNavi* that He would atone for all those who participate in a *Bris* so they would be holy and pure at that special time. May Hashem help us merit true holiness and purity and we will fulfill the mitzvos of Hashem with joy always, until we merit to see the redemption and salvation of Israel swiftly in our days. *Amen v'amen.*

5

Seuda Shlishis, Parshas Vayera 5766

At the third Shabbos meal, Mohorosh Shlit"a, spoke inspiring words based on the words of Rebbe Nachman in Lekutei Mohoran, Part I, Lesson 124, which speaks about prayer that can, so to speak, "conquer" Hashem.

Mohorosh began: Rebbe Nachman says, "It is written in Tehillim (88): 'Shir Mizmor Lam'natzeach' and our Sages explain (Pesachim 119a), 'Sing to the One Who we conquer and He rejoices.' When a person speaks out before Hashem all that is in his heart, pleading his case with logical arguments, claims and supplications, he wants to, so to speak, "conquer" Hashem. And Hashem has pleasure from this. Therefore, He sends this person words that can "conquer" Him in order to receive the pleasure. For without this, it would certainly not be possible for a human being to "conquer" the Holy One Blessed is He. But, Hashem Himself sends and arranges for the person words and arguments to "conquer" Him." (These are the words of Rebbe Nachman.)

Mohorosh explained that we see from this that when a person clearly expresses his problems before Hashem, pleading his case with logical arguments and excuses, and he wants to "conquer" Hashem, so to speak, with his prayer, Hashem has great pleasure from this. Hashem sends the person the right words with which he can "conquer" Him, because Hashem desires that a person reveal what is inside his heart to Him with complete sincerity and simplicity, and ask Him for all that he lacks spiritually and materially. Hashem wants us to even use strong and compelling arguments before Him and not to be embarrassed, because it is His pleasure that a person in this lowly world recognizes clearly that all that he needs depends only on Hashem. And since we are totally dependent on Hashem, there is no other way – besides asking Hashem and putting forth strong and compelling arguments before Him – to receive everything we need. And therefore, there is nothing wrong with this "conquering" at all. On the contrary, Hashem derives great pleasure from it, as Shimon ben Shetach said to Choni Hamagel, who spoke to Hashem in this manner while praying for rain (Berachos 19a): "What can I say? You speak to Hashem and He fulfills your wishes, like a son who speaks to his father and he fulfills his wishes. About you the verse says (Mishlei 23:25): 'Let your father and mother be glad, and let her who bore you rejoice.'" For this is the will of Hashem; that a person should "conquer"

Him with his prayer. We see this frequently in Tehillim where the Psalm begins "Lam'natzeach". Dovid HaMelech is arousing a person to "conquer" Hashem with his prayer (see Lekutei Halachos, Birkas Re'iah, Halacha 5:12). And as our holy Sages have said (Pesachim 119a): "What is the meaning of the verse, 'Lam'natzeach Mizmor L'Dovid'? It means, 'Sing to the One Who we conquer and He rejoices.' Come and see that Hashem's ways are not like the ways of human beings. A human being, if you are victorious over him, will be sad. But the Holy One Blessed is He, if you are victorious over Him, rejoices, as it says (Tehillim 106:23): 'And He said that He would destroy them, had not Moshe, His chosen one, stood in the breach before Him, to turn back His wrath from destruction.'" Rashi (Pesachim ibid.) comments on the word 'Lam'natzeach' that since it is not written 'Le'natzeach' this teaches us that He gave the power to people to "conquer" Him, and this is what Rebbe Nachman teaches us here. Hashem sends a person words that can "conquer" Him and wants to hear these words. Especially when a person prays on behalf of others and feels the pain of their burdens and troubles and pleads their case before Hashem with all kinds of compelling claims and arguments – this gives Hashem great pleasure. Because it is His will that people pray to Him on behalf of His children, as Moshe Rebbeinu did when he prayed that Hashem should forgive the people of Israel after the sin of the Golden Calf. And Hashem accepted Moshe's prayer. This is the verse mentioned above: "Had not Moshe, His chosen one..." Rashi writes (ibid.) that the verse praises Moshe by referring to him as 'His chosen one' because he turned back Hashem's wrath. So we see that a victorious prayer is very sweet and pleasant to Hashem. Therefore, happy is the one who merits to always speak out to Hashem all that is bothering him until he "triumphs" over Him with his prayer. For then he will be very beloved in the eyes of Hashem and he will accomplish all that he needs spiritually and materially. Happy is he and fortunate is his lot!

Mohorosh tied this idea to the Parsha in a most wonderful way. It is written (Shemos 6): "Elokim spoke to Moshe and said to him, 'I am Hashem (yud-kay-vav-kay)'". And Rashi explains that He took Moshe to task because he had spoken critically when he said, (v. 22) "Why have You done evil to this people?" We need to understand why Moshe Rebbeinu spoke in this fashion to Hashem, which made it appear as if Moshe was criticizing His ways, G-d forbid. But according to the words of Rebbe Nachman, we can understand why – it is the will of Hashem that a person should pray to Him specifically in a way of trying to win. When one tries to "conquer" Hashem with his prayer, Hashem sends him the words to do this, especially when a person prays for

2

others and is pained over their troubles. We see this trait of Moshe Rebbeinu as it is written (Shemos 2:11): "He (Moshe) went out to his brethren and observed their burdens." All of Moshe's argumentation and pleading came from his great love for the Jewish people, as our holy Sages have said (Menachos 65a): "Moshe Rebbeinu was a lover of Israel", therefore, even though he spoke strongly, and it appeared as if he were using the attribute of strict justice, it was revealed afterwards that this was Hashem's will and that Hashem Himself sent Moshe the words with which to "conquer" Him. And through this, Hashem's attribute of strict justice was transformed into the attribute of compassion. It is thus written: "Elokim spoke to Moshe", Elokim is the trait of strict justice. At first Hashem's attribute of strict justice was revealed to Moshe but afterwards, "And He said to him (to Moshe), 'I am Hashem (yud-kay-vav-kay)." This is the Name of compassion. That is, He revealed to Moshe that He Himself was within the words that Moshe spoke, and through this, the attribute of strict justice was transformed into the attribute of compassion. As it is brought in the Midrash (Shemos Rabbah, 6:1): "The attribute of justice sought to attack Moshe, as it is written, 'Elokim spoke to Moshe" but because Hashem saw that it was for the sake of Israel's pain that Moshe spoke this way, He therefore turned and dealt with him with the attribute of compassion, as it says, 'And He said to him, "I am Hashem (yud-kay-vav-kay)." For when a person prays in a fashion of trying to win his case, in the end Hashem will change the justice into compassion, and he will draw upon himself complete kindness and mercy.

We see that the main claim of Moshe Rebbeinu was (Shemos 5:22): "Why have you done evil to this people?" i.e. he was asking about the great harshness of the enslavement of the Jews in Egypt. We need to understand how Hashem answered him and specifically how the verse, "And I have also heard the groaning of the Children of Israel whom Egypt enslaves," was an answer to Moshe's question. It is explained in the commentaries (Sefer Prashas Derachim, Derech Mitzrayim, Drush 5) that the decree of exile in Egypt should have been 400 years as it was said to Avraham Avinu at the "Bris Bein HaBesarim" when he asked (Bereishis 15:8): "How shall I know that I will inherit it (the Land)?" Hashem said to him, "Know with certainty that your offspring will be strangers in a land not their own, and they will serve them and they will oppress them 400 years." But in actuality, the Jews were only in Egypt for 210 years. How did they make up for the other 190 years? Many answers are given for this, and one of them is that the great harshness of the slavery made up for the time (Sefer Prashas Drachim, ibid.). Therefore, at the time that Moshe made the claim before Hashem, "Why have

3

you done evil to this people?" i.e., why are the Jews suffering such a harsh enslavement, Hashem answered him (Shemos 6:5): "Moreover, I have heard the groan of the Children of Israel whom Egypt is enslaving..." That is, the great harshness of the slavery that you, Moshe, are asking about, is exactly what will fulfill the allotted time of the exile, so the Children of Israel can leave before the period of 400 years.

With regard to the harshness of the slavery, it is brought in the book "Techeiles Mordechai" by the brilliant and holy Maharsham z"l, that the essence of the harshness was that the Children of Israel were the slaves of slaves. An analogy: A rich man who had a servant, lost his wealth, became poor and was forced to become a servant to another rich man. It would have been much worse had he been forced to serve his servant. There would have been no greater disgrace than this. We see that Cham was cursed by his father Noach (Bereishis 9:25): "A slave of slaves he will be to his brothers," and from him Mitzrayim (Egypt) was born. And when the Children of Israel became their slaves, this was for them a great disgrace up to the heavens, since they became slaves to slaves. Therefore, even though it was decreed against them, "Know with certainty that your offspring will be strangers in a land not their own (for 400 years)," however, this 400 years was possible had it been a different nation who weren't servants to Israel. Not so, if they were exiled to Egypt. This is a very great disgrace. And this was the essence of the harshness of the slavery. This is also, "I have heard the groan of the Children of Israel whom 'Egypt' enslaves," because it was Egypt in particular who were enslaving them, and not another nation. And this was the essence of the harsh slavery. Therefore they are already fit to be redeemed.

In the book, "Ksav Sofer", by the brilliant and holy Rabbi Avraham Shmuel Binyomin Sofer from Pressburg z"l (Parshas Shemos) it is written that the essence of the harshness of the subjugation was the Egyptians' trait of ingratitude, because it was only proper for them to be grateful to the Jews for Yosef Hatzaddik who saved them from starvation and destruction. It was bad enough that they were ungrateful, that they acted as if they didn't know Yosef, but to even pay them back evil for good is a situation that would greatly pain anyone. If one knows that he was good to another person, and not only does the person he helped not show gratitude but even afflicts and subjugates him, this situation causes tremendous pain. This was the essence of the harsh subjugation – that it was specifically "Mitzrayim" that subjugated them instead of another nation, because Mitzrayim paid them back evil for

4

good, and because of this (Shemos 6:5): "…and I have remembered My covenant" and they are already fit to be redeemed.

And my father and teacher, Harav Hatzadik Rav Menachem Zev Schik z"l, may his merit protect us, in his book, "Minchas Zev" explains according to the above idea the words of the Midrash (Shemos Rabbah, 6:2): "Hakadosh Baruch Hu said to Moshe, 'you are particular about My words, by your life, you should know that it says (Koheles 7): 'The end of a matter is better than its beginning' – Israel's end is better than their beginning when I had first placed them in Egypt.'" This needs explanation. What did Hashem say to Moshe with this? But according to everything we learned above, we can understand it very well. For Moshe Rebbeinu asked about the harshness of the subjugation. And Hashem said to him, "Israel's end is better than their beginning," that they will leave before the time that was originally decreed for them". For "In the beginning, I placed them in Egypt," i.e., they were in Egypt and became the slaves of slaves (as the Maharsham writes) or they suffered from the Egyptians' ingratitude (as the Ksav Sofer writes), and through this, they had a good ending and were redeemed before the time that was originally decreed for them. And Hashem should help that we should soon go out from all of our troubles and it should be fulfilled with us, "As in the days of your going out from Egypt I will show you wonders," speedily in our days. Amen V'Amen.

5

Friday Night, Parshas Chayay Sarah, 5767

Friday night, at the first Shabbos meal, Mohorosh *Shlit"a* spoke inspiring words on the great importance of the trait of *hischadshus* (self-renewal), based on *Lekutei Mohoran*, Part I, Lesson 261.

Rebbe Nachman says: "When a person falls from his level, he should know that it came from heaven, for "distancing is the beginning of drawing near". Therefore, if he fell it is in order that he should be aroused to draw closer to Hashem. And the advice for him is to begin entering the service of Hashem anew as if he had never begun before. This is a great rule in serving Hashem – every day one needs to literally begin anew."

Mohorosh explained that this teaching of Rebbe Nachman's is an essential principle for a person's entire lifetime. And this principle is the trait of *hischadshus* – which means that every day one needs to start again from the beginning as if one had never before begun, not thinking about yesterday at all. For most of a person's falls stem from his thinking about yesterday, for example, how he didn't succeed in learning and praying properly. And as a result, he becomes discouraged and thinks that again today things will most likely go the same way and he loses hope of ever seeing any good in his life.

But when he accustoms himself to the trait of *hischadshus*, not thinking about yesterday at all, but only focusing his attention entirely on today, then he will see much success in his life. He will strive to fill every day with much true and eternal good and snatch for himself an abundance of Torah, prayer, mitzvos and good deeds. And then he will amass great wealth for the sake of his eternal home in the world to come. For the reward they pay a person in the upper worlds for every mitzvah and every good point is beyond calculation – "No eye has seen it, G-d, except for You (*Yeshayahu* 64)." And we receive entire worlds in the merit of the Torah and mitzvos we do, as our holy Sages have said (end of Tractate *Uktzin*): "In time to come, Hashem will cause each and every Tzaddik to inherit 310 worlds." Likewise, it is written in the *Tikkunei Zohar* (introduction 14a): "One who learns one tractate is given one world, two tractates two worlds and so on".

So we find that when a person merits the trait of *hischadshus* and every day he snatches good points of Torah and mitzvos, then there is no way to measure the amount of holy riches he acquires for himself. Therefore, happy is the one who guards each and every day of his life and toils to fill them with as many good points of Torah and mitzvos as possible. He will then merit to enjoy the fruits of his labors and to delight in the pleasantness and radiance of the *Shechinah*. Happy is he and fortunate is his lot.

Mohorosh connected the above ideas to our parsha in the following way. It is written (*Bereishis*, Ch. 23): "And the life of Sarah was a hundred years and twenty years and seven years – the years of the life of Sarah." Rashi points out in the name of our Sages that the word "years" is written after each number (the 100's, 10's and 1's), whereas in all previous chapters of the Torah – in *Bereishis* and *Noach* – we don't find this regarding anyone else's lifespan. The Sages explain this unusual wording as follows: "The reason the word 'year' is written at every group of years is to tell you that every one is to be explained by itself. [When she was] 100 years old she was like a 20 year old regarding sin. Just as when she was 20 she was not considered as having sinned since she was not yet subject to punishment, so, too, at 100 she had not sinned. And when she was 20 she was like a seven-year-old, regarding [her] beauty." And on the apparently redundant words at the end of the verse - "the years of the life of Sarah" - the Sages say that this tells us that "they were all equally good."

Reb Nosson explains (*Lekutei Halachos, Tefillin, Halacha* 5:38) that this verse is hinting to the teaching of *hischadshus*. For the root of man's achieving wholeness (*shleimus*) is to begin to live a new life with every new day. And even when one reaches old age, he should see himself as a complete newborn, as if he has not even begun to live and serve Hashem yet, and now he begins to live in the service of Hashem as a brand new creature. And this is the verse: "When she was 100 years old she was like a 20 year old… and when she was 20 she was like a 7 year-old….they were all equally good", for not one day of her life went by without her adding on some new holiness and vitality into her life. And our mother Sarah bequeathed to us this trait of *hischadshus* so that we could merit to perpetually live new life and fill our days and years with goodness and sweetness.

According to what we have said above, we can taste the sweetness of the following interesting *Midrash* (*Bereishis Rabbah* 58:3): "Rabbi Akiva was sitting and teaching but noticed that his listeners were dozing off. He wanted

2

to perk them up so he said to them, 'What did Esther see that encouraged her to rule over 127 countries? She saw that she was the descendant of Sarah who lived 127 years." This is very puzzling! What is the connection between Ester's ruling over 127 countries and our mother Sarah's 127 years? And why did Rabbi Akiva choose this particular teaching with which to rouse them from their slumber? Let's try to answer this according to the above words of Rebbe Nachman.

When Rabbi Akiva saw his audience falling asleep in the middle of his lecture, he understood that they were lacking the attribute of *hischadshus* and that their divine service had become old to them, as it is brought in the words of Rebbe Nachman (*Lekutei Mohoran*, Part I, Lesson 60): "There are people who are sleeping away their days, and even though it may appear to the world that they are serving Hashem and involved in Torah and prayer, Hashem has no pleasure from all their service, as their minds are asleep and all of their service remains down in the lower world and they cannot elevate themselves to the upper worlds." Therefore, Rabbi Akiva wanted to rouse them from their sleep by planting within them the trait of *hischadshus*. And this is why he said to them, "What did Esther see that encouraged her to rule over 127 countries? She saw that she was the descendant of Sarah who lived 127 years." For the idea behind Esther reigning over 127 countries was that this was her reward for her tremendous self-sacrifice to sanctify the name of Hashem and His holy Torah. Therefore, she received her reward both spiritually and physically by ruling over 127 countries which are the holy worlds that were created through the power of her divine service and self-sacrifice. And she learned this trait from her grandmother Sarah who lived 127 years, all of which equaled each other in goodness due to her powerful *hischadshus* each and every day.

Therefore, it was precisely with this teaching that Rabbi Akiva tried to awaken his audience, for he revealed to them that with the power of their Torah and mitzvos they could acquire entire countries and worlds for themselves in both a spiritual and physical sense and how it would be such a pity to waste their days and years with unnecessary sleep. And when they heard this, they surely woke up right away, for they understood the enormous preciousness and importance of every single moment of serving Hashem and learning His holy Torah. And then and there, they made a brand new start in serving Hashem. May Hashem help us to renew ourselves in His service and to fill all our days and years with Torah, prayer, mitzvos and good deeds until we merit to ascend and be included in Him completely for now and evermore. *Amen v'amen.*

3

Friday Night, Parshas Toldos, 5767

On Friday night, Mohorosh Shlit"a spoke inspiring words on the verse (*Bereishis*, Ch. 27): "And he said: See now, I am old, I do not know the day of my death. And now please take your weapons....and make for me delicious food such as I love....so that my soul may bless you before I die."

Let's try to understand why Yitzchak wished to bless Esav right before his death and not at some earlier point in his life. Also, why did Yitzchak command Esav to prepare delicious food for him before he blessed him? Apparently, Yitzchak wanted Esav to do something in order for the blessing to be able to rest on him. It is possible to say concerning all this that our holy Sages have made known to us the tremendous preciousness of the mitzvah of *Kibud Av v'Eim* (honoring ones parents) to the extent that they have said (*Kidushin* 30b) "their honor is compared to the honor of Hashem: And Hashem said: 'If you honor your father and mother, it's as if you are honoring me.'" Therefore, our holy Sages called the mitzvah of *Kibud Av v'Eim* (*Midrash Rabba Parshas Ki Saytsay*): "The most severe of all mitzvos", for there is nothing more severe than degrading the honor of one's father and mother as well as showing ingratitude to them despite all the acts of kindness they have done with their child since he was born – for they are the ones who brought him into the world and raised him, and it is only through their strength and merit that he is alive; and through them he has the chance to fulfill the Torah and mitzvos to merit the world to come.

Therefore, it is a tremendous obligation to honor them as much as possible. Our holy Sages have already said (*Kidushin* ibid.): "Honor them in their lifetime and honor them in their death." For even after they have departed for life in the world to come, there is still a great mitzvah to honor them with every kind of honor, for instance, to learn Torah and give *tzedaka* for the elevation of their souls. It is explained in *Zohar Chadash* (Ruth) that all of the souls in the upper worlds are very jealous of someone who has left behind a son in this world who is involved in Torah and mitzvos as this causes a tremendous elevation and delight to the soul of his father and mother who are in the upper worlds. Therefore, happy is the one who merits to be very careful in fulfilling the mitzvah of *Kibud Av v'Eim*. And this will cause one's parents every sort of pleasure and delight in this world and the next. And through this mitzvah, the child will draw upon himself all of the blessings in the world. And he can be assured that his own children will always honor *him*. Happy is he and fortunate is his lot.

In light of these teachings about the mitzvah of *Kibud Av v'Eim* we can now try to answer the questions we asked above, namely, why did Yitzchak call for Esav specifically before his death and command him to bring him delicious food, as it is written: "See now, I am old, I do not know the day of my death." Yitzchak *Avinu* wanted to be assured that Esav would be involved with good things even after his death for the sake of Yitzchak's soul in the upper worlds. Therefore, the first thing he did was command him in the mitzvah of *Kibud Av v'Eim* and he said to him: "And now please take your weapons…" in order to hint to him that all of the good deeds that he does now as well as after his father's death will be a source of delight for his father and an elevation for his soul in the upper worlds. Also, through the power of the mitzvah of *Kibud Av v'Eim* that he fulfills *now*, a blessing will rest upon Esav which are the words "And **now** please take your weapons and make for me delicious food."

It is brought in the *Tikunei Zohar* (52b): "'Make me delicious food such as I love' – this allude to the positive commandments of the Torah that are done out of love." For by Esav preparing a meal for his father Yitzchak, he thereby fulfills the positive commandment of *Kibud Av v'Eim* which is the most severe of all mitzvos. And this will give Esav the strength to continue to fulfill other mitzvos. And this is the verse: "So that my soul may bless you before I die", by this Yitzchak was telling Esav, "Your performing the mitzvos causes blessing for my soul, and death will not be able to touch me", as our holy Sages have said (*Bereishis Rabbah Parsha* 49:8): "Whoever has a son who toils in Torah it's as if he hasn't died." Therefore, at the time Yitzchak was giving out the blessings, he said (*Bereishis*, Ch. 27) to Yaakov, thinking that he was Eisav: "And may G-d give you of the dew of heaven and of the fatness of the land and abundant grain and wine." And our holy Sages have commented on this verse (*Bereishis Rabbah Parsha* 66:3)": "'The dew of the heaven' is the written Torah and 'the fatness of the land' is the Mishnah; 'an abundance of grain' – this is Talmud; and 'wine' – this is *Agadata* (Midrash)." For Yitzchak blessed him that he should merit to learn the four parts of the holy Torah every day which correspond to the Four Worlds. And through this, he will draw down a great light upon his soul from all of the Four Worlds, as explained in the writings of the Ariz"l that the written Torah corresponds to our world, the world of Action; Mishnah

2

corresponds to the world of Formation; Talmud to the world of Creation; and *Agadata* which includes the Zohar and the secrets of the Torah to the world of Emanation. And through his learning the four parts of the Torah every day, he thereby fulfills the mitzvah of *Limud Torah* (learning Torah) and this causes great pleasure and delight to the soul of his father and mother in the upper worlds. Now we understand why Yitzchak summoned Esav specifically before his death and commanded him in these matters. It was because he wanted to show him the special importance and preciousness of the mitzvah of *Kibud Av v'Eim*. May Hashem help us to occupy ourselves in Torah and mitzvos all the days of our lives and we will give pleasure to Hashem and to all of the souls of those who are alive and those who have departed this world, until we merit to see the redemption and salvation of Israel swiftly in our days. *Amen v'amen.*

3

Seuda Shlishis, Parshas Toldos, 5766

At the third Shabbos meal, Mohorosh *Shlit"a* spoke inspiring words on the subject of joy and the nullification of sorrow, based on *Lekutei Mohoran*, Part II, Lesson 23.

Rebbe Nachman says: "Concerning the matter of joy, an analogy: sometimes when people are dancing in a state of joy, they will grab hold of someone standing on the side who is obviously sad and bitter, and pull him into their dance circle, and force him to rejoice with them. So too, regarding the matter of joy within the person himself. When a person is happy, then the bitterness and suffering stand off to the side. But it is an even greater level to specifically chase after the bitterness and bring it into the joy in a way that the bitterness will transform itself into joy just as when a person is pulled into a circle of joy. And then, the greatness of the joy and delight will transform all of his worries, sadness and bitterness into happiness. Grabbing hold of the bitterness and bringing it against its will into a place a joy, as in the above analogy, is all an aspect of the verse (Isaiah, Ch. 35): "Joy and happiness will overtake [catch] and sorrow and groaning have fled", that is, the sorrow and groaning flee from happiness, for at the time of joy it is the way of sorrow and bitterness to stand on the sidelines. But, one must specifically go after them and grab them and bring them precisely *within* the joy. And this is the meaning of "Joy and happiness will overtake…" for joy and happiness will grab hold of the sorrow and bitterness which are trying to flee from the happiness, and bring them into the joy against their will. For there is a type of sorrow which is from the *sitra achara* (side of spiritual impurity), and it does not want to be associated with holiness. Therefore, it flees from joy. And this is why it is necessary to force it into holiness, i.e. into joy against its will, and transform it into hapiness." (These are the words of Rebbe Nachman.)

Mohorosh explained that the trait of *simcha* comes from being attached to Hashem, as it is written (*Divrei HaYamim* I, Ch. 16): "Might and joy are in His place" which means that whoever is close to Hashem's place and feels His G-dliness resting in his midst, such a person will have joy and happiness, for Hashem is the source of *simcha*. And whoever is attached to Hashem is always happy. This is not the case when a person is suffering from feelings of self-importance and arrogance. Such a person is far from Hashem's place. For Hashem says about such a person (*Talmud Sotah*, 5a): "He and I cannot dwell in the same world together." And as a result, bitterness and sadness enter him. But the main service is to reveal the light of Hashem to such an extent that the sadness and bitterness will be completely nullified. From the abundance of the revelation of the *Shechinah* and from much joy, the sadness and bitterness will flee completely. And not only will they flee and be nullified, but the *simcha* will pursue them and transform them into *simcha*. As a result of the great revelation of G-dliness it will be made known to them that even the sadness and bitterness were only due to the concealment of Hashem's presence. But in truth, even within the concealment, Hashem's G-dliness is treasured away. And now that he has come to a state of true joy, it has become known to him that there is no source or place for sadness and bitterness at all.

And this is the tremendous level and importance of one who merits to bring joy to others and to transform their sorrow and groaning into happiness and joy. This is the greatest *tzedaka* and *chesed* that we can do for another person. Greater than giving someone money is making him happy, to bring him out of his bitterness and sadness. For someone who falls into bitterness and despair and begins to have thoughts of suicide, G-d forbid, all of the silver and gold in the world mean nothing to him. His life means nothing to him. But when someone comes and makes him happy and brings him out of his depression, there is no *tzedaka* greater than this, as it is written (*Tehillim*, Ch. 32): "Praiseworthy is the one who deals intelligently with a poor person." And Rebbe Nachman explains this to mean (*Lekutei Mohoran*, Part I, Lesson 106): "Praiseworthy is the one who shines knowledge and wisdom into the poor who lack knowledge and wisdom", that is, to strengthen and gladden him. And with the power of this mitzvah alone, one merits the world to come, as Rabbi Baroka (*Talmud Taanis*, 22a) asked Eliyahu as they were walking through the marketplace together, "Who in this marketplace is destined for the world to come?" And Eliyahu pointed to two comedians who were bringing joy to people and making **shalom** between them. For this is the greatest mitzvah, and through it one fulfills the verse: "Joy and happiness will overtake – sorrow and groaning have fled" since he has chased after the sadness and bitterness and transformed them into *simcha*.

Therefore, an exceedingly important service is to strive to reach a state of total *simcha* in one's service of Hashem. And one merits this by recognizing Hashem's divine supervision over the smallest details of everything in

2

creation and by banishing all thoughts of "*My* strength and the might of *my* hands have made for me this wealth" which the Torah warns us about (*Devarim* 8:17). For the moment a person attributes his success to the work of his own hands, he falls into sadness and bitterness and he derives no vitality and happiness from all of his money, as it is written (*Tehillim*, Ch. 115): "Their idols (lit. 'their sadness') are silver and gold, the work of man's hands." When is there sadness from silver and gold? When it is the work of man's hands, that is, when one thinks that the work of his hands was what produced the silver and gold for him and he forgets that Hashem is the One "Who gives him strength to make wealth (*Devarim* ibid.)" and without Him he would have absolutely nothing. And when a person forgets this and it seems to him that everything is just Nature, chance and *mazal*, he should know that his forgetfulness comes from feelings of haughtiness and arrogance which cause him to think that he is able to bring something into existence by himself. In this way, he pushes Hashem away from himself, G-d forbid. And then all of the curses and suffering come, G-d forbid, as it is written (*Yayikra*, Ch. 26): "And if you walk with me with *keri* (casualness/chance/happenstance)…I will break the pride of your strength." For the moment a person walks with *keri*, that is, with chance, Nature and *mazal*, he should realize that this is only due to the arrogance within him. Therefore, measure for measure: "I will break the pride (or arrogance) of your strength" – Hashem will break his pride and arrogance.

And so we find that the main rebuke comes only from a lack of happiness in serving Hashem, as it is written (*Devarim*, Ch. 28): "Because you did not serve Hashem, your G-d, with *simcha* and goodness of heart despite an abundance of everything." For if he would have been happy in serving Hashem and fulfilling His mitzvos, this would have guarded him from all harm, and he would have drawn down upon himself all the blessings in the world, for sadness and bitterness would have fled from him completely and joy and happiness would have pursued them until they would have been transformed into a mighty joy. Therefore, praiseworthy is the one who merits to always be happy and to know that all benefits come to him only from Hashem alone. And through this, he will be protected from the negative traits of self-importance and arrogance. The *Shechinah* will always rest upon him and all of the blessings, both spiritual and material, will be drawn upon him. Happy is he and fortunate is his lot.

Mohorosh connected the above ideas to our parsha in the following way. It is written (*Bereishis*, Ch. 26): "Avimelech said to Yitzchak, 'Go away from us

3

for you have become much stronger than us.' " And after Yitzchak went away from there, he dug wells and built an altar as it is written: "And he built an altar there, and called out in the name of Hashem [i.e., he revealed and publicized the truth of Hashem's existence], and pitched his tent there; and there Isaac's servants dug a well." And then Avimelech returned to him and said: "We have surely seen that Hashem has been with you." We need to understand why Avimelech returned to Yitzchak and made a covenant with him when he had originally driven Yitzchak away? Let's try to answer this according to the above words of Rebbe Nachman.

Avimelech was a man filled with arrogance; and his name "Avi-Melech" means that "I want to rule and take the kingship for myself" and separate myself from the Kingship of Hashem. ("Ava" in Hebrew is to want and "Avi" denotes "I want" – see *Lekutei Mohoran*, Part I, Lesson 10)." Therefore, he was surely very far from the trait of *simcha*. For the moment a person separates himself from Hashem, the source of *simcha*, sadness and bitterness seize him. But Yitzchak was named for laughter (*tzchok*) and *simcha* in serving Hashem, as it is written (*Bereishis*, Ch. 21): "G-d has made *tzchok* for me [Sarah]; all who hear about it will laugh (*yitzchak*) for me." Therefore, Avimelech was unable to bear Yitzchak's presence, for light and darkness, holiness and defilement are unable to mix together. Therefore, "Avimelech" – the arrogant man – "said to Yitzchak" – the Tzaddik and man of joy – "go away from us" – for we cannot tolerate you at all. For the arrogant man is completely distant from *simcha* to the ultimate degree.

And the main reason for his hatred and jealousy of Yitzchak was due to Yitzchak's great wealth and property which he used only for holy purposes and this prevented sadness and bitterness from seizing him. Therefore, Avimelech told Yitzchak "You have become much stronger than us" i.e. in wealth and possessions, as it is written (in verse 14): "And he had livestock, sheep, herds and many servants, and the Philistines envied him." And Rashi comments: "People would say: '[Better] The dung of Yitzchak's mules than the silver and gold of Avimelech.' " For the wealth and property of an arrogant man is absolutely worthless. In fact, it only serves to increase his sadness and bitterness. So Avimelech greatly envied the wealth and happiness of Yitzchak and was therefore completely unable to tolerate him. And so it is explained by the Ohr HaChaim (on verse 27) that hatred that stems from jealousy will never be nullified. But Yitzchak was not at all fazed by this – "And Yitzchak went away from there and encamped by the stream of Grar and he dwelled there." And here is where he began to involve himself with

4

digging wells. And wells are a metaphor for the revelation of G-dliness and for drawing down explanations of the Torah (*Lekutei Mohoran*, Part I, Lesson 20). This was done specifically in the land of the Philistines which then caused the fulfillment of the verse: "Joy and happiness will overtake and sorrow and groaning will flee". For *simcha* will grow so strong due to the revelation of G-dliness to the point that it will run after the sorrow and bitterness and transform them into *simcha*. This is the reason for Avimelech's return to Yitzchak and his request that they should forge a covenant together as it is written: "We have surely seen that Hashem has been with you; and we said: 'Let there now be an oath between us and we shall make a covenant with you.' " For the moment the light of Hashem is revealed – which is the source of *simcha* – then sorrow and bitterness make a covenant with and become transformed into the light of *simcha*. May Hashem help us to acquire the trait of true *simcha*, and may we merit to draw down upon ourselves all kinds of heavenly abundance both spiritually and materially, until we merit to see the *simcha* and salvation of Israel with the coming of our righteous redeemer swiftly in our days. *Amen v'amen.*

5

Friday Night, Parshas Vayetzey, 5764

Friday night at the first Shabbos meal, Mohorosh *Shlit"a* spoke inspiring words on the subjects of remembering the world to come and the power of imagination, based on *Lekutei Mohoran*, Part I, Lesson 54.

Rebbe Nachman says: "We must guard our faculty of memory so we do not fall into forgetfulness, which is the category of 'demise of the heart'. The main focus of one's memory should always be to remember the world to come, and not think, G-d forbid, that there is only one world. It is a fitting custom of G-d-fearing people that as soon as one awakens in the morning before doing anything else, he should immediately remember the world to come. To guard one's memory one must guard himself from falling into the category of 'a bad eye', which is also an aspect of the 'demise of the heart'…and one must also guard the eye from the power of imagination. Even one who has a good eye needs to guard himself from this…and the power of imagination comes about through speaking *loshon hara* (slander). The power of imagination is the power of animalism, for an animal also has this power of imagination. And the one who speaks *loshon hara* falls into animalism…and a dream is an aspect of the power of imagination." (This is a condensed version of the words of Rebbe Nachman).

Mohorosh explained that our faculty of memory is truly called "memory" only insofar as it is used to remember the world to come, that is, to remember Hashem and to always remember that there is another world and that this world is only an antechamber before the world to come. To remember material things and the vanities of this world is not referred to as "memory" in the true sense at all, rather it is in the category of 'demise of the heart' in that a person completely forgets his eternal goal, G-d forbid, and how he needs to prepare himself for eternal life in the world to come. For all of this world does not amount to the blink of an eye compared to the life of the world to come, for "the days of our years are seventy years and if with strength eighty years, and they are all cut off quickly and we fly away (paraphrase of *Tehillim*, Ch. 90)", as Rebbe Nachman says (*Lekutei Mohoran*, Part II, Lesson 61): "All seventy years are only like a quarter of an hour". Opposite this, the life of the world to come is eternal life without interruption.

So we find that remembering something of this world is not considered "memory" at all. The main thing is to remember the world to come, that there is another world, and it is our obligation to prepare ourselves for it always and at every moment and not to mislead ourselves by making this world into an independent entity and a separate existence. Therefore, a fitting custom of the G-d-fearing is that as soon as one wakes up in the morning he should remember the world to come and say, "*Modeh ani lifanecha* (I gratefully acknowledge and thank You..." with deep concentration, to thank Hashem for returning his *neshama* to him so that he can fill today with much true and eternal good whose fruits he will enjoy in this world while its capital will remain for him in the world to come.

The main cause of forgetting this is the trait of having a "bad eye", which means that a person has a begrudging eye regarding the affairs of his fellow and he envies him for everything he has. This causes him to forget his eternal goal of the world to come and he falls under the control of Nature and the times of this world. For as soon as a person begins to envy his fellow and to look at him with a bad eye, he thus makes this world into an independent entity and existence and he completely forgets the goal of the world to come. For had he thought about his goal in the world to come, he would not have become bothered by his friend's business at all, and he would have placed his full attention on amassing Torah, prayer, mitzvos and good deeds so that it should be treasured away for him for the world to come. Therefore, the first condition one must fulfill in order to remember the world to come is to acquire the trait of a good eye, and to place one's entire attention and focus on seeing the G-dly vitality and the good that exists in everything.

Even one who already has a good eye needs to guard himself from the power of imagination. The power of imagination within a person is what causes one to see illusions, i.e. to see only the physical shell of things, to imagine that they are independent entities separate from Hashem, and to love only the physical shell and not the G-dliness within. We see how a person with very good vision can be mistaken about something when he looks at it from far away and it may appear to him to be the very opposite of what it really is. Therefore, one needs extra watchfulness in this area, for the imagination works powerfully on a person to implant within him all sorts of fantasies and illusions. For instance, he thinks that someone who walks with his head bent down is a true humble man and a true servant of Hashem. But the truth may be that it's all a show and the ultimate in arrogance (*Lekutei Mohoran*, Part I, Lesson 197). The power of imagination can confuse a person's mind to the

2

point that he sees elevated people as lowly and the lowly as elevated, as the Sage said to his son who saw this himself while he was temporarily unconscious during an illness: "My son, you have seen a clear world (*Talmud Pesachim*, 50a)". What he saw while he was unconscious was what looked like an upside down world - those who he had imagined to be great when he was conscious were on the bottom rungs in his vision and those who he had imagined to be lowly were the leaders. But his father told him that he had in fact seen a right side up world in his vision.

The way things appear to people according to the power of their imagination is for the most part the exact opposite of the truth. The one who people consider to be a humble man may really be a *baal gaavah* (arrogant); and the one considered a *baal gaavah* may actually be a true humble man, as it is brought in the Zohar (*Parshas Chayei Sarah*, 122b): "The one who is great is small and the one who is small is great", meaning that the one who holds himself great is actually very small, while the small one is really the great one. The imagination confuses a person's mind to such an extent that the *yetzer hara* itself is called the "the power of imagination (*Lekutei Mohoran*, Part I, Lesson 25)", for the imagination engenders all kinds of fantasies of lust and sin in a person until it seduces him to carry it out in actuality, G-d forbid. Therefore, we need to escape from the imagination, which is the power of animalism within a person, and elevate ourselves to the intellect. It is referred to as the power of animalism because an animal is deeply sunken in the power of imagination and illusion, in that they are only drawn after their physical drives and senses and are therefore only interested in the physical shell (i.e. the touch, taste and smell of things). Likewise, a person who does not fix his eyes and heart on the eternal goal will also be sunken in the power of imagination. And what he sees before his eyes is also a world of imagination. Therefore, he needs to guard himself very much from the power of imagination and ascend to the divine intelligence and wisdom that Hashem has implanted in everything.

The power of imagination is fueled mainly by speaking *loshon hara*. Shlomo HaMelech wrote (*Mishlei*, Ch. 10): "And he that speaks slander is a fool." When a person's intellect departs from him he falls from the love of Hashem into the love of animalism, i.e. the love for imagination. For the one who allows himself to speak evil about his fellow and to spread *loshon hara* and strife, uproots himself from true wisdom and falls into animalism until his power of imagination overpowers him exactly as it overpowers an animal. But the one who's mind is complete and whole, that is, he who places his

3

heart and eyes to gaze at the good that exists in everything, will not speak evil of any creature in the world, for our holy Sages have said (*Pirkei Avos*, Ch. 2): "Do not judge your fellow until you have reached his place." And who really knows what his fellow has gone through in life and has reached his place? But, as soon as one falls from the "mind of Man" into animalism, the power of imagination begins to overpower him and he is liable to imagine all sorts of falsehood and vanity as he wanders this world as if in a dream.

A dream also comes from the power of imagination. When a person is sleeping, his intellect departs from him and he enters the world of imagination. Therefore, what a person sees in his dreams cannot affect a halachic dispute (*Sanhedrin*, 30a), for most people's dreams are only imaginary and contain no truth. They dream about what they have contemplated and imagined during the day. And when they sleep and their intellect departs from them they continue to see these images. Not so the Tzaddikim who cleave to Hashem with a true attachment, and all day their heart and eyes gaze upon the goal of the world to come. When they sleep, lofty matters and secrets of the Torah are revealed to them and their dreams are accurate and true. Therefore, happy is the one who merits to bind his thoughts to Hashem and to always remember the world to come, for then he will merit the trait of a having a good eye and to look at the good that is in everything. He will be guarded from the power of imagination and have holy and pure dreams until he will be included in Hashem completely. Happy is he and fortunate is his lot.

Mohorosh connected the above ideas to our parsha in the following way. It is written (*Bereishis*, Ch. 28): "He dreamt and behold, a ladder standing on the earth and its top (lit., 'its head') reaching heavenward." We need to understand why Yaakov saw in his dream this particular vision of a ladder that stood on the ground and whose top reached heavenward. Let's try to answer this question according to the above words of Rebbe Nachman.

The dream of Yaakov *Avinu* was completely pure and separated from the power of imagination and, therefore, he had dreams that were holy, trustworthy and true. Therefore, he saw in his dream the matter of remembering the world to come, as mentioned above, how a person is placed here in this world with his feet on the ground, which is an aspect of "a ladder standing on the ground" but "its head reaches into heaven", that is, his head and thoughts are bound to the heavens above – to the world to come – and he is always thinking about Hashem. Therefore, the moment he awakens in the

4

morning he performs the custom of the G-d fearing – "and Yaakov awoke from his sleep and he said, 'Indeed, Hashem is in this place...'" – i.e., he reminded himself of the world to come and contemplated the G-dliness that exists in everything. And with this, he taught us for all generations how every person has the power to raise himself up from the earth to the heavens with his thoughts. For everyone can merit to purify his power of imagination until he will always see this ladder standing before his eyes - its feet standing on the earth and its head reaching up into the heavens.

And the main way to accomplish this is by means of the "ladder (*sulam*)" whose gematria (136) is the same as the word *kol* (voice), as it is brought in the *Tikunim* (pg. 83a) as well as in the Baal Haturim on this verse. For through a person's voice – when it is guarded from evil words of *loshon hara* – his power of imagination undergoes a purification and clarification until he is able to perceive the G-dliness that exists in everything. The memory of the world to come will always be before his eyes and he will ascend and attach himself to Hashem from all aspects and details of his life. May Hashem help us to sanctify our minds until we are bound to Him in truth, and we will merit to be included in Him completely for now and evermore. *Amen v'amen.*

5

Friday Night, Parshas Vayishlach, 5761

Friday night, at the first Shabbos meal, Mohorosh *Shlit"a* spoke inspiring words on the subject of "elevating the *Shechinah* (the Divine Presence of Hashem that rests in the world)", based on *Lekutei Mohoran*, Part I, Lesson 89.

Rebbe Nachman says: "It is written (*Tehillim*, Ch. 8): 'And You have made him [man] lack, it has [so to speak] diminished G-d's glory [*Elokim*]; and with honor and splendor You have crowned him.' It is known that whatever a person is lacking spiritually or physically, this lack is in the *Shechinah*, as the Shechinah rests within each and every person. And if 'You have made him lack' – then there is a lack in the *Shechinah*. However, when a person knows this, that the lack is not only below in the physical sense but also Above in the *Shechinah*, he will surely have great pain and sadness and he will not be able to serve Hashem with *simcha*. Therefore, he needs to tell himself: 'Who am I and what is my life worth that the King Himself should tell me what He is lacking? This is a tremendous honor for me!' And from this, he will come to great *simcha* and his frame of mind will be renewed and rejuvenated. And this is the meaning of the rest of the verse: 'with honor and splendor You have crowned him.' This means that from the honor and glory that one has because the King Himself tells him what He is lacking, 'You crown him' with a new mind. (These are the words of Rebbe Nachman.)

Mohorosh explained that the tremendous level that a Jew can attain is impossible to describe or estimate at all. His makeup is composed of aspects from all of the worlds. He has a holy and pure *neshama* that comes from the highest world - *Olam HaAtzilus* (The World of Emanation). Therefore, the entire creation is dependent upon him. And if he has some pain or lack, whether it is spiritual of physical, the pain and lack is also in the holy *Shechinah*, for the dwelling place of the *Shechinah* is within each and every member of Israel, as it is written (*Shemos*, Ch. 25): "They shall make for Me a sanctuary and I will dwell within them." And our holy Sages have said (brought in the Shelah on tractate *Taanis* 60): "'It doesn't say 'within it', but rather 'within them'. This teaches us that Hashem rests His *Shechinah* within each Jew. So we find that if there is some lack in an individual Jew, the lack is in the *Shechinah*. And the *Shechinah* grieves over the pains of Israel, as it is written (*Tehillim*, Ch. 91): "I am in pain with him." And it is also written (Isaiah, Ch. 63): "In all of their distress *He* is in distress." Therefore, this is the explanation of the words of our verse: "And You have made him lack" – if one has a certain lack, this causes a lack in the *Shechinah* which is called "*Elokim*". The revelation of the *Shechinah* within Nature is referred to as "*Elokim*" for "*Elokim*" has the same gematria (86) as the word for Nature – *HaTeva*. Although it might appear to our eyes as though the pain and lack are only Nature, chance and *mazal*, the truth is that G-d is hidden within the pain and lack, for the holy *Shechinah* is found there and it grieves together with Israel in their pain. We must fill the *Shechinah's* lack.

When a person has this knowledge, and it has become crystal clear to him that whatever happens to him also happens to the holy *Shechinah* (as he recognizes the level and holiness of his *neshama*, which is actually a part of G-d above, and that there is no such thing as independent forces of Nature at all), then he will surely feel great pain and sadness when he experiences some lack, for it is not enough that he must bear this suffering and lack himself, but the holy *Shechinah* Itself also grieves over this suffering with him. This thought can make a person so broken that he will be unable to serve Hashem with *simcha*. And the wholeness of one's divine service comes about only through *simcha*, as it is written (*Devarim*, Ch. 28): "Because you did not serve Hashem, your G-d, with *simcha* and goodness of heart despite an abundance of everything." So how can one ever raise his state of mind and attain real *simcha*?

A person needs to tell himself: "Who am I and what is my life worth, that the King Himself should tell me of His lack?" When a person sees himself with a certain pain or lack, Hashem is telling him that this very lack is actually in the holy *Shechinah*. This is a tremendous honor for a person that the King Himself would confide in him and tell him what He is lacking. The King would only share His pain with someone who is truly close to Him. He would certainly not share this with a commoner. So we see, by telling himself these things, a person can come to great *simcha*. For this is a very awesome *simcha* that the King would tell him about His pain. And through this *simcha* his mind becomes renewed and rejuvenated. And with this *simcha* itself all of his lacks are filled. For when a person is in a state of joy and recognizes with clear and true knowledge that there is no absolute existence at all besides Hashem, he thereby lacks nothing, as it is written (*Devarim*, Ch. 2): "[This forty year period] Hashem, your G-d, was with you, you did not lack a thing."

2

And so our holy Sages have said (*Talmud Nedarim* 41a): "You have acquired wisdom, what do you lack?" With this recognition, one crowns oneself with a new consciousness and mindset, which is an aspect of the words "with honor and glory You have crowned him". And this is the essence of "elevating the *Shechinah*". It turns out that he has transformed the ultimate fall into the ultimate elevation. For from the sadness and the pain, he has come to *simcha* and pleasure and he has brought himself very close to Hashem. And this is the true basis of cleaving to Hashem. Happy is the one who merits to attain this!

Mohorosh said that we need to be so very careful to ensure that the *Shechinah* is able to rest in our shuls and *batei medrash* (study halls); that there should be no lack or blemish in these places, G-d forbid, for in this way we shame and disgrace the Holy *Shechinah*, G-d forbid, as it is brought (Zohar, *Parshas Trumah* 131b) "Woe is the person who profanes the *Shechinah* by degrading the sanctity of the *Beis Haknesses* (shul)". We need to be very careful not to speak idle chatter in shul or the *beis medrash* and how much more so forbidden words, G-d forbid, for this is a very great blemish. Even "gezundheit" is forbidden to be said in the *beis medrash* (*Shulchan Aruch, Yoreh Deah*, 246). In a place where the *Shechinah* rests we must be exceedingly careful not to cause any pain or lack to the *Shechinah*. The Ariz"l has already revealed to us that the honor of the synagogue is very much needed for the perfection and wholeness of a man and for acquiring understanding, as it is brought (*Shaar Hakavannos, Drushei Kavannos habrachos, hakdama aleph*): "One who enters a synagogue needs to detain himself a little at the doorway before entering and to show that he is filled with awe and trembling to enter the chamber of the King of the world. Doing this greatly helps a person to acquire perfection (*shleimus*) and understanding." Therefore, happy is the one who merits to always be careful with the holiness of the synagogue and the *beis medrash*.

Mohorosh recounted that in his youth he merited to know one of the great Breslover Chassidim who was a kabbalist and a great expert in the books of the Zohar. Once Mohorosh noticed that this great man was about to enter a certain synagogue but before he walked through the door he became filled with trembling and fear; his entire body was literally shaking and his face turned white. Afterwards he entered the shul. Mohorosh understood that what had happened was that this kabbalist exerted himself to fulfill the words of the Ariz"l mentioned above. And this made a great impression on Mohorosh.

3

Mohorosh also recounted that once he prayed in a Breslover shul in Jerusalem and one of the Chasidim stood by the door and motioned to Mohorosh with his hand to leave the shul and come outside with him. It turned out that this man had something to tell Mohorosh. But Mohorosh did not want to leave the shul at that time. Therefore, Mohorosh motioned back to him with his hand that he wasn't ready to leave yet. After a short time had passed Mohorosh left the shul and encountered this man standing outside. The man spoke words of honor to Mohorosh and gave him thanks and acknowledgment for his holy books, how they are his whole vitality and strength. And then he asked Mohorosh for forgiveness for having signaled to him with his hand to leave the shul, but that because of his great desire to speak with him and because he had accepted upon himself for many years already not to speak in shul, he had to motion to Mohorosh to leave the shul. Mohorosh said that it was very clear to him how much care this man took not to speak in shul – not even proper and important speech. Therefore, happy is the one who merits to treat the holiness of the shul with the proper care.

Mohorosh connected all of these ideas to our parsha in the following way. We find in our parsha the episode of Dina, the daughter of Yaakov, and how Shechem the son of Chamor violated her. This was an atrocity that certainly caused great pain to the holy *Shechinah*. For whatever occurred in Yaakov *Avinu's* household, which is the root of the souls of Israel, has an effect throughout history on all of the souls of Israel in general and on the holy *Shechinah* in particular. Therefore, it is written (*Bereishis*, Ch. 34): "And Yaakov's sons came in from the field when they heard; the men were distressed and were very angry because he [Shechem] had committed an outrage in Israel..." They were in very great pain after hearing what had happened. And this caused them sadness and anger for they felt intensely not only the pain of their sister Dina but also that of the holy *Shechinah*. But afterwards, they employed the advice mentioned above that we must certainly serve Hashem with *simcha* and that we must repair and fill the lacks of the *Shechinah*. Therefore, they immediately decided how they would take revenge against the people of Shechem, and the plan was fulfilled specifically through Shimon and Levi as it is written (*Bereishis*, Ch. 34): "Two of Yaakov's sons – Shimon and Levi, the brothers of Dina – each took his sword and came to the city confidently..." For Shimon and Levi allude to the two categories mentioned above – feeling the pain of the holy *Shechinah* and feeling it's happiness and consolation. For Shimon means "hearing" which is (*Bereishis*, Ch. 29): "For Hashem has heard (*shema*) that I am unloved [when Leah named her son Shimon]. So "Shimon" alludes to "hearing" and

4

understanding the pain of the holy Shechinah. And Levi means attachment and cleaving, as in (*Bereishis*, ibid): "This time my husband will become attached (*yi'laveh*) to me..." Therefore, "Levi" alludes to attaching and binding oneself to the holy *Shechinah* through *simcha*; i.e. a person makes himself happy by realizing that the King feels so close to him that He would tell him about His lack. And there is no *simcha* greater than this. And in this way one merits to bind oneself to Hashem to a very great degree and to come to a state of renewed and expanded consciousness. Therefore, the revenge taken against Shechem was specifically through Shimon and Levi, for both of them together allude to the two categories mentioned above of empathizing with and sharing the pain of the *Shechinah* as well as rejoicing together in its *simcha*. May Hashem help us to be bound to him in truth and to fill the lack of the *Shechinah* at all times until we merit to see the redemption and salvation of Israel swiftly in our days. *Amen v'amen.*

5

Parshas Vayeshev 5764

On Friday night at the first Shabbos meal, Mohorosh Shlita spoke inspiring words on the concept of "a descent which ultimately leads to an ascent", based on Lekutei Moharan part II, Lesson 12.

Mohorosh began by saying that Rebbe Nachman teaches that even when a person falls into a state of doubt, G-d forbid, and the fall could be so great that he falls into doubting Hashem Himself, nevertheless, the fall and descent can ultimately lead to a supreme ascent. And this is implied in the word *Breishis*, which is referred to as "a hidden utterance". This "hidden utterance" hints to the idea of G-d's presence that exists but in a state of concealment even in very lowly and dark places. And this is the concept of the verse in the Torah, "Where *(Ahyeh)* is the lamb for the *Olah* (an elevation or completely burnt offering; the word *Olah* literally means 'ascent')", which Yitzchak asked his father Avraham when they were climbing Mount Moriah together on their way to the *Akeida*. That is to say, when a person falls to great depths, and yet he asks, "Where *(Ahyeh)* is G-d", this very asking "Where *(Ahyeh)*" is itself "the lamb for the elevation offering". It is considered for him as if he had offered an *Olah* to Hashem. See all this in Lekutei Mohoran, Lesson 12.

Mohorosh then explained that Rebbe Nachman reveals to us in this lesson a very awesome and wondrous secret – how there is no such thing in the world as despair, and even if a person falls to the lowest level, a terrible descent G-d forbid, exactly from there he can rise to the ultimate heights and transform all the darkness to light. For it is known that there is no absolute existence besides Hashem Himself, and even in unclean places far from Hashem's Glory, Hashem's life-force and existence are there, as it is written (*Malachi* chapter 1): "And in every place they offer incense to My Name." And it is written (*Tehillim* 103): "His Kingship rules over everything." For without His life-force and existence, there would be no existence for anything in the world. Therefore, our holy Sages said (Talmud *Yerushalmi Taanis* chapter 1): "If someone asks you, 'Where is your G-d?' say to him, 'He is in a great city in Rome'" – which means that Hashem can be found even in a place of impurity, albeit in a greatly concealed state. Certainly, these are filthy places and it is forbidden to enter them. However, if a person has already descended to these places for whatever reason, G-d forbid, he should know that he can find Hashem even there and if he cries out and asks, "Where is Hashem?" and sincerely searches and seeks Him out, then it will be revealed to him how even from that place he has the ability to return to Hashem. It turns out that he has transformed a terrible descent into a supreme ascent, for it was specifically through his descent that he came to recognize how Hashem is found everywhere.

And this is the idea behind the verse, "And where is the lamb for the *Olah*?". If a person asks, "*Ayeh*?" – Where is Hashem? – *this* question itself is the "lamb for the elevation offering" and it is considered as if he had offered an *Olah* that is completely consumed on the altar for the sake of Hashem. And a person ascends (lit. *Olah*) to the utmost heights by the very asking of this question. And therefore our Sages say, "the word *Bereishis* is a hidden utterance", for there are ten utterances through which the world was created. These are the ten times the word "*Vayomer* (and He said)" appears in the account of creation. But in truth, there are only nine utterances – nine times that the word *Vayomer* appears! However, the word "*Bereishis*" itself is also an utterance, but it is a "hidden utterance", as it doesn't say explicitly, "*Vayomer*"; rather the utterance (the *Vayomer*) is hidden within the word *Bereishis* in a state of great concealment and this hints to the fact that Hashem is found, so to speak, even in unclean and lowly places. And this is the word, "*Bereishis*" whose letters make up the words "*Bara tayish*" ('He created a sheep'), that is, the lamb for the *Olah* that had already been created from the time of the six days of creation. For the matter of asking "Where?" which transforms a descent into a supreme ascent was already established at the beginning of creation and without it the world could not exist at all. There are times when a person may, G-d forbid, find himself in very lowly places and situations, but when he knows that even there he can find Hashem Who gives continued existence to the entire Creation, happy is he! Fortunate is the person who doesn't mislead himself by falling into despair over anything at all. Precisely when he is lowly and fallen does he begin to seek out Hashem until he finds Him. And then he will ascend to the utmost heights and transform all of the darkness to light. Happy is he and fortunate is his lot.

Mohorosh connected the above ideas to our parsha in the following way. We find in our parsha the descent of Yosef HaTzaddik to the most immoral place on earth in his time – *Mitzrayim* - by being sold by his brothers until he arrives at the house of an Egyptian. What a terrible descent! It is impossible to describe. For Yosef was a young lad who found refuge in the shadow of his father's wings, always sitting within the walls of the *beis medrash*. And suddenly he is thrown into the tremendous immorality of *Mitzrayim*. And

2

there he went through what he went through. The Egyptians even suspected him of committing evil deeds. But what was the source of his strength and endurance? It was the above teaching of "Where (*Ahyeh*) is the place of His Glory"?! Through our asking and searching for Hashem even in lowly places we transform the descent into a tremendous ascent, as it was with Yosef HaTzaddik that in the end he was made second to the King, and he ruled over the entire land of Egypt. And this is what it says in the Torah (*Bereishis* 39): "And Hashem was with Yosef, and the man was successful and he was in the house of his Egyptian master (Potifar)." This verse reveals to us how Yosef HaTzaddik merited this great level – that Hashem was always with him and he was successful – it was due to the fact that "he was in the house of his Egyptian master (Potifar)." This means that through Yosef HaTzaddik's very difficult situation and because it seemed as if there was no hope, he was able to transform the descent into a supreme ascent and Hashem was revealed to a very great extent.

And this is the concept of the holy days of Chanukah. In the days of the *Hashmonaim* it appeared as if a great darkness had descended upon the world and that there was no way to save oneself from it, as our holy Sages have said (*Bereishis Rabbah* chapter 2): "And darkness was upon the deep" – this is the Greek exile which darkened the eyes of the Jews. However, through the Tzaddikim of that generation who sought out and searched for Hashem from within the darkness, the Jewish people found the light, and the descent was transformed for them into a supreme ascent. And what came out of the *klippah* (impure shell) of Greece were the holy days of Chanukah during which great miracles were performed – the military victory and the lights of the menorah. Through these miracles the hidden light of the six days of Creation shined. And this teaches us that it is possible to merit the ultimate ascent precisely from the utmost descent. And this is why we find that the one remaining pure jar of olive oil was found buried in the earth. It was in order to protect the oil from impurity. This shows us that a salvation of the utmost ascent will sprout forth exactly from a descent into the ground. And may Hashem cause to be drawn upon us the holiness of these days and may we merit to truly cleave to Hashem until we are included in Him completely for now and evermore. *Amen and Amen.*

3

Friday Night, Parshas Mikaitz, Second Shabbos of Chanukah 5764

At the Friday night meal, Mohorosh Shlit"a spoke awesome and wondrous words based on the teachings of Rebbe Nachman Z"l in Lekutei Mohoran, part I, lesson 218, which discusses the concept of a person being spontaneously inspired to travel to a faraway place.

Mohorosh began: Rebbe Nachman says, "Know, that sometimes when a harsh decree has been decreed upon a person, G-d forbid, 'even though he is not aware of it, his soul is aware of it (*Megillah* 3b)'. Sometimes there is a spontaneous urge to travel to some faraway place in order to hide oneself from the decree. And even though he does not know why he suddenly wants to travel, nevertheless, his soul knows why. This is where the inexplicable desire to journey to a certain place comes from. And sometimes, when he arrives at that place, his identity becomes publicized and he becomes famous. This fame can harm him very much, G-d forbid. In this way, a great Tzaddik passed away after suddenly getting the urge to travel to the Land of Israel. He himself was consciously aware of the spiritual process that prompted him to go away and hide himself. But on his way to Israel, he passed through a certain country, where people learned of his greatness and he became famous. Soon after, he passed away in that place. This happened very recently in our time, may Hashem save us. (These are the words of Rebbe Nachman.)"

Mohorosh explained that Rebbe Nachman revealed to us in this lesson why a person sometimes has a sudden desire to travel without a clear reason for doing so. And this is because he wants to hide himself from the Satan that wants to pursue and accuse him. He needs to take great care to remain inconspicuous throughout the entire journey. His presence must not become publicized as this could harm him greatly as happened in the case of the brilliant Tzaddik, Rabbi Naftali Katz (author of *Smichas Chachomim*), may his merit protect us. He wanted to go to the Land of Israel and on the way he had to pass through the city of Istanbul in Turkey. And there his greatness was discovered and his fame spread. He then passed away and was buried there. Rebbe Nachman, on his journey to the Land of Israel, passed through Istanbul and was at Rabbi Naftali's grave on one *Erev Shabbos*. While he was at the gravesite, he fainted. Only with great difficulty did they succeed in reviving him. Rebbe Nachman related afterward that if they hadn't tried to wake him up he would have died, because the great Tzaddik, Rabbi Naftali, said to Rebbe Nachman at the gravesite that he was very lonely there and he wanted Rebbe Nachman to be buried there next to him. Rebbe Nachman was in great danger of passing away there. But thanks to people reviving him, he was saved from death. And that which Rebbe Nachman mentions in this lesson, "and this happened very recently in our time", is a reference to Rabbi Leib Z"l, who was the father-in-law of Rabbi Yudel Z"l, a student of Rebbe Nachman's. Rabbi Leib was a very great Tzaddik and he wanted to go to the Land of Israel. When he was on the boat, a huge and very strange sea creature came and wanted to swallow the boat. He went up to the ship's mast and showed the sea creature the sign of the *Bris Kodesh* and the creature fled. From this it became publicized to everyone his great holiness, but it caused him to pass away there on the boat. They placed him on a plank of wood in the ocean, out of fear that the body would decompose, and the plank floated next to the boat the entire trip until it reached a certain island. And on that island they buried him with great honor. These are the two stories that Rebbe Nachman refers to in this lesson.

Rebbe Nachman reveals to us that through a person's hiding himself from others, and not desiring fame, he will be saved from the accusations of the Satan, and he can continue to serve Hashem in this life. This is an important idea for an upright person involved in serving Hashem – that he should not have the desire and the will to become famous, because this could harm him very much, G-d forbid. Rather, the important thing is to be involved in serving Hashem with simplicity and modesty. And if Hashem should want him to become famous, then against his will, he will become famous. But he will not strive for this himself and he will therefore be able to accomplish all he needs to do in order to fulfill his mission. Happy is he, and fortunate is his lot.

Mohorosh tied all of this to our weekly parsha in a most wondrous way as follows: We find regarding *Yaakov Avinu*, that he operated with the above advice and commanded his children to hide themselves as much as they could, as it is written (Bereishis, ch. 42), "And Yaakov saw that there was food to buy in Egypt. And Yaakov said to his children, 'Why do you act conspicuously and draw attention to yourselves?'" For Yaakov Avinu saw that they would need to journey to Egypt because there was food to buy there. The word for "food for sale" that is used in this verse is *shever*. The word *shever*, besides meaning "food that can be purchased", also means

2

expectation and hope. But Yaakov did not see clearly how and through what means the salvation from the famine and his pain would come about. This is exactly the concept discussed above – although he himself was not conscious of it, his soul knew that there was more than food to be bought in Egypt – there was great expectation and hope for salvation there. Therefore he said to his children, "why do you draw attention to yourselves?" That is, do not draw the attention of the children of Eisav and Yishmael as if you are fully satiated and not suffering from the famine. As *Rashi* states on this verse, that they should not appear conspicuous and strange to other people so that the *yetzer hara* should not stir up accusations against them. Therefore, he told them not to enter Egypt through a single gate, in order not to draw attention to themselves due to their beauty and greatness. And this attention would in turn cause the Evil Eye to harm them. As it is written (Bereishis 42:5), "The children of Israel came to buy food among the other people who came." And *Rashi* explains that they hid and spread themselves out among the crowd in order not to be recognized. All of this was in order to hide and protect themselves from being harmed by spiritual accusations. And when they came before Yosef, he understood well that they needed to feel regret and to rectify the wrongs they did to him – how they wanted to kill him by throwing him into a pit full of snakes and scorpions and how they ended up selling him as a slave. And all of these wrongs came about because they envied and hated him. But Yosef wanted to show them the way to do *teshuva* – that although they envy and hate someone, it is forbidden to kill him or to leave him to die or to sell him into slavery. Therefore, he also utilized the above advice, i.e. to hide oneself and to comport oneself modestly as it is written (Bereishis 42:7), "He acted like a stranger to them and spoke harshly to them." And he accused them of being spies, until they confessed to each other (Bereishis 42:21), "But we are guilty…" But this was still not enough. He then arranged the incident with the silver goblet until they returned and said to him (Bereishis, ch. 43), "What can we say to our master, what can we speak, how can we justify ourselves, G-d has found the sin of your servants, here we are slaves to our master…" in order to rectify their selling him as a slave, but at this point they still didn't know he was Yosef. Therefore the main rectification finally came after the death of *Yaakov Avinu*, when they came before Yosef and flung themselves down before him (Bereishis, ch. 50): "And they said, we are now your slaves." Then Yosef revealed to them the secret of teshuva, "And Yosef said to them, do not fear, am I in place of G-d? You thought to do evil to me, G-d meant it for good in order to save alive a great people." That is, we have to know that every cause is from Hashem. He is the Cause of all causes. And we only have to give ourselves over completely to Him. In this way, Yosef

3

wanted to instill in them true knowledge: that it is forbidden to pursue any Jew, to hate him, and to leave him to perish. May Hashem help us merit to integrate into ourselves true love for our fellow Jews and we will thereby merit to unite with all Jewish souls until we merit to see the redemption of Israel speedily in our days. Amen and amen.

4

Friday Night, Parshas Vayigash, 5765

On Friday night, at the first Shabbos meal, Mohorosh Shlita spoke awesome and wondrous words based on the teachings of Rebbe Nachman Z"l in Lekutei Mohoron, Part I, Lesson 34, which discusses the topic of purity of the mouth and heart.

Rebbe Nachman says that in each and every Jew there is a "Tzaddik point" as it is written (Isaiah 60:21): "And your people are all tzaddikim". The "Tzaddik point" is the capacity to express the attribute of Yesod (the Sefira of Foundation) which is also Shmiras HaBris (Guarding of the Covenant). Kabbalistically, the four-letter name of Hashem that is associated with the Sefira of Yesod is spelled in a special way - with a melapum. A melapum is a vowel sign formed from the letters yud and vav. It is a vav with a yud in it, i.e. a dotted vav. The letters of the word melapum spell the words malei (full) and pum (mouth). For the mouth of the Tzaddik (the Tzaddik is most closely associated with the Sefira of Yesod) is filled with G-dliness. The letter yud stands for wisdom. It also represents the mouth as it is written (Tehillim 49:4), "My mouth shall speak wisdom." The letter vav represents the heart as it written (ibid.), "And the meditation of my heart shall be of understanding." The heart is an aspect of the Tablets of the Covenant (the Tablets that Moshe Rebbeinu brought down from Mt. Sinai). The Tablets are also represented by the letter vav, for the Tablets were six cubits long by six cubits wide (Bava Basra 14). (The letter vav has the numerical value of six.) There are also "tablets" in the heart as it is written (Mishlei 3:3), "Bind them about your neck, write them upon the tablet of your heart." The main thing is to draw the speech coming from the mouth towards the heart, so that one's mouth and heart are the same. And one should bind the heart to those concerns that are most pressing and important right now. Then, the disgraceful things that rest on the heart will be nullified. These are all the lusts and negative character traits. A person will thus merit to circumcise the foreskin of his heart, and his heart will be aroused to the love of Hashem (See all of this in lesson 34 in Lekutei Mohoron).

Mohorosh explained how Rebbe Nachman revealed to us in this lesson the greatness of the faculty of speech and how through the power of speech we can purify the heart and awaken it to the love of Hashem. For the mouth and the heart are closely connected to each other. And when a person connects both of them to Hashem, then "the Tzaddik point" which is Shmiras HaBris, comes out from potential to actuality. Then a person will merit a pure heart and holy speech until at the highest level all the words that come from his mouth are established and make an impression in the upper worlds. He will even be able to perform miracles in this world according to his will. For it is explained in the writings of the Arizal that the aspect of Hashem's four letter name which shines in the Sefira of Yesod (Shmiras HaBris Kodesh, is the four letter name of Hashem spelled with a melapum. And melapum has the form of a vav with a yud in it, which is the heart and the mouth respectively, as explained above. Also, the letters of the word melapum spell the words malei (full) and pum (mouth), which teaches that the mouth of the Tzaddik is filled with G-dliness because he is always speaking about Hashem or to Hashem. And through a multitude of holy words, he draws his mind towards his heart, bringing his mouth and heart into synch, his heart also becoming full of G-dliness which in turn causes all of the shameful things – the negative loves and lusts - that rest on his heart to become nullified. His heart is left clean and pure for cleaving to Hashem. The primary way to make the mouth and heart equal is to always attach oneself to that which is bothering one's heart the most right now. In other words, a person should plumb the depths of his heart to try to understand what is really bothering him now, what he is lacking, and the goals he yearns and desires to attain. He should bring forth these desires from his mouth in prayer and supplication to Hashem. Then, with these very words, he will circumcise the foreskin of his heart. And slowly but surely, he will merit purity of heart until he rises to the level of cleaving to Hashem. Then, his speech will also become holy and he will be granted from above holy power and dominion, as well as the ability to perform miracles in the world which is an aspect of the verse (Tehillim 114:2), "Israel, His dominion." For through purifying the "tablet of his heart" and sanctifying his words, everything that comes from his mouth makes an impression in the upper worlds. And he rises up and delights in the pleasantness of the glow of Hashem's presence. Happy is he!

It is explained in the words of Rebbe Nachman (Lekutei Mohoran, Part I, Lesson 19) that this is called "Loshon HaKodesh", the Holy Tongue. That is, when a person utilizes his speech to speak to Hashem or about Hashem, even when he is speaking a foreign language, as long as his words are spoken with holiness, words of faith and awe of Heaven, they are called Loshon HaKodesh. On the other hand, when one speaks ugly words of loshon hara, rechilus and profanity, G-d forbid, even if one is using the letters of Loshon HaKodesh (Hebrew), he is actually speaking Loshon HaAmim, a foreign language. These kinds of negative speech are a sign of the blockage of the uncircumcised heart and a sign of negative thoughts. As it is brought in Sefer HaMidos (ch. Profane Speech, Part I), "One who speaks profanity, it is certain that his heart is contemplating sinful thoughts." We find that everything depends on the spoken word. Happy is the one who takes care to speak with the proper level of holiness.

This is what is written in Mishlei (18:21), "Death and life are in the power of the tongue." If a person wants a good life, a life of eternity, in this world and the next, then he should use his tongue to speak only "Loshon HaKodesh", that is, holy words of Torah, prayer, faith, and awe of Heaven. Then he will merit eternal life, for tzaddikim in their death are called alive (Brochos 18:). Even after their passing, if they have left behind holy words of faith and awe of Heaven, it is considered as if they are still alive and "their lips speak in the grave" (Yevamos 97.) On the other hand, when a person blemishes his speech, G-d forbid, with evil and forbidden words, he brings death upon himself also in this world, G-d save us. As our holy Sages have said (Brochos 18:), "The wicked are considered dead even when they are alive." We find that death and life are literally in the power of the tongue. Fortunate is the one who sincerely sanctifies his tongue.

This is the power of going to receive a blessing from the mouth of a Tzaddik at any time. Since the Tzaddik has sanctified his speech with a great amount of holiness, and his mouth and heart are equal in their cleaving to Hashem, he has power and dominion in the world to perform miracles according to his will, and his every blessing is fulfilled. As the Tzaddikim have explained the verse (Bamidbar, 30:3), "He shall not desecrate his word; according to whatever comes from his mouth shall he do": If a person does not desecrate his words, but always speaks in Loshon HaKodesh (as explained above), and his mouth is filled with G-dliness, then, "according to whatever comes from his mouth shall he do", that is to say, all that comes from and is decreed by his mouth will be done and fulfilled. For, just as he did not make his words profane in this world, Heaven will not make his words profane in the upper worlds and all his blessings are fulfilled. Happy is the one who merits to sanctify his speech with great holiness and to purify his heart with the light of G-dliness. In this way, he will merit a good life, a life of eternity, in this world and the next. Happy is he and fortunate is his lot.

Mohorosh tied the above ideas to this week's parsha in a wonderful way. It is written regarding the revelation of Yosef to his brothers (Bereishis, 45:12): "Behold! Your eyes see as do the eyes of Binyamin that it is my mouth that is speaking to you." Rashi explains this verse as follows: "And behold, your eyes see my glory, and that I am your brother, that I am circumcised as you are, and further, that it is my mouth that is speaking to you in Loshon HaKodesh." In tractate Megillah (16:), it is brought that when Yosef said to his brothers, "that it is my mouth that is speaking to you", he was also saying to them, "like my mouth, so is my heart". We should try to understand the connection between all of these messages that Yosef gave to his brothers when he revealed himself to them- "your eyes see my glory", "I am circumcised like you are", "I am speaking to you in Loshon HaKodesh" and "like my mouth, so is my heart." According to the words of Rebbe Nachman the connection is clear. For Yosef HaTzaddik showed them how he merited to bring out the "Tzaddik point" from potential to actuality, how he became a righteous ruler who feared G-d, and how his every command is fulfilled in the Land of Egypt. This is the meaning of "your eyes see my glory": I have dominion over all and can make things happen as I see fit. For Yosef sanctified both his speech and the "tablet of his heart" to the extent that he completely circumcised the foreskin of his heart, which is the meaning of "that I am circumcised like you are." And he sanctified his tongue and speech, which is the meaning of "I am speaking to you in Loshon HaKodesh." He made his mouth and heart equal and they were both filled with G-dliness, which is the meaning of, "like my mouth, so is my heart." We find that all of these attributes are closely related and interdependent. May Hashem help us merit to perfect our speech and to purify our heart until we merit to return to Him in perfect repentance, to be included in Him completely for now and forever. Amen and Amen.

1

Friday Night, Parshas Vayechi, 5765

On Friday night, at the first meal, Mohorosh Shlita spoke inspiring words based on the teachings of Rebbe Nachman in Lekutei Mohoron, Part I, Lesson 97, on the topic of Menashe and Ephraim.

Mohorosh began: Rebbe Nachman says there are two types of impediments in the service of prayer. One is prior to praying, that is, one stands ready to pray with a feeling of greatness because he knows he has very good ancestry or because he has toiled very much in the service of the Creator. Because of this, it is impossible for there to be complete devotion to his prayer. Therefore, he needs to forget all of this, and it should seem to him as if he had just been created today and as if he were the only one in the world. This is the concept of Menashe, from the word "neshiyon" – to forget – as it is written (Bereishis 41:51): "For G-d has made me forget (*neshani*) all my toil and all my father's household." "All my father's household", this is yichus or excellent ancestry. And "all of my toil," this is previous toil in the service of the Creator.

The second impediment is during prayer - that because of prior intentional sins, or having willfully entertained evil thoughts - foreign thoughts enter his mind during prayer. And because of these foreign thoughts, it is also impossible for him to be totally devote in his prayer. Therefore, he needs to break the foreign thoughts by means of holy thoughts of prayer and through this, the willful sins, that is, the foreign thoughts, become for him like merits. And this is the concept of Ephraim as it is written (Bereishis 41:52): "For G-d has made me fruitful in the land of my suffering (*anyi*)," which means the things that had been impoverished (*aniyus*) before – desolate and dried up – by means of holy thoughts become like merits (i.e. fruitful). See all this in the words of Rebbe Nachman in Lesson 97).

Mohorosh explained that what comes out of Rebbe Nachman's words in this lesson is that Menashe and Ephraim hint to two different ways of serving Hashem. Menashe is the concept of forgetting and driving away – to forget and cause to be forgotten the evil and the negative character traits, such as arrogance and pride – and to humble oneself before

2

Hashem. Ephraim is the concept of being fruitful and multiplying the holy and pure thoughts, mitzvos and good deeds, through which the bad traits and the sins will automatically become nullified. When one does true Teshuva, the sins are transformed into merits. These two types of divine service are alluded to in the verse (Tehillim 34:15): "Turn from evil and do good." "Turn from evil, " is the concept of Menashe, to turn from evil, to do battle with it and to cause it to be forgotten. "Do good," is the concept of Ephraim, to do good, to be fruitful in good deeds, and to turn the bad into good. We find in the words of the Tzaddikim, a difference of opinion regarding which of these two modes of service takes precedence. The masters of Mussar held that "Turn from evil" comes first, for one has to do much work in breaking bad character traits, and to cause the evil to be forgotten from oneself, before he comes to the gates of holiness. For it is written (Tehillim 50:16): "But to the wicked, G-d said, 'what does it avail you to recount My statutes, while you bear my covenant (only) upon your mouth, " that is, if you do not nullify the evil first, this will blemish and invalidate the good. Therefore, one needs to first stop the evil and to turn from it. Afterwards, one can come to "do good," to be fruitful and multiply in mitzvos and good deeds. On the other hand, the masters of Chassidus and students of the holy Baal Shem Tov, held that if a person occupies himself first with "turn from evil," he will not complete it because the war is very heavy and long. Therefore, the primary thing is to begin with "do good", to be fruitful and multiply in mitzvos, good deeds, and holy and pure thoughts. And then, though the power of these mitzvos and thoughts, the evil and impurity will of itself fall away and be nullified. From the greatness of the light, the evil husks will flee, as Rebbe Nachman once said to someone (Chayei Mohoron #447): "You do much good. Your bad will automatically fall and be nullified." Therefore, certainly, both of these paths of serving G-d are proper and holy. The difference of opinion between the Tzaddikim was only over which one of them should have priority in order for a person to be successful in his service.

According to this, we can understand very well the dispute between Yaakov and Yosef in this week's Parsha, when Yaakov blessed Ephraim and Menashe. Yaakov Avinu blessed Ephraim before Menashe and placed his right hand upon him to show his importance. But Yosef HaTzaddik wanted his father's right hand to rest upon

3

Menashe's head, to give priority to Menashe with regard to the blessings. Seemingly, it is hard to comprehend what the dispute between them was and what we are supposed to learn out from it. But according to all of the above we can understand it well. Yosef HaTzaddik who was tested in the power of the immorality of Egypt, and there he fathered Menashe and Ephraim, held that certainly the mode of service of "Menashe" has the status of the firstborn, as he actually called his firstborn Menashe (Bereishis 41:51:) For he first needed to forget all the evil and bad character traits – the concept of "turn from evil" and to assure that the evil and impurity of Egypt would not enter into him. Only afterwards could he be fruitful and multiply in mitzvos and good deeds in the proper way, which is the concept of "Ephraim", the concept of "do good". But Yaakov Avinu who saw the tremendous length of the exile, and the greatness of the tests that pass over people when they are doing battle with evil and impurity, and that not everyone merits to properly subdue the impurity – if so, when will a person begin to do good. Therefore, he placed Ephraim before Menashe and placed his right hand upon Ephraim, to teach the subsequent generations that they must begin with "do good", to be fruitful and multiply in mitzvos and good deeds. And then all the evil and impurity will fall away by itself and he will merit the proper holiness and purity. And may Hashem help us merit to occupy ourselves in His service in truth and simplicity all our days till we merit to be "Turn from evil and do good" in truth, rising and cleaving to Him with a true and eternal attachment now and forever. Amen and amen.

Friday Night - Parshas Shemos 5766

On Friday night, at the first Shabbos meal, Mohorosh Shlit"a spoke inspiring words on the topic of how Torah brings grace and wisdom to a person, based on the teachings of Rebbe Nachman in Lekutei Mohoran, Part I, Lesson I.

Mohorosh began: Rebbe Nachman says that a Jew needs to always contemplate the Divine intelligence in everything and to attach himself to this wisdom and Divine intelligence, so that the Divine intelligence that is in each thing will be a light for him, enabling him to draw closer to Hashem via that detail of the world. This is the idea of Yaakov. For Yaakov merited the bechora – the birthright – the status of the firstborn. The bechora is the same concept as the word reishis (first or beginning). And the word reishis denotes wisdom. However, because the light of Divine intelligence is very great, one needs to first make use of the concept of Malchus (Kingdom) before one can become enlightened by the Divine intelligence that exists in everything. And Malchus is Emunah (faith). But one who does not attach himself to the Divine intelligence, wisdom and vitality that exist in everything, includes himself in the concept of Eisav who despised the birthright, as it is written (Bereishis 25:34): "And Eisav despised the bechora" i.e., he despised Divine wisdom. And despising Divine wisdom is the concept of Malchus HaRisha (the Kingdom of evil). Each one of us needs to give strength to Malchus d'Kedusha (the Kingdom of Holiness) to overpower the Kingdom of evil, as our Sages have said (Berachos 5a): "A man should always incite his good inclination to fight against his evil inclination." And how do we give power to the Kingdom of Holiness? Through the Torah that we learn with strength and effort, as our Sages have said (Kidushin 30b): "If this lowlife (the evil inclination) bumps into you, drag him to the house of learning." For through the Torah, one gives power to the Kingdom of Holiness. (See all of this in the words of Rebbe Nachman.)

Mohorosh explained that the essence of the divine service of each Jew lies in contemplating the wisdom and intelligence that exist in everything, i.e., to contemplate the G-dliness in everything that continuously gives it life and sustenance. For Hashem clothes his G-dliness in all the details of Creation, in all earthly, physical things. Within all of the details of the inanimate, plant, animal and human worlds we can find His G-dliness and this makes it possible for us to draw closer to Hashem through that detail of the world. This is called

2

Wisdom of Holiness, since the essence of wisdom is only to recognize Hashem. This Wisdom of Holiness is represented by Yaakov who took the birthright – the bechorah – which is the "Reishis Chochmah" (Tehillim 110:10) "the beginning and source of wisdom", that exists in everything. However, since the light of wisdom is so great, one needs to precede it with Malchus (Kingdom), which is Emunah - to believe beforehand with complete faith that certainly there is G-dliness in each and every detail of Creation. And as soon as a person has this clear and complete faith, slowly but surely, he penetrates the wisdom that exists in each thing, until the G-dliness becomes revealed to him from every detail of the world. All of this is referred to as "raising up the Kingdom of Holiness" – the concept of Yaakov who accepted upon himself the Holy Kingdom of Hashem from all the details of Creation.

The flip side of the coin of all this is the Kingdom of evil – the Kingdom of the wicked Eisav who despised the Divine wisdom and intelligence in everything, as it is written (Bereishis 25:34): "And Eisav despised the bechora." He says that everything is nature, chance and luck, G-d forbid. And for this reason he was called Eisav, since to him everything was already made (Asui), finished and completed and it's only according to the fixed and "done" laws of nature that the world operates. And from him comes the wisdom of Nature and philosophy, which denies the wisdom of G-dliness and the Kingdom of Holiness. They have no emunah (faith). Therefore, we need to give strength to the Kingdom of Holiness to overpower the Kingdom of evil. And how is this done? Through learning Torah, because the Torah reveals to us how in every earthy, physical thing there is G-dliness. We see how all the laws of the Torah are connected to the inanimate, plant, animal or human in this physical world. And the Torah teaches us how there is Torah and G-dliness in each and every detail of this physical world. Therefore, the more a person increases his learning and involvement in the Torah, the more he causes the Kingdom of Holiness to overpower the Kingdom of evil and subdue it completely. Only through the power of the Torah can we win the war against the evil inclination which wants to strengthen the Kingdom of evil, as our Sages have said (Kiddushin 30b): "If this lowlife encounters you, drag him to the beis hamidrash." They also said (ibid.): "Said HaKadosh Baruch Hu, I created the evil inclination, and I created the Torah as its antidote." And (Berachos 5a): "A person should always incite his good inclination to fight against his evil inclination…if it goes away, good; if not, he should engage in Torah study." For only with the power of the Torah is it possible to subdue the Kingdom of evil completely. And because of this, the evil inclination strengthens itself very much to prevent a person from learning Torah. And it

3

clothes itself in all kinds of disguises that look like mitzvos, but really aren't, all to prevent a person from learning Torah. Therefore, one needs to be a mighty warrior against it and occupy himself in Torah with great strength. And through this, one will subdue it completely and always be attached to wisdom and the Kingdom of Holiness. Happy is he and fortunate is his lot!

Mohorosh tied the above ideas to our Parsha in a wonderful way. It is written (Shemos 1:10): "Come, let us outsmart him (the Jewish people) lest he increase and it may be that if a war will occur, he, too, may join our enemies, and wage war against us and go up from the land." Perhaps we can say that this verse encompasses all of the above ideas of Rebbe Nachman. For the wicked Pharaoh, who was the Kingdom of evil, decreed and said, "Come, let us outsmart him", i.e., let us outsmart the Jewish people with the wisdom of the Kingdom of evil to cancel out the learning of Torah and the wisdom of holiness from Jewish souls; this is necessary "lest he increase", i.e., we are worried that Jewish souls will increase in their learning of the holy Torah, i.e., with the holy scrolls that were in their hands from their forefathers, the scrolls that they learned and delighted in every Shabbos, as our Sages have said (Shemos Rabbah, Parsha 5: 18) on the verse (Shemos 5:9) 'Let the work be heavier upon the men': "This teaches that they were in possession of scrolls which they delighted in from Shabbos to Shabbos and which said that the Holy One Blessed be He would redeem them, etc." Pharaoh was afraid that if Jewish souls would occupy themselves in the words of Torah, then, "it may be that if a war will occur", i.e. if Jewish souls go out to meet the battle of the evil inclination and they incite the good inclination to fight against the evil inclination then, it, too, may join our enemies and "wage war against us", i.e. they will win the war against us, and "go up from the land", because even from the "land" – the earthy and the physical - they will rise up and cleave to Hashem. Pharaoh realizes that the Torah will reveal to them how the Kingdom of Holiness also rests literally on earth, and then his kingdom will be completely nullified. And when we study Torah with strength and diligence that is exactly what we do. May Hashem help us to occupy ourselves in the holy Torah with great strength, and may we merit to see the establishment of the Kingdom of Holiness and the redemption of Israel speedily in our days. Amen and Amen.

Seuda Shlishis, Parshas Vayera 5766

At the third Shabbos meal, Mohorosh Shlit"a, spoke inspiring words based on the words of Rebbe Nachman in Lekutei Mohoran, Part I, Lesson 124, which speaks about prayer that can, so to speak, "conquer" Hashem.

Mohorosh began: Rebbe Nachman says, "It is written in Tehillim (88): 'Shir Mizmor Lam'natzeach' and our Sages explain (Pesachim 119a), 'Sing to the One Who we conquer and He rejoices.' When a person speaks out before Hashem all that is in his heart, pleading his case with logical arguments, claims and supplications, he wants to, so to speak, "conquer" Hashem. And Hashem has pleasure from this. Therefore, He sends this person words that can "conquer" Him in order to receive the pleasure. For without this, it would certainly not be possible for a human being to "conquer" the Holy One Blessed is He. But, Hashem Himself sends and arranges for the person words and arguments to "conquer" Him." (These are the words of Rebbe Nachman.)

Mohorosh explained that we see from this that when a person clearly expresses his problems before Hashem, pleading his case with logical arguments and excuses, and he wants to "conquer" Hashem, so to speak, with his prayer, Hashem has great pleasure from this. Hashem sends the person the right words with which he can "conquer" Him, because Hashem desires that a person reveal what is inside his heart to Him with complete sincerity and simplicity, and ask Him for all that he lacks spiritually and materially. Hashem wants us to even use strong and compelling arguments before Him and not to be embarrassed, because it is His pleasure that a person in this lowly world recognizes clearly that all that he needs depends only on Hashem. And since we are totally dependent on Hashem, there is no other way – besides asking Hashem and putting forth strong and compelling arguments before Him – to receive everything we need. And therefore, there is nothing wrong with this "conquering" at all. On the contrary, Hashem derives great pleasure from it, as Shimon ben Shetach said to Choni Hamagel, who spoke to Hashem in this manner while praying for rain (Berachos 19a): "What can I say? You speak to Hashem and He fulfills your wishes, like a son who speaks to his father and he fulfills his wishes. About you the verse says (Mishlei 23:25): 'Let your father and mother be glad, and let her who bore you rejoice.'" For this is the will of Hashem; that a person should "conquer"

Him with his prayer. We see this frequently in Tehillim where the Psalm begins "Lam'natzeach". Dovid HaMelech is arousing a person to "conquer" Hashem with his prayer (see Lekutei Halachos, Birkas Re'iah, Halacha 5:12). And as our holy Sages have said (Pesachim 119a): "What is the meaning of the verse, 'Lam'natzeach Mizmor L'Dovid'? It means, 'Sing to the One Who we conquer and He rejoices.' Come and see that Hashem's ways are not like the ways of human beings. A human being, if you are victorious over him, will be sad. But the Holy One Blessed is He, if you are victorious over Him, rejoices, as it says (Tehillim 106:23): 'And He said that He would destroy them, had not Moshe, His chosen one, stood in the breach before Him, to turn back His wrath from destruction.'" Rashi (Pesachim ibid.) comments on the word 'Lam'natzeach' that since it is not written 'Le'natzeach' this teaches us that He gave the power to people to "conquer" Him, and this is what Rebbe Nachman teaches us here. Hashem sends a person words that can "conquer" Him and wants to hear these words. Especially when a person prays on behalf of others and feels the pain of their burdens and troubles and pleads their case before Hashem with all kinds of compelling claims and arguments – this gives Hashem great pleasure. Because it is His will that people pray to Him on behalf of His children, as Moshe Rebbeinu did when he prayed that Hashem should forgive the people of Israel after the sin of the Golden Calf. And Hashem accepted Moshe's prayer. This is the verse mentioned above: "Had not Moshe, His chosen one..." Rashi writes (ibid.) that the verse praises Moshe by referring to him as 'His chosen one' because he turned back Hashem's wrath. So we see that a victorious prayer is very sweet and pleasant to Hashem. Therefore, happy is the one who merits to always speak out to Hashem all that is bothering him until he "triumphs" over Him with his prayer. For then he will be very beloved in the eyes of Hashem and he will accomplish all that he needs spiritually and materially. Happy is he and fortunate is his lot!

Mohorosh tied this idea to the Parsha in a most wonderful way. It is written (Shemos 6): "Elokim spoke to Moshe and said to him, 'I am Hashem (yud-kay-vav-kay)'". And Rashi explains that He took Moshe to task because he had spoken critically when he said, (v. 22) "Why have You done evil to this people?" We need to understand why Moshe Rebbeinu spoke in this fashion to Hashem, which made it appear as if Moshe was criticizing His ways, G-d forbid. But according to the words of Rebbe Nachman, we can understand why – it is the will of Hashem that a person should pray to Him specifically in a way of trying to win. When one tries to "conquer" Hashem with his prayer, Hashem sends him the words to do this, especially when a person prays for

2

others and is pained over their troubles. We see this trait of Moshe Rebbeinu as it is written (Shemos 2:11): "He (Moshe) went out to his brethren and observed their burdens." All of Moshe's argumentation and pleading came from his great love for the Jewish people, as our holy Sages have said (Menachos 65a): "Moshe Rebbeinu was a lover of Israel", therefore, even though he spoke strongly, and it appeared as if he were using the attribute of strict justice, it was revealed afterwards that this was Hashem's will and that Hashem Himself sent Moshe the words with which to "conquer" Him. And through this, Hashem's attribute of strict justice was transformed into the attribute of compassion. It is thus written: "Elokim spoke to Moshe", Elokim is the trait of strict justice. At first Hashem's attribute of strict justice was revealed to Moshe but afterwards, "And He said to him (to Moshe), 'I am Hashem (yud-kay-vav-kay)." This is the Name of compassion. That is, He revealed to Moshe that He Himself was within the words that Moshe spoke, and through this, the attribute of strict justice was transformed into the attribute of compassion. As it is brought in the Midrash (Shemos Rabbah, 6:1): "The attribute of justice sought to attack Moshe, as it is written, 'Elokim spoke to Moshe" but because Hashem saw that it was for the sake of Israel's pain that Moshe spoke this way, He therefore turned and dealt with him with the attribute of compassion, as it says, 'And He said to him, "I am Hashem (yud-kay-vav-kay)." For when a person prays in a fashion of trying to win his case, in the end Hashem will change the justice into compassion, and he will draw upon himself complete kindness and mercy.

We see that the main claim of Moshe Rebbeinu was (Shemos 5:22): "Why have you done evil to this people?" i.e. he was asking about the great harshness of the enslavement of the Jews in Egypt. We need to understand how Hashem answered him and specifically how the verse, "And I have also heard the groaning of the Children of Israel whom Egypt enslaves," was an answer to Moshe's question. It is explained in the commentaries (Sefer Prashas Derachim, Derech Mitzrayim, Drush 5) that the decree of exile in Egypt should have been 400 years as it was said to Avraham Avinu at the "Bris Bein HaBesarim" when he asked (Bereishis 15:8): "How shall I know that I will inherit it (the Land)?" Hashem said to him, "Know with certainty that your offspring will be strangers in a land not their own, and they will serve them and they will oppress them 400 years." But in actuality, the Jews were only in Egypt for 210 years. How did they make up for the other 190 years? Many answers are given for this, and one of them is that the great harshness of the slavery made up for the time (Sefer Prashas Drachim, ibid.). Therefore, at the time that Moshe made the claim before Hashem, "Why have

3

you done evil to this people?" i.e., why are the Jews suffering such a harsh enslavement, Hashem answered him (Shemos 6:5): "Moreover, I have heard the groan of the Children of Israel whom Egypt is enslaving…" That is, the great harshness of the slavery that you, Moshe, are asking about, is exactly what will fulfill the allotted time of the exile, so the Children of Israel can leave before the period of 400 years.

With regard to the harshness of the slavery, it is brought in the book "Techeiles Mordechai" by the brilliant and holy Maharsham z"l, that the essence of the harshness was that the Children of Israel were the slaves of slaves. An analogy: A rich man who had a servant, lost his wealth, became poor and was forced to become a servant to another rich man. It would have been much worse had he been forced to serve his servant. There would have been no greater disgrace than this. We see that Cham was cursed by his father Noach (Bereishis 9:25): "A slave of slaves he will be to his brothers," and from him Mitzrayim (Egypt) was born. And when the Children of Israel became their slaves, this was for them a great disgrace up to the heavens, since they became slaves to slaves. Therefore, even though it was decreed against them, "Know with certainty that your offspring will be strangers in a land not their own (for 400 years)," however, this 400 years was possible had it been a different nation who weren't servants to Israel. Not so, if they were exiled to Egypt. This is a very great disgrace. And this was the essence of the harshness of the slavery. This is also, "I have heard the groan of the Children of Israel whom 'Egypt' enslaves," because it was Egypt in particular who were enslaving them, and not another nation. And this was the essence of the harsh slavery. Therefore they are already fit to be redeemed.

In the book, "Ksav Sofer", by the brilliant and holy Rabbi Avraham Shmuel Binyomin Sofer from Pressburg z"l (Parshas Shemos) it is written that the essence of the harshness of the subjugation was the Egyptians' trait of ingratitude, because it was only proper for them to be grateful to the Jews for Yosef Hatzaddik who saved them from starvation and destruction. It was bad enough that they were ungrateful, that they acted as if they didn't know Yosef, but to even pay them back evil for good is a situation that would greatly pain anyone. If one knows that he was good to another person, and not only does the person he helped not show gratitude but even afflicts and subjugates him, this situation causes tremendous pain. This was the essence of the harsh subjugation – that it was specifically "Mitzrayim" that subjugated them instead of another nation, because Mitzrayim paid them back evil for

4

good, and because of this (Shemos 6:5): "...and I have remembered My covenant" and they are already fit to be redeemed.

And my father and teacher, Harav Hatzadik Rav Menachem Zev Schik z"l, may his merit protect us, in his book, "Minchas Zev" explains according to the above idea the words of the Midrash (Shemos Rabbah, 6:2): "Hakadosh Baruch Hu said to Moshe, 'you are particular about My words, by your life, you should know that it says (Koheles 7): 'The end of a matter is better than its beginning' – Israel's end is better than their beginning when I had first placed them in Egypt.'" This needs explanation. What did Hashem say to Moshe with this? But according to everything we learned above, we can understand it very well. For Moshe Rebbeinu asked about the harshness of the subjugation. And Hashem said to him, "Israel's end is better than their beginning," that they will leave before the time that was originally decreed for them". For "In the beginning, I placed them in Egypt," i.e., they were in Egypt and became the slaves of slaves (as the Maharsham writes) or they suffered from the Egyptians' ingratitude (as the Ksav Sofer writes), and through this, they had a good ending and were redeemed before the time that was originally decreed for them. And Hashem should help that we should soon go out from all of our troubles and it should be fulfilled with us, "As in the days of your going out from Egypt I will show you wonders," speedily in our days. Amen V'Amen.

5

Seuda Shlishis, Parshas Bo, 5766

At the third Shabbos meal, Mohorosh Shlit"a spoke inspiring words based on Lekutei Mohoran, Part II, Lesson 7, which discusses the topics of compassionate leaders and the importance of leaving behind children and students in the world.

Rebbe Nachman says, it is written (Yeshayahu 49:10): "For he that has compassion on them will lead them." That is to say, the one who is merciful, is the one who can be a leader. One needs to know how to conduct oneself with compassion. For upon the wicked or upon murderers and thieves it is forbidden to show mercy. The main compassion is when Israel, the holy nation, falls, G-d forbid, through their sins. This is the greatest compassion of all. For all harsh afflictions in the world are as naught compared to the heavy burden of sin, G-d forbid. In truth, where do sins come from? – only from lack of knowledge, since, "a person doesn't sin unless a spirit of folly enters him (Sotah 3a)." And this is the greatest act of compassion – to cause knowledge to enter a person and save him from sin. This is the concept of the verse (Tehillim 41): "Happy is the one who intelligently considers a poor person," i.e., the one who teaches intelligence to a person lacking it. As our Sages teach us "the only poor person is the one who lacks knowledge (Nedarim 41a)." The true leader needs to have mercy on him and to put knowledge into him. When he does this, then even when the leader's time to leave the world arrives and his Neshama rises and cleaves to his place in the upper worlds, at the same time, he is still here below, accomplishing great feats. For the goal and ultimate perfection is not that the Neshama merely be in a state of cleaving Above. Rather the main perfection of the Neshama is: when the Neshama is Above, it is at the same time here below. Therefore, a person needs to leave behind a blessing in this world – a son or a student – in order for his knowledge to remain below at the same time that he rises Above. As our Rabbis said (Bava Basra 116): "Who is referred to in the Posuk (Tehillim 55:20) *'Asher ain chalifos lamo'* – 'those for whom there is no substitute'? One opinion says it refers to the person that leaves no son, and one opinion says it means the one that leaves no student." Because when one leaves behind a son or a student who absorbed his knowledge, it is considered as if he has left a substitute in the world. Surely, there is no virtue in leaving behind a wicked son, G-d forbid. The ultimate purpose is to leave a son behind who will also be in the category of a student – through receiving his father's mind and knowledge. As to the opinion that says it only has to be a student, since the main thing is to leave behind one's knowledge in the world, it is sufficient to leave only a student. *This* is the essential perfection – that a person leaves his knowledge in this world at the same time his Neshama ascends Above. And every person can fulfill this – not only a teacher – for when two people speak together about Awe of Heaven, and one of them illuminates his friend with a good word, his friend is considered to be in the category of his student. (See all of this in Lekutei Mohoran II: 7.)

Mohorosh explained that we see from this lesson that the primary virtue of a leader of Israel is that he be a true man of compassion and that his entire aim is to have compassion upon his fellow Jews and to take them out from their sins, for there is no greater compassion in the world like the compassion for a person who has fallen through his sins. The souls of Israel, in their root, are completely removed from sin, and sin has no relationship to them at all. Therefore, if, G-d forbid, they fall into sin, the main compassion is to take them out from their sins. And Rebbe Nachman begins by saying, "The leaders need to know how to conduct themselves with compassion, for upon the wicked, the murderers and the thieves it is forbidden to have mercy." And even though Rebbe Nachman says in another place (Lekutei Mohoran I:182) that even the completely wicked should be judged favorably – to find in them something good – even so, he also says (Sefer Hamidos, Merivah #88) that we do not judge favorably one who incites others to sin, for one who seduces his friend to leave the straight path, there is no judging him favorably. This is the intention of Rebbe Nachman here: that upon the wicked who are seducers and inciters, it is forbidden to judge them favorably; they should be judged unfavorably and we must separate ourselves from them totally. However, upon the Holy Nation who falls into sins, G-d forbid, we certainly need to show very much compassion, to bring them out of their sins and to do anything possible to bring the souls of Israel closer to their Father in Heaven.

Therefore, it is a great mitzvah to speak words of Faith and Awe of Heaven with every person, because people are wandering about in this world filled with sadness and bitterness and their hearts are full of doubts and confusion about Faith. And they have no one to pour out their bitter hearts to. And when they see a happy person with a cheerful expression on his face, they are drawn to him like a magnet because they want to hear a good word from him. Therefore, Rebbe Nachman once said to his close followers that if they would be happy it would be a great favor for the whole world. And why? Because

2

when the people of the world see a happy person whose joy is on his face, they will open up and pour out the bitterness in their hearts to him and they will receive from him words of Faith and Awe of Heaven. There is no greater mitzvah than this – to revive a fellow Jew and to bring him out from his doubts and confusion. This is the true compassion that is mentioned above. A person should not say, "I am not a leader of Israel, and I have no connection to these things," because these things relate to every person at every time. There is an obligation on every individual to raise sons and students. And when one speaks to others words of Faith and Awe of Heaven, he is literally raising students! And sometimes if the other person can't take in his words, the words will bounce back and go into himself and he himself will be positively affected by his own words (Lekutei Mohoron, I:184). Therefore, it is a great mitzvah to speak words of Faith and Awe of Heaven with all of one's acquaintances and close friends. And this is literally included in the mitzvah of Tzedakah, as it is written (Tehillim 41:2): "Fortunate is he who intelligently considers ("*maskil*") the poor", i.e., fortunate is he who shines intelligence ("*seichel*" - same root as "*maskil*") into the person who is worse off and poorer than himself, for "a poor person is only one who is poor in knowledge (Nedarim 41a)." And if we shine knowledge and intelligence into him, what a great act of tzedakah this is (Lekutei Mohoran, I:106)!" And sometimes a storeowner or a businessman can fulfill this better than anyone else – because he is constantly speaking and dealing with people. And when he speaks words of Faith and Awe of Heaven with them, he thereby performs a tremendously great act of tzedakah! And he reveals and publicizes the truth of Hashem's existence throughout the entire world.

We see that when a person merits raising up sons and students, his memory will be perpetuated for all generations. However, the essential purpose of having children and raising up students is that faith should continue from generation to generation. And a son is like a student because he receives the parent's knowledge and keeps it going after him. And a student is like a son, because he who teaches Torah to his friend's son, the Torah considers it as if he had fathered him (Sanhedrin 19b). When a person instills Faith and Awe of Heaven into his children and students when he is alive, he is fulfilling the main goal of Creation and he is considered alive even after his demise. As our Sages said (Bava Basra 116b): "*Asher ain chalifos lamo* – 'those for whom there is no substitute' – one says a son, and one says a student." And they are both true, because when a person raises a son or a student and instills Faith and Awe of Heaven into him, he continues to exist in the world through his son or his student, and he doesn't vanish or pass away at all. Therefore, happy

3

is the one who merits speaking with all of his friends and acquaintances words of Faith and Awe of Heaven, for in this way, he will reveal and publicize Hashem's presence in the world to all people and he will bring the world to its eternal rectification. Happy is he and fortunate is his lot.

Mohorosh tied these ideas to our Parsha in a wonderful way. We find in the Parsha (Shemos 13:8) the mitzvah of "You shall tell your son on that day, saying…" i.e., the mitzvah of telling over the story of the Exodus from Egypt. And our Sages said (Pesachim 116a): "If he has a son, the son asks. If he has no son, his wife asks. If he has no wife, he asks himself. Two Torah scholars ask each other." We need to understand, why is it, that only when it comes to the Exodus is there a mitzvah to "tell it over to others" – to a son or to a wife or to a friend. Furthermore, why is this mitzvah not like the mitzvah of "Remembering the Exodus every day" for which a person only needs to tell himself? According to the words of Rebbe Nachman mentioned above, we can understand it very well. For at the moment of the Exodus from Egypt, the souls of Israel rose up to become Hashem's Chosen Nation. And from that moment on, they have been perpetuating Faith in Hashem from generation to generation. Therefore, we were commanded precisely *then* to tell the story of the Exodus to our children and to others – because beginning exactly at that moment – we need to be engaged in raising sons and students who will perpetuate Faith in Hashem from generation to generation. Thus, the Torah commands us to fulfill the mitzvah of telling over the story of the Exodus to all categories of children – wise, wicked, simple and the one who doesn't know how to ask. As our Sages said (Yerushalmi Pesachim 70b): "The Torah speaks regarding four sons," because we need to bring them all close to Hashem and to speak to each and every one according to his individual needs. When the wise son asks (Devarim 6): "What are the testimonies and the decrees, etc.," we must answer him according to his own way. When the wicked son asks (Shemos 12:26): "What is this service to you?" and he has doubts, we must answer him according to *his* own way. When the simple son asks (Shemos 13:14): "What is *this*?" – this also denotes a question arising from doubts about Faith as it is written in the Tikunai Zohar (Tikun 22) that the word "*this*", in many verses, alludes to Faith - so we must also speak to the simple son according to *his* way and to conduct ourselves with compassion towards him in order to bring him close to Hashem. And when the son who doesn't know how to ask says nothing, then we should initiate the dialogue (Shemos 13:8): "And you shall tell your son on that day, saying…" We find that it is precisely on the festival of Pesach, which is the beginning of the revelation of holy Faith – as many of the mitzvos are

4

"*Zeicher le'Yitziyas Mitzrayim*" (a memorial of the Exodus) – that the mitzvah is to be deeply involved with raising sons and students and passing down to them pure and clear Faith. For through this there will be a continuation of the light of Faith for infinite generations to come. And Hashem should help us to always be occupied with revealing and publicizing Faith until we merit to see the redemption and salvation of Israel, swiftly in our days. Amen V'Amen.

5

Friday Night, Parshas Beshalach, Shabbos Shira, 5766

On Friday night, at the first Shabbos meal, Mohorosh Shlit"a spoke inspiring words based on Lekutei Mohoron, Part I, Lesson 272, which discusses the verse "Today, if you would listen to His voice".

Rebbe Nachman says, "It is written (Tehillim 95), 'Today, if you would listen to His voice.' This is a great rule in serving Hashem, to place before one's eyes only this day. In respect to earning one's livelihood and obtaining one's other needs, it is necessary not to think about tomorrow. The same thing goes for serving Hashem – to only place before one's eyes this day and this moment. Because when one wishes to begin serving Hashem, it seems to a person as if it is a heavy burden and that it is impossible for him to carry such a heavy load. However, when he will consider that he only has this day, then it will not be a burden at all. Moreover, he should not push off until tomorrow what he can do today, saying to himself, 'I will start tomorrow. Tomorrow, I'll pray with concentration and with the proper strength.' The same thing applies to all other forms of Divine service. For a person only has in his world this day and this moment in which he is standing. For tomorrow is another world completely. '*Today*, if you would listen to His voice,' – precisely *today.*" (These are the words of Rebbe Nachman.)

Mohorosh explained that we see from Rebbe's Nachman's revelation to us that all of a person's success, both spiritual and material, depends only on a person's integrating within himself this idea – that he has only today, and that he shouldn't confuse himself with what happened yesterday or with what will be in the future. In this way, he will merit success in all of his endeavors and he will live a truly good and sweet life. Because the main reason for all of the stumbling blocks in a person's life is that he is always thinking about what was, about what has already happened to him – the mighty waves and breakers that have passed over him – and it seems to him that the same things will happen again today. And even if he has already merited seeing some salvation in his life or some other good thing happen to him today, he will immediately begin to worry about and fear what will happen tomorrow. And this confuses him completely and he is unable to be happy with today. But, when a person absorbs into his mind very well that all he has is today – "*Today*, if you would listen to His voice" – then he will greatly succeed in all of his endeavors. In spiritual matters, he will do everything he can to learn, pray and fulfill mitzvos on this day, and he will not confuse himself with the past or the future at all. The same thing applies to material matters - his being involved in making a living and in all of his other physical needs – he should only worry that he will have enough for today and not to confuse himself with worrying about tomorrow at all. He will then be very successful in every matter and live a truly good life.

We see that the idea of "*Today*, if you would listen to His voice," is also a secret of success in finding one's spouse, as well as in making a living. And even though our holy Sages said (Sotah 2a): "Finding one's wife is as difficult as splitting the Red Sea," and they also said (Pesachim 118a): "Making a living is as difficult as splitting the Red Sea," the main difficulty is only when a person confuses himself with his past and his future, and he hangs everything on nature, chance and fate and he says to himself, "You see that I still haven't found a wife, and I still have no livelihood, and chances are that it will stay like this for me." As a result, it will really be difficult for him and he'll be completely broken. But, when a person absorbs into himself the trait of Holy Faith and says, "I only have today," and he stands up and prays before Hashem, "Master of the Universe, everything depends only on Your hand. If it is Your will, I will find my spouse today, and if it is Your will, I will have my sustenance for today." Then, he will not be confused at all by what has already happened to him and he will strengthen himself greatly. And even if the day of his salvation is pushed off for a short while, he will not become disheartened at all, for he knows that it was Hashem's will. And then certainly, the day of his salvation will eventually arrive. As Rebbe Nachman says (Lekutei Mohoran, I:9): "Just as one gives 'sustenance' to his Father in Heaven through his prayer, so too will they [Heaven] grant him *his* sustenance; and just as he causes a union (*zivug*) [between Hashem and His Shechinah] to happen through his prayer, so too will he merit to find his own match (*zivug*), because everything depends on prayer. The Red Sea was split into twelve parts (Pirkei d'Rebbe Eliezer, ch. 42) one for each of the twelve different prayer liturgies, since each tribe has its own heavenly gate and special liturgy through which to elevate their prayers. And when a person focuses only on today and what needs to be done today, and doesn't confuse his mind with the past or the future or with what others are doing, searching only for his own gate and path, he will then merit to receive a wondrous salvation, literally as great as the splitting of the Red Sea. He will be saved from all oppressive and constricting forces surrounding him and an

2

abundance of heavenly blessings, both spiritual and physical, will be showered upon him. Happy is he and fortunate is his portion.

Mohorosh tied these ideas to our parsha in a wonderful way. It is written (Shemos 14): "And Hashem saved Israel *on that day* from the hand of Mitzrayim, and Israel saw Mitzrayim dead on the seashore." We can ask ourselves, why are the words "*on that day*" necessary? At first glance, these words seem to be superfluous (as this question is also raised in the holy book "Kedushas Levi"). However, according to the words of Rebbe Nachman, we can understand it very well. The main salvation of Israel in all generations which is to be saved from all of those things which press them down and make their lives narrow, spiritually and physically, is accomplished through attaining the trait of "On that day" – i.e., not to place before one's eyes anything but today and to strive to serve Hashem according to what needs to be done "On that day". As my master, my father, may his merit protect us, brings in his book "Minchas Zev" (Parshas Beshalach) the explanation of the "Yismach Moshe", may his merit protect us, in Parshas Nitzavim on the verse (Devarim 29): "You are standing *today* all of you…": that if a person truly thinks that he only has today to live, he will surely fill that day with Torah and Mitzvos and the service of Hashem. Likewise, with regard to earning a living and finding one's spouse, which also includes having family harmony, it all depends on actualizing the trait of "On that day." For when a person will think that he has only today, he will not worry about his sustenance for tomorrow, and he will not start an argument with his wife and hurt her feelings, G-d forbid. Rather, he will be a person who is a master of "giving in" and "yielding" in his home and he will do whatever in the world is possible to be at peace with her. Does it really pay to destroy his home just for "that day", G-d forbid? And this alluded to in the verse, "And Hashem saved Israel "*on that day*" from the hand of Mitzrayim." The word Mitzrayim includes all of the exiles and afflictions which pass over Israel. All of these troubles are referred to as "*Mitzrayim*" since they all press down upon and constrict Israel (the Hebrew word *meitzar* means to press down upon and to constrict as Rebbe Nachman teaches in Lekutei Mohoran, I:4). But when a person has reached the level of "On that day", he is saved from all forces which press on him and make his life narrow. And this is the verse, "And Israel saw Mitzrayim dead on the seashore" – also those things that constrict and press down on a person which are in the category of "the seashore", i.e. the issues of a livelihood and marital life, which are both as difficult as the Splitting of the Red Sea, also these constricting and repressive forces will completely perish and nullify themselves before him by means of the trait of

3

"On that day". For when a person places before himself only today and continually prays to Hashem that He should help him find a livelihood, a spouse and family harmony, in this way, great heavenly abundance, both spiritual and physical, will be showered upon him. And he will lack nothing at all. And Hashem should help us to attach ourselves to Him anew each and every day, not thinking about any day but today until we merit to ascend and be included in Him completely, now and forever. Amen v'Amen.

4

Friday Night, Parshas Yisro, 5762

On Friday night, at the first Shabbos meal, Mohorosh Shlit"a spoke inspiring words based on Lekutei Mohoran, Introduction to Part II, which discusses the verse, "One was Avraham."

Rebbe Nachman says, "It is written (Yechezkel 33): 'One was Avraham.' Avraham served Hashem only through his being 'one', i.e. he considered himself to be the only one in the world, paying no attention at all to the rest of humanity who turned away from Hashem and who tried to hinder him, not even to his father or to the rest of his opponents – rather, he served Hashem as if he were the only one in the world. This is the meaning of the verse, 'One was Avraham.' So too, anyone who wishes to enter into the service of Hashem will not be able to do so without utilizing this concept. He must think that there is no one in the world besides himself – just one individual in the world. And he should pay no attention to anyone who tries to hold him back – neither his father or mother, father-in-law or mother-in-law, wife or children. He should disregard all hindrances that come from all of the people in the world who mock, seduce and try to prevent him from serving Hashem. He should not be pained or pay any attention to them. Rather, he should be in the category of 'One was Avraham' – as if he were the only one in the world." (These are the words of Rebbe Nachman.)

Mohorosh explained that for a person to merit entering into the service of Hashem properly, he is required to devote himself entirely to Hashem and to think that he is the only one in the world – serving Hashem with real self-sacrifice. Even though the rest of humanity does not understand him at all, and are unable to comprehend the depth of his thinking – how his whole desire and will is to attach himself to Hashem – nevertheless he should not stop at all. For behold, there is only himself with Hashem alone. And the purpose of his being created is only to recognize Hashem, as it is brought in the Holy Zohar (Parshas Bo, 42b): "*B'gin diyishtamodin ley* (in order that we recognize Him)." Therefore our Holy Sages said (Sanhedrin 37a): "Everyone is obligated to say, 'The world was created for my sake'." For in truth, the world *was* created for *his* sake, and all of humanity toils to help him reach his eternal goal. There is not even a grain of arrogance in this at all. Just the opposite – this is the ultimate in humility – since he is not gazing at other people at all and neither does he wish to rule or lord over them, G-d forbid. Rather, his entire aim and focus is to recognize Hashem and to be attached to Him completely. This was the level of *Avraham Avinu*, who was the foremost of all the believers. He understood that it is impossible to succeed in serving Hashem unless one considers oneself to be alone in the world, which is the concept of (Yechezkel 33): "One was Avraham." Idolators were numerous in his days, even in his father's house. And all of his acquaintances were idolaters. So he was forced to adopt the thinking that he was alone in the world since he knew that his purpose in life was to recognize Hashem and to reveal and publicize Him to all of humanity. And then *his* oneness would be included in Hashem's oneness. This is the root of Faith: "Hear O'Israel, Hashem is our G-d, Hashem is one." When a person serves Hashem with the concept of "one" in mind, he ascends and is included in Hashem's oneness, and becomes one with Him, so to speak, which is the concept of "He is one, and there is no second" (from the Adon Olam prayer). His entire intention is only to attach himself to Hashem and to reveal His oneness to all of humanity. And then he rises and cleaves to Hashem properly and merits to delight in the pleasantness of the glow of the Divine Presence. Happy is he and fortunate is his portion.

Mohorosh tied these ideas to our Parsha in a wonderful way. We find in our Parsha that Moshe Rebbeinu also served Hashem through the concept of "one". He paid no attention to the fact that people alienated him and drove him away from where he lived. He became isolated from other people when he was forced to flee from Egypt and from his father's home. And he found his spouse in a remote place in Midyan and named his firstborn son "Gershom" after his being forced to live as a foreigner in a strange land (Shemos 18): "For he said, I have been a stranger in a strange land." And also there, he found himself among idolaters, as our holy Sages have said (Mechilta, ch. 18): "'I have been a stranger *in a strange land* (*b'eretz nachriya*) – *nechar ya* – among people who were estranged from Hashem. Moshe said, 'Since the whole world are idolaters, I will serve the 'One Who spoke and the world came into being.'" He also named his son Gershom, as the idolaters banished (were *m'gareish*) his father-in-law, Yisro, from his own home (see the commentary of the Ohr Hachaim on this verse). We see that *Moshe Rebbeinu* served Hashem through the concept of being "one", that is, by not paying attention to anyone, by viewing oneself as being alone in the world and by realizing that it is one's duty to serve and recognize the 'Only One' may His name be blessed. And because Moshe Rebbeinu served

2

Hashem through the concept of "one", he merited to bring down the Torah to the Children of Israel and to teach them about Hashem and His oneness for all times.

And this is what we find in our Parsha: that the *Aseres Hadibros* (the Ten Commandments) were said in the singular, as it is written (Shemos 19): "I am Hashem *your* (singular form of you) G-d Who has taken *you* (singular you) out from the land of Egypt, from the house of slavery, etc." The commentators have already remarked on why it was said in the singular. The Ramban on verse 2 explains that it comes "to warn that each individual is responsible for the mitzvos, for He spoke to and commanded each individual that they should not imagine that they can simply follow the crowd and be saved with them." And this follows the above words of Rebbe Nachman – that each person needs to serve Hashem as if he were the only one in the world and not pay attention to others at all. Rather, he should know that the entire Torah was given to him alone, and he is responsible for all of it. And then he will be very successful.

Rashi (Shemos 19:2) gives another reason for why the *Aseres Hadibros* were said in the singular – in order to give Moshe Rebbeinu an opening for the future to defend the Jewish people for the incident of the Golden Calf: Moshe said to Hashem, 'You did not command them in the plural, i.e., 'There shall not be to you (*la'chem* – plural) other gods', but You only commanded me alone [when You spoke in the singular]. This explanation is also in line with the above words of Rebbe Nachman. For the true Tzaddik receives his strength to judge Israel favorably and to defend them precisely because he serves Hashem in the manner of "one" and he is self-effacing and unassuming to the extent that he has no desire at all to rule over others. Rather, he only wants to see the success of each and every individual, as it is brought in the words of Rebbe Nachman (Lekutei Mohoran, I:79): "Because Moshe Rebbeinu recognized his own lowliness, he was able to recognize the importance and virtues of Israel, and he was able to sacrifice his very soul for them." Therefore, precisely because Moshe Rebbeinu served Hashem in the manner of "one", combined with his his great humility, he knew that all of the *Aseres Hadibros* were said to him alone. And this is how he was able to judge favorably even the lowliest member of Israel and to save them from all evil.

At the end of our Parsha it is written (Shemos 20): "You shall not go up by steps on my altar, that you not expose your nakedness upon it." This verse warns each and every person about the trait of humility - that a person should

3

not ascend to levels that are too far above him, and that he should not indulge in self-praise and pride in his service of Hashem as if he were greater and more important than his fellow. "That you not reveal your nakedness upon it" – that you should not reveal your disgrace in public – for the destiny of one who is haughty towards others is that his disgrace will be exposed in public and everyone will see that, in truth, he is nothing. Therefore, a fundamental rule of divine service is to serve Hashem in the manner of "one", i.e., to include oneself only in Hashem's oneness, to not pay attention to others at all, and certainly not to desire to rule over them. Then, one will walk on a secure path, and wherever he turns he will find success. And Hashem should help us to serve Him in truth and simplicity all the days of our lives until we merit to ascend and be included in Him completely, now and forever. Amen v'Amen.

4

Seudah Shlishis, Parshas Mishpatim, 5765

At the third Shabbos meal, Mohorosh Shlit"a spoke inspiring words based on Lekutei Mohoran, Part I, Lesson 51, which discusses the virtues of Truth and of keeping away from falsehood.

Rebbe Nachman says, "Falsehood harms the eyes, physically and spiritually, and this is an aspect of the verse (Yeshayahu 3): '*U'misakros einayim* [literally 'winking eyes', but it is spelled the same way as 'lying eyes']. For when the eyes are weak they 'lie', since they don't see a thing the way it really is, i.e. something big will appear small, or one object will appear to be two. Furthermore, impurity of the blood comes about through falsehood for it is impossible to speak falsehood until one has polluted his blood. And it is impossible to speak the Truth unless one has first purified his blood. Falsehood, which is evil and impure, comes about as a result of being far from 'One' – for Truth is 'One'. An analogy: To say that a silver vessel is silver is the truth, but to say that it is any other type of vessel is false. We see that the Truth is 'One'. For it is only possible to state the truth in "one" way. But falsehood is many: It is possible to say that it is a vessel of gold or brass or any other material. So we see that falsehood is in the category of "many", as alluded to in the verse 'They have sought "many" calculations' (Koheles 7). Accordingly, in the future, evil and falsehood will be annihilated, for everything will be "One" unity. This is an aspect of the verse (Zechariah 14): 'On that day, Hashem will be One and His Name One." (These are the words of Rebbe Nachman.)

Mohorosh explained that Rebbe Nachman reveals to us in this lesson the great power of Truth as well as the great disgrace of falsehood. For the Truth comes from being attached to the One Hashem as well as by purifying one's blood from its impurities by fulfilling the will of Hashem through the mitzvos of the Torah. This causes one's eyes to shine with the light of Truth and helps one to ascend and cleave to Hashem, Who is the very essence of Truth, as it is written (Yirmiyahu 10): "Hashem G-d is Truth". Our Sages teach us (Shabbos 55a) that Truth is the seal of Hashem, and a seal symbolizes a name. Hashem and His Name are One, as it is written (Zecharia 14): "Hashem is One and His Name is One"; and He is one with the Torah, as it is brought in the Holy Zohar (Bereishis 24a): "Hashem and the Torah are one." Therefore, the more a person attaches himself to the Holy Torah and fulfills the mitzvos of the Torah, the more he is attached to Hashem Who is the essence of Truth. And then, the status of the world "before creation" or "after creation" will be no different to him, i.e. whether he has money and honor and other material possessions or whether he has none of them, it makes no difference to him. For just as before the creation, Hashem was One, and there was absolutely nothing else besides Him, so too after the creation, Hashem is One and there is no absolute existence at all other than Him. Therefore, a person like this is not fazed by anything at all. And because he only wants Hashem and nothing else, he automatically has it all, for "Hashem is good for everything" (*Tehillim* 145) and "The seekers of Hashem will lack no good" (*Tehillim* 34). This is not the case for one who is far from the Torah and mitzvos and is distanced from Hashem. He is being held tight in the grips of falsehood and his polluted blood, which is caused by his sins, blinds his eyes from seeing the Truth. He falls into the category of (Yeshayahu 3): *"Misakros einayim"* and it is very difficult for him to see the Truth. Also the aspect of "Many calculations" hovers over him, as it is written (Koheles 7): "G-d made man straight, but they seek 'many' calculations," which means that he has all kinds of plans and desires for amassing money and honor and other vanities of this world, but in actuality he is always lacking very much. Because he has distanced himself from the Truth, which is the divine unity of all creation where there is no need for anything other than Hashem, therefore all he has left are many plans for obtaining all of the vanities of this world, and he forgets his eternal goal completely. Therefore, the word Truth – *EMeS* – (spelled *Aleph-Mem-Saf*) is the acronym: *E-Mes*, i.e. I remember that "I will be dead *(mes)*" and will have to give up this physical world and return to Hashem Who is the essence of Truth. And the closer a person brings himself to the Truth, the more he clings to Hashem's Oneness. And then he lacks nothing at all, for with Hashem there is everything, which is not the case with one who pursues falsehood. Into this man of falsehood enters *Sinah* (hatred), *Kinah* (jealousy) and *Retzicha* (murder), the first letters of which spell *SheKeR* (falsehood). Because he has distanced himself from the Truth, therefore, hatred, jealousy and murder against the people of truth – the *Tzaddikim* – enter into him and he simply cannot tolerate them; they are thorns in his eyes. He is like a blind man groping in the dark and it seems to him as if there is no light at all. He has no comprehension whatsoever of the virtues of the *Tzaddikim* who cling to the light of Hashem Who is the essence of Truth. Therefore, happy is the one who doesn't mislead himself at all, who merits reaching the light of Truth, the light of the *Tzaddikim* who cling to the

2

Truth, for then he will merit a good and pleasant life in this world and the next. Happy is he and fortunate is his portion.

Mohorosh tied these ideas to our Parsha in the following way: A warning about falsehood is written in our Parsha (Shemos 23): "Keep far away from a false thing *(M'davar sheker tirchak)*, and the innocent and the righteous do not kill, for I will not exonerate a wicked person." We can ask, why is this warning written in this particular way: "*M'davar sheker tirchak* (keep far away from a false thing)", rather than simply "Do not speak falsehood (*Lo ti'daber sheker*)", which is the way the other negative commandments of the Torah are written? Another question: what does the second part of the verse – "and the innocent and the righteous do not kill, etc." have to do with the beginning of the verse – "*M'davar sheker tirchak?*" According to the words of Rebbe Nachman we can understand it very well. The Holy Torah reveals to us the great disgrace of falsehood and how "speaking falsehood" ("*M'daber sheker*") "distances" ("*tirchak*") a person from Hashem [note: the word "*M'daber*" – "to speak" – is spelled exactly the same way as the word "*M'davar*" – "from a thing"]. By speaking falsehood the person distances himself from Hashem's Oneness – Hashem being the essence of Oneness. And the closer a person brings himself to falsehood, the more he distances himself from Hashem Who is the essence of Truth. And this causes him to argue with the *Tzaddikim* and to purse them, G-d forbid, which is alluded to in the end of the verse, "the innocent and the righteous do not kill, etc...", for falsehood causes hatred, jealousy, and murder to enter into a person, as mentioned above. And then he is liable to commit all of the evils in the world, G-d forbid. Therefore, we must distance ourselves completely from the trait of falsehood and draw closer only to Hashem Who is the essence of Truth, as well as to the *Tzaddikim* who are attached to Hashem in truth. In this way, everyone can merit to the Truth and live a *truly* good life forever.

And this is likewise alluded to in the verse (Shemos 23:1): "Do not accept a false report ('*shema shav*'), do not help a wicked person by being a false witness for him." And Rashi explains it to mean: "This is a warning against accepting gossip [*Loshon Harah*]; it's also a warning to a judge that he should not hear the claims of one litigant before the other litigant arrives; and it warns all of us not to help a wicked person by being a false witness for him against the other litigant." We need to understand why the commentators explain the words "false report (*shema shav*)" to mean Loshon Harah and why they say that a judge who hears one side without the other side being present is committing a falsehood? We know that Loshon Harah includes

3

even a report that is true! And the prohibition against a judge hearing only one side even refers to a judge who hears a true report! So why do the commentators refer to these "true" things as being "false?" But according to the words of Rebbe Nachman we can understand it very well. As soon as a person is prepared to hear *Loshon Harah* or to listen to one litigant without the second one being present, he thus demonstrates that he is far from Hashem's Oneness Who commanded us concerning these prohibitions. So we see that this person is attached to falsehood and is therefore prone to accept *Loshon Harah* about the *Tzaddikim* who are attached to Hashem in truth. He will justify the wicked who pursue the *Tzaddikim*, G-d forbid, or he will listen to the one who is pursuing the righteous litigant without both parties being present together. Such a judge is already unfit to make a true judgment. This is why the cases in our verse (Shemos 23:1) of *"Loshon Harah"* and "a judge hearing one side" are both explained to be referring to falsehood – *sheker* – and why they are both included in the prohibition "*M'davar sheker tirchak*" – the command to distance ourselves from falsehood completely. For falsehood causes a person to distance himself from Hashem, G-d forbid. May Hashem help us to aquire the trait of Truth in all our ways, and may we merit to ascend and cleave to His light until we are included in Him completely, now and forever. Amen v'amen.

4

Friday Night, Parshas Terumah, 5766

Friday night, at the first Shabbos meal, Mohorosh Shlit"a spoke inspiring words based on Lekutei Mohoran, Part II, Lesson 12, which discusses the concepts of *temimus* (wholeheartedness) and *peshitus* (simplicity).

Rebbe Nachman says: "The main principle of Judaism is just to walk with *temimus* (wholeheartedness) and *peshitus* (simplicity), without any sophistication, and to see Hashem in everything one does and not to concern oneself at all with one's own honor. Rather, if what one is doing will bring some honor to Hashem, then it should be done, and if not, one should not do it. Then, surely one will never stumble." (These are words of Rebbe Nachman.)

Mohorosh explained that the traits of *temimus* and *peshitus* surpass everything and that they are signs that a person recognizes his true status and knows that it is impossible in any way to totally understand the ways of Hashem. Therefore, he fulfills everything Hashem has commanded him with *temimus* and *peshitus*. He doesn't ask cynical questions or look for scientific proofs. Rather, in everything he does, he only seeks that Hashem should be there, and if Hashem will not be there, then he will not do it. However, we need to understand how a person is able to see whether or not Hashem is there in what he is doing. Is it not written *(Shemos 33)*: "For a person cannot see Me and live"? If so, who can boast that he sees Hashem, so to speak, in what he does? However, it is brought in the *Zohar (Acharei 73a)*: "The Holy One Blessed is He and the Torah are one." Hashem is one with the Torah. If so, the main thing is to see that in everything one does the Torah should be there and that all of one's deeds should be appropriate and with integrity according to the Torah. Then, it will be considered as if he sees Hashem in everything he does. And this is called true *deveikus* (cleaving) to Hashem, that a Jew conducts himself in all of his ways in accordance with the Holy Torah with complete *temimus* and *peshitus* and without any sophistication at all. Then he will cling to Hashem, for Hashem is simple to the ultimate degree of simplicity, as Rebbe Nachman says elsewhere *(Sichos HaRan #101)*: "We need no sophistication in the service of the Creator, only wholeheartedness, simplicity and Faith. He further said, that simplicity is higher than anything, for Hashem is higher than anything and He is simple with the most perfect simplicity." We see from this that the most essential thing is to conduct oneself with complete simplicity, without showing outwardly anything special at all, as Rebbe Nachman once said, "Someone who knows me can testify that there is absolutely no movement in me of a 'famous tzaddik'." For the more a *Tzaddik* is attached to Hashem, the more he conducts himself with simplicity, and then people cannot see anything unusual about him. Therefore, Rebbe Nachman said (*Lekutei Mohoran*, Part II, Lesson 116) that, "People make a mistake and think that it is possible to recognize a *Tzaddik* from the outside, but in reality it is totally impossible to recognize a *Tzaddik* from the outside, for he seems to be like any other man with the same body and limbs. But on the inside, he is an entirely different matter." So we see that the main service is to attain the trait of true *temimus* and *peshitus* until nothing will seem different about a person on the outside. And this is a sign that one has entirely nullified one's feelings of self-importance and greatness to the point where he is completely included in Hashem. Happy is the one who has merited attaining this awareness.

Mohorosh connected these ideas to our Parsha in the following way: We find in our Parsha that the Ark of the Covenant was covered on top by the *Kapores* (the golden Ark Cover), as it is written *(Shemos 25:17)*: "And you shall make a *Kapores* of pure gold, two and half cubits its length, and one and half cubits its width." Rashi explains: "*Kapores* - a cover for the Ark which was made open on top. He laid it upon the Ark like a slab." We can ask ourselves why a cover needed to be made for the Ark, while a cover was not needed for any of the other holy vessels in the Tabernacle. According to the words of Rebbe Nachman we can understand it very well. The Ark alludes to the holiness of the *Tzaddikim* who cleave to the light of the Torah, for within the Ark were the Tablets which encompass and include the entirety of the Torah (as Rashi explains on *Shemos* 24:12). And the essence of the wholeness of the *Tzaddikim* comes about through the traits of *temimus* and *peshitus* - they fulfill all the words of the Torah with complete wholeheartedness and as a result, people cannot detect in their outward appearance and movements anything different about them. And this is the idea of the cover that was upon the Ark. For even though the *Tzaddikim* are in a state of intense cleaving to the light of the Torah and in everything they do they are able to see the Torah, even so, since all of their deeds are with *temimus* and *peshitus* it is impossible to see on them any outward signs of this at all. And this is due to their great humility and self-effacement to Hashem. All of this is hinted to in the Torah's measurements of the Ark and the *Kapores* (the Ark's golden cover): two and a half cubits its (the Ark's) length, one and a half cubits its width, and one and a half cubits its height. All of the dimensions are "half" measurements to hint

2

to the traits of humility and lowliness – that a person feels himself to literally be a "half". When the measurements are calculated in handbreadths instead of in cubits (six handbreadths to a cubit according to Rebbi Meir in Talmud Bava Basra 14a), two and a half cubits are the same as fifteen handbreadths; and the number fifteen alludes to one of the names of Hashem spelled *Yud-Hay* (numerical value also equal to fifteen), the letters of which represent the holy intellectual faculties of *Chochmah* (Knowledge) and *Binah* (Understanding) respectively, as explained in Kabbalah. Through these holy intellectual powers, a person has the ability to nullify his feelings of self-importance and arrogance. For as soon as a person has *Chochmah* and *Binah*, his arrogance is automatically and completely nullified. Therefore, it is brought in the writings of the Arizal *(Shaar Ruach Hakodesh)* that concentrating on the name **Yud-Hey** is a remedy for removing arrogance, for the numerical value of *gaivah* (arrogance) is fifteen like the Divine name *Yud-Hey*. Similarly, the height and width of the Ark - one and a half cubits - is equal to nine handbreadths, and the number nine alludes to the traits of *anavah* (humilty) and *shiflus* (lowliness) in the following way: the secret of the letter *Hey* is that it is formed by two letters: first, by the letter preceding it in the aleph-beis – the *Dalet*– and afterwards by combining the letter *Yud* (the smallest letter) with the *Dalet,* making it a *Hey (Tikunnei Zohar, Tikun 21)*. This means that initially one feels himself to be impoverished *(Dalet)* to the utmost degree of lowliness. But afterwards, when he draws into himself the small *Yud*, representing *Chochmah* (knowledge), this small point combines with the *Dalet* to make the letter *Hey* (*Lekutei Mohoran*, Part I, Lesson 49). So we find that the letter *Dalet* and *Hey* allude to lowliness and self-effacement (*shilflus*) and the numerical value of *Daled* (4) and *Hey* (5) when added together is nine, which are the nine handbreadths of the height and width of the Ark and of the width of the *Kapores*. It comes out, that all of the measurements of the Ark and the *Kapores* allude to *anavah* (humility) and *shiflus* (lowliness), to show us that the light of the Torah rests only on a person who is humble and that upon such a person a covering from above will surely rest – the *Kapores* – and people will not be able to see anything different about him in his outward appearance. Rather, only one who observes carefully and wants to find Hashem and the Torah in everything the Tzaddik does will merit seeing the light of the *Shechinah* (Divine Presence) and hearing the voice of prophecy emanating from between the "two *Keruvim* (cherubs) on top of the *Kapores*" of the Tzaddik. And may Hashem help us to always be attached to the light of the Torah until we return to Him wholeheartedly and are included in Him completely, now and forever. Amen v'Amen.

3

Seudah Shlishis, Parshas Tetaveh, Shabbos Zachor 5766

At the third Shabbos meal, Mohorosh Shlit"a spoke inspiring words based on Lekutei Mohoran, Part II, Lesson 12, which discusses the traits of *temimus* (wholeheartedness) and *peshitus* (simplicity).

Rebbe Nachman says: "The main point of Judaism is just to walk with *temimus* and *peshitus* without any sophistication, to see in everything one does that Hashem will be there, and to not concern oneself at all about one's own honor. Rather, if there is honor for Hashem in this, one will do it, and if not, not. Then, one will surely never stumble."

Mohorosh explained that we see from this teaching that the ways of *temimus* surpass everything and that when a person trains himself to serve Hashem with complete temimus and peshitus and in everything he does he sees that Hashem will be there, then he will never stumble; rather, he will succeed in all his endeavors. However, we need to understand what Rebbe Nachman means when he says that a person should see Hashem in everything he does. How can a person boast that he sees Hashem in what he is doing? It is brought in the Holy Zohar (Acharei 73a), "The Holy One Blessed is He and the Torah are one." Hashem is one with the Torah. So, it comes out that a person needs to see in everything he does that the Torah will be there, which means that what he is doing should be appropriate and upright according to the Torah. It is thus considered as if he sees Hashem in what he is doing. And then, he will never stumble. Therefore, we need to learn much Shulchan Aruch and the other Codes, as Rebbe Nachman strongly urged us to do (Sichos HaRan #185): "Each Jew is obligated to learn the Codes every day, as a rule not to be broken, for through this learning he will merit to become expert in all of the laws which apply to him every day. And all of his ways will be proper according to the Codes. This is the way of true temimus."

It is certain that the foundation of *temimus* is *Emunas Chochamim* (faith in the Sages), for without faith in the words of our holy Sages (i.e. the Oral Torah), we cannot know a thing about how to fulfill the Torah and the mitzvos, for most of the mitzvos are written in the Torah in a generalized fashion and by way of hints and so we need the words of our Sages to explain to us all the details of the mitzvos. Therefore, clear and pure faith in Hashem is impossible to attain without clear and pure faith in the words of the Sages, as it is brought in the Midrash (Mechilta Parshas Beshalach) on the verse (Shemos 14) "And they had faith in Hashem and in Moshe, His servant": "This comes to teach you that whoever believes in the Faithful Shepherd is as if he believes in the words of the One Who spoke and the world came to be." For it is impossible to come to perfect faith without Emunas Chochamim. Therefore, the main point and foundation on which everything depends is to attach oneself to a true Tzaddik and to accept his Torah guidance (Lekutei Mohoran, Part I, Lesson 123). We see with our own eyes, that the philosophers and scientists who are completely removed from the trait of temimus all scoff at the true Sages, and they mock and scorn their words, for they cannot tolerate the trait of temimus at all. All of their strength flows from the klipa (the impure spiritual realm) of Amalek who was a philosopher and a heretic, as it is written (Devarim 25): "And he did not fear G-d," which means that he lived and behaved only according to the secular wisdoms of the world, completely devoid of any fear of G-d. He is the stumbling block that exists within all of the seven wisdoms of the world, which is an aspect of the verse (Mishlei 24): "For a Tzaddik falls seven times and yet rises up again." The last letters of each of the Hebrew words in this verse ("Ki sheva yipol tzaddik v'kam") spell Amalek (Lekutei Mohoran, Part II, Lesson 19), for he wants to infuse his atheism into all of the wisdoms and detach these wisdoms from the wisdom of the Torah. (note: There are seven wisdoms of the world, and the Tzaddik is able to descend into these wisdoms and connect them to the Torah while remaining strong in his faith in Hashem.) Therefore, Amalek is called a *leitz* (a scoffer) by our holy Sages (Shemos Rabbah, the beginning of parshas Yisro), because he scoffs at the words of the Sages and weakens people's faith in the Sages by raising doubts in their minds about the Sage's words. Therefore, the gematria (numerical sum of the letters) of Amalek equals the gematria of *sefeik* (doubt). And the main war against Amalek is waged by Moshe Rebbeinu, peace be upon him, about whom it is written (Shemos 17): "And his (Moshe's) hands were steady until sunset (the Hebrew word used here for "steady" is "*emunah* - faith"; literally, "his hands were faith")." Through *emunah*, he weakened Amalek (the sophistication and skepticism), and he infused peshitus and temimus into the souls of Israel. This is the meaning of the verse, "His hands were *emunah* (faith)" – specifically his **hands**, which represent the performance of the practical mitzvos, which a person does with his hands and with total *temimus* and *peshitus*, without any sophistication or academic research. And when the souls of Israel cast aside their own understanding and wisdom, and believe in the words of Moshe Rebbeinu, they thereby subdue Amalek, which is what our holy Sages have said (Talmud Rosh HaShanah 29a): "Was it really Moshe's hands which won

2

or lost the war? Rather, as long as the people of Israel looked heavenward and subjugated their hearts to their Father in Heaven they would gain the upper hand, and if not, Amalek would gain the upper hand." Moshe Rebbeinu's standing on top of the hill with his hands spread out toward heaven signaled and directed the Jewish souls that they should turn towards the heavens and subjugate their hearts to Him (as explained in the words of the Tosfos Yom Tov on tractate Rosh Hashanah, ch. 3, mishna 5). For sometimes it is impossible for a Tzaddik to speak explicitly about what is in his heart; he can only make gestures and hint with his hands in the sea of wisdom; but through these hand motions, people will understand his intention (Lekutei Mohoran, Part II, Lesson 7). As soon as a person casts aside his own understanding and begins to rely on the understanding of a true Tzaddik, he is saved from all doubt and confusion, which is Amalek, and he will merit to the ways of true temimus, which is the mishna (Pirkei Avos 1): "Accept a teacher upon yourself and remove yourself from doubt." If you accept upon yourself a teacher and have true *Emunas Chochamim*, you will remove yourself from Amalek, the gematria of which equals *safeik* (doubt), and merit to the ways of true *temimus*. Therefore, happy is the one who merits to humble himself before the true Tzaddikim of the generation, inculcating within himself Emunas Chochamim, for in this way he will merit to the traits of *temimus* and *peshitus* which in turn will enable him to be attached to Hashem *b'emes* (with truth) and with his whole heart. Happy is he and fortunate is his portion.

Mohorosh tied these ideas to our Parsha in the following way: We find in our Parsha the mitzvah of making the Ephod (an apron-like garment) worn by the Kohein Gadol (High Priest) as it is written (Shemos 28): "You shall make the Me'il (Robe) of the Ephod entirely of *techeiles* (turquoise wool).... It must be on Aharon in order to serve and his kol (this word has two meanings: voice and sound) will be heard when he enters the Sanctuary before Hashem and when he exits, so that he not die." [note: Dangling from around the entire hem of the Ephod were pomegranate-shaped tassels; and in between every two pomegranates was a golden bell, each with a ringer. There were seventy-two bells and seventy-two pomegranates.] Our Sages said (Talmud Eruvin 16b) "The Ephod atones for the sin of Loshon Harah (evil speech): let an object with a kol come and atone for an act done with the kol." We need to understand what is the Divine attribute of "measure for measure" in this: how does hearing the kol of the Kohein while he is performing the service atone for the kol of Loshon Harah? But according to the words of Rebbe Nachman we can understand it very well. The main Loshon Harah of the wicked, who come from the impure spiritual realm of Amalek, is the evil words they speak

3

about the Tzaddikim of the generation, to scoff at and mock them and their upright ways. In this way, they cool off people's desire to come close to the Tzaddikim as well as their desire to acquire the trait of *temimus* in serving Hashem. This is what is written about Amalek (Devarim 25): "That he happened (*karcha*) upon you on the way" [note: the word "*karcha*" has two meanings: "to happen upon you" and "to cool you off"] – therefore it was necessary to make the special priestly garments for Aharon the Kohein, the great Tzaddik - "for glory and splendor" (Shemos 28) – so that people will see the greatness and the splendor of the Tzaddik – and then "his *kol* will be heard when he enters the Sanctuary before Hashem" (ibid) – that is to say, people will listen to his voice and accept upon themselves his upright words of temimus until they too will serve Hashem with temimus. And this will contradict and nullify the evil words of Loshon Hara that the wicked speak about the true Tzaddik and his followers. Therefore, it is fitting that it is precisely a garment like this – a garment through which is fulfilled the verse, "His voice shall be heard" – that should atone for the voice of Loshon Harah, for the essential purpose of the priestly garments is to inspire the people to listen to and accept the words of the Kohein, the Tzaddik.

And this is also the connection to Parshas Zachor and the holy days of Purim. It is brought in the Baal HaTurim on our parsha that the word "*v'nishma* (will be heard)" is found three times in the entire Torah, Prophets and Writings: 1). In this week's parsha – "**v'nishma** kolo b'vo'o el hakodesh (his voice **will be heard** when he enters the Sanctuary before Hashem)", 2). (Shemos 24) "Col asher dibeir Hashem na'aseh **v'nishma** (Everything that Hashem has said we will do and **we will hear**", 3). (Ester 1) "**V'nishma** pisgam hamelech (And when the king's decree which he shall make **will be heard**)." We need to understand what the connection is between all three of these instances. According to the words of Rebbe Nachman it is clear. By implementing a means by which people will come to listen to the Kohein's voice – "**His voice will be heard** when he enters the Sanctuary before Hashem" – the people will merit to receive and accept all the words of the Holy Torah – both the Written and Oral Torah – with complete *temimus* and *peshitus*, which is the verse– "Everything that Hashem has said **we will do and we will hear**", and then all of the evil words of the wicked Haman, which he speaks against the Tzaddik Mordechai and against all Israel, will fall and evaporate like smoke, as our Sages said (Talmud Megillah 13b): "There was no one who knew how to speak *loshon hara* like Haman: He said to the king that Israel has no time to serve the king because they are always occupied with their religion, saying 'Today is Shabbos. Today is Passover'." These are days on which they go to

4

the Tzaddikim to learn from them the ways of *temimus*. Haman wanted to disgrace the honor of the Tzaddik in the eyes of Israel, until even Mordechai would end up bowing to him. But, Mordechai the Tzaddik was not fazed by him and he held fast to the ways of *temimus* until he subdued Haman completely. And the following words were fulfilled (Ester 1): "And when the king's decree which he shall make **will be heard** throughout his entire kingdom." (note: When the word "king" appears in the Megillah it refers to the King of the World, Hashem.) And Mordechai revealed and publicized the yoke of His Kingdom to everyone. Therefore, it was at that time that the Torah was first accepted by Israel out of love, as it is written (Ester 9): "The Jews confirmed and accepted upon themselves." And our Sages say on this verse (Talmud Shabbos 88a): "They confirmed what they had already accepted." And Rashi explains this to mean that they accepted the Torah with love when they saw the miracle of Purim. And this is the verse: "Everything that Hashem has said we will do and we will hear," and then they listened well to the voice of the Tzaddik, as it is written (Ester 9): "And his fame was spreading throughout all the provinces," thereby fulfilling the verse in our parsha, "His voice will be heard when he enters the Sanctuary before Hashem." We find that all three of these verses are closely intertwined and that they all reveal how Israel merited to hear the voice of the Tzaddik and to receive from him the ways of temimus. And Hashem should help us get close to the true Tzaddikim and to always listen to their holy voices until we see the blotting out of the name of Amalek and the flourishing of the glory of Israel, swiftly in our days. Amen v'amen.

5

Friday Night, Parshas Ki Sisa Shabbos Parah, 5766

Friday night, at the first Shabbos meal, Mohorosh Shlit"a spoke inspiring words based on Lekutei Mohoran, Part I, Lesson 133, which discusses the topic of "the light of the Tzaddik."

Rebbe Nachman says: "It is written (Mishlei 4): 'The path of the righteous is like the glow of sunlight that grows steadily brighter until the height of noonday.' For the sun itself, in its own place, is always shining the same, at the start of the day and at mid-day. The obscuring [of the light] is only due to the earth's intervening between people and the sun. Therefore, the light does not spread out so much at the beginning of the day, but only little by little, until it is spread out over the land. It is the same with regard to the Tzaddik. By himself he is always shining. The obstruction is due to those who receive the light and it is due to the intervening earth, namely, this world. For people are sunk in this world. Therefore, they are unable to receive the light of the Tzaddik. And this is the verse: 'The path of the righteous is like the glow of sunlight,' literally 'like the glow of sunlight': like the sun that is always shining, only that the obstruction is due to the earth blocking the light. So too, the Tzaddikim are always shining. It is only the earth – this world – that gets in the way of seeing their great light. And even though their light is very great, and the whole of this world is small and very inferior compared to their great light, nevertheless, it gets in the way and blocks us from seeing their light, as in the analogy of a small coin: if you hold it right against your eye, it will prevent you from seeing a great mountain, even though the mountain is thousands of times bigger than the small coin. But since the coin stands in front of your eyes, it blocks your vision until you do not see an object many times bigger than the coin. So too, when a person comes to this world, he remains sunk there in the vanities of the world, and it seems to him that there is nothing better for him than this. This small and puny world prevents him from seeing the great and exalted light of the Torah that is "many thousands of times bigger" than this world. And this is literally the metaphor of the sun: the earth blocks a person from seeing the great light of the sun, even though the sun is many times bigger than the earth. And all of this is because the world stands before his eyes and blocks him until he is unable to see the light of the Torah and the Tzaddikim, which is "thousands of times greater" than the world. However, if he moves the small obstruction away from his eyes, that is, he turns his eyes away from the [vanities of] the world and does not gaze at the world, but raises his head and lifts up his eyes and contemplates what is above this world that blocks and obstructs, then he will merit to see the great and exalted light of the Torah and the Tzaddikim, for truly, their light is "thousands and tens of thousands of times greater" than all of this world and its vanities, as stated before. It is only that this world stands before his eyes and does not allow him to turn his eyes upward to gaze upon the light of the Torah and the Tzaddikim, literally as in the analogy of the small coin that stands in front of his eyes and stops him from seeing a great mountain, etc. However, with just a little effort he can remove the coin from his eyes, and immediately, he will see the mountain that is bigger [than the coin]. It is literally the same with regard to the world and the Torah: just by moving something away, he can cause the world to move away from before his eyes and then he will merit to see the great light of the Torah and the Tzaddikim that shines in all the worlds with a very great light. Understand this well. Similarly, I have heard in the name of the Baal Shem Tov that he said, 'Oy! The world is filled with wondrous and awesome lights and secrets, and the small hand stands before the eyes and prevents a person from seeing great lights." (These are the words of Rebbe Nachman.)

Mohorosh explained that the light of the Tzaddikim shines in this world with a very sweet and wonderful radiance. And the person who merits to taste some of this light, his eyes will be opened with the blessed light of Hashem. And he literally experiences the taste of the Garden of Eden. When the first Man was created, the hidden light of the six days of creation was shining. And as long as he lived in the Garden of Eden, he was able to enjoy this light. He would look into this light and see from one end of the universe to the other. It was only after he sinned and was driven out of the Garden that this light was hidden and the world became dark for him. Since then, all following generations need to fix his sin and draw down the hidden light to this world once again. This is the service of the Tzaddikim in every generation, who give themselves over completely to finding Hashem in each and every detail of life until they once again draw down the hidden light to this world. This service is an aspect of the verse (Mishlei 4): "The path of the righteous is like the glow of sunlight that grows steadily brighter until the height of noonday." And the person who merits to draw close to them will also have some of this light drawn upon him and the days of his life will begin to shine with the blessed light of Hashem and he will experience a wondrous taste all the days of his life.

2

However, there are two factors which cause this light to be concealed from a person, namely, the two things mentioned above in the words of Rebbe Nachman: the small coin and the small hand "The small coin" is the pursuit of money. As soon as a person invests all of his mind and knowledge in the pursuit of money, and all of his activities are only aimed at increasing his wealth and possessions, it is already very difficult for him to see the light of the Tzaddik. For even the smallest coin placed in front of one's eyes will cause even the greatest mountain to be hidden from him. Of course, the money of a Jew is a very important thing, since he can perform mitzvos and acts of kindness with it, which expand the boundaries of holiness in the world; and if a person uses his money for holiness, he can do very great things with it. But, as soon as a person looks at money as something of substance with an existence independent of holiness, and wants to hoard his riches and stuff his pockets and becomes jealous and begrudging of other people's wealth, then the "small coin" blinds his eyes, making it impossible for him to see the light of the Tzaddik. Therefore, the first pre-requisite to opening one's eyes to the light of the Tzaddik is to raise one's vision above the money and to move the "small coin" away from one's eyes. Then, he will be able to truly see and comprehend the light of the Tzaddik.

The second obstruction is the "small hand". This is the phenomenon of scoffing at and mocking the words of the Tzaddik. This scoffing can be accomplished with a slight movement of the hand, for example, by making a slight waving motion with the hand, a person can convey the message that what he is hearing is sheer nonsense. This hand movement, which is the "small hand", is very dangerous for the following reason. When a person hears words of inspiration from the mouth of a Tzaddik and his heart is burning with passion for Hashem, he makes up his mind that from now on he will definitely be an *ish kasher* (an upright and honest person), and then he goes outside and bumps into a scoffer who asks him, "Where were you?" He says to him, "I was with a certain Tzaddik." And the scoffer asks him, "What did you hear there?" And he says, "I truly heard the words of the living G-d." And then the scoffer waves his "small hand" as if to say, "This is nothing but nothing." In this way, he cools the person down from all of the holy inspiration and passion that he received from the Tzaddik. We see that the "small hand" is a powerful way to cause the light of the Tzaddik to be hidden from the world. A person needs to be very strong not to be fazed at all by anyone who wants to discourage him and cool him down from drawing close to the Tzaddik. He shouldn't let it enter his ears nor let his eyes see any

3

attempt to draw him away from the Tzaddik. Then he will walk on a secure path and merit to enjoy the light of the Tzaddik.

On the other hand, we need to know with regard to drawing close to the Tzaddik, that we must also guard our "eyes" from being "blinded" by the greatness of the Tzaddik's light, just as we are careful not to be blinded by the light of the sun. Just as it is impossible to gaze at the light of the sun when it is blazing at noon, so too, in drawing close to the Tzaddik, it is impossible to look at everything he does without some kind of "covering" or "hiding-place", otherwise one's "eyes could be blinded", G-d forbid and he will no longer be able to "see" anything. Rather, one needs to know that he will not be able to understand all of the Tzaddik's ways. Neither must one do everything exactly the same way the Tzaddik does it. The Tzaddik has very lofty intentions in everything he does, and someone who tries to imitate him can end up "blinding his own eyes", G-d forbid. About this and similar matters the Sages say (Talmud Chagiga 113a): "Do not seek what is beyond you." The main thing is to walk with simple faith and wholeheartedness, to believe that all the words of the Tzaddik are not simple and to observe and contemplate all of the revealed ways of the Tzaddik, such as his Torah and prayer and to emulate him in these ways, e.g. to be very diligent in learning Torah and to increase in prayer and hisbodedus. And then the great light of the Tzaddik will be drawn upon him and his eyes will shine with the light of Hashem "that grows steadily brighter until the height of noonday." Happy is he and fortunate is his lot.

Mohorosh connected the above ideas to our Parsha in the following way: At the end of the Parsha, it is written that the skin of Moshe Rebbeinu's face had become radiant when Hashem had spoken to him on Mt. Sinai immediately before he came down with the second Tablets. This is the matter of the revelation of the light of the Tzaddik as discussed above, as it is written (Shemos 34): "Aharon and all the children of Israel saw Moshe, and behold! - the skin of his face had become radiant; and they feared to approach him." Moshe Rebbeinu merited this radiance when Hashem placed him in a cave on Mt. Sinai and then shielded him with His "hand". (Rashi on verse 29: From where did Moshe merit this radiance? Our Sages say [Midrash Tanchuma 37] that it resulted from the cave when Hashem placed His hand upon Moshe's face [Shemos 33:22].) For when the Divine presence was revealed to Moshe in the cave, he merited a supreme cleaving to Hashem until he was completely included in Him, as it is brought in the words of Rebbe Nachman (Lekutei Mohoran, Part I, Lesson 54) that the word for 'cave' – **ma'arah** – is

4

the language of cleaving as in the verse (Kings I, 7:36) *"k'ma'ar ish v'loyos* as one is attached to his compainon And this drew upon Moshe the supernal light until his face shone with the light of the Shechinah (Divine Presence). And whoever drew close to Moshe merited to see this light. But, the wicked and the scoffers in Israel, who were ruled by "the small hand", did not merit to see this light, for if they had seen it, they would have been completely nullified by it. Only those who humbled themselves before Moshe Rebbeinu with wholeheartedness and simplicity, and believed that all of Moshe's words were not simple, merited to see this light. And this is the allusion in Hashem placing His "hand" upon Moshe's face and from this, Moshe's face became radiant. It was precisely the "hand"; for it was revealed to Moshe how "the supernal hand" nullifies the "small hand" of this world that hides the light of the Tzaddik. And when a person moves the "small hand" away and always contemplates the "hand of Hashem" which is found in everything, he receives the ability to overcome the wicked and the scoffers and to see the light of the Tzaddik. And Moshe Rebbeinu received the rays of light precisely with the second set of Tablets, which was immediately after he succeeded in gaining forgiveness for Israel for the sin of the Golden Calf. For this sin was due to the great abundance of silver and gold they had, which is the "small coin", as our holy Sages have said (Talmud Berachos 32a) on the verse (Devarim 1) *"V'Di zahav* (zahav is Hebrew for gold)": "Moshe said before the Holy One Blessed is He, 'Master of the world, it was the silver and gold that you bestowed upon Israel until they said '*Di* (enough)' that caused them to make the calf." But, as soon as they removed from their eyes the "small coin", they could see the great light of the Tzaddik that shone throughout the entire world. This is also the allusion in the beginning of the parsha regarding the mitzvah of the Half Shekel, as it is written (Shemos 30): "This they shall give". And Rashi explains: "He showed Moshe a kind of coin made of fire, the weight of which was half a shekel and said to him, 'Like this shall they give.' " For Hashem showed Moshe Rebbeinu that the rectification for the "small coin" which blinds the eyes from seeing the light of the Tzaddik who is the *Rosh B'nei Yisrael* (the Head of the Children of Israel) which is hinted to in the verse (ibid) *"Ki sisa es 'Rosh B'nei Yisrael'* (When you take a census of the Children of Israel; literally, "When you lift up the head of the Children of Israel"), the first letters of which spell *"Rebbe"* (Lekutei Mohoran, Part I, Lesson 111) - the rectification for this is "the coin of fire", which changes the physical *kesef* (money) into spiritual money, that is, the *kisufim* (yearning and longing) for Hashem, and then a person will merit to see the light of the Tzaddik in truth. [Note: The word for money – *kesef* – comes from the word *kisufim* which means "longing or yearning" as in the

5

verse (Bereishis 31): "Because you have greatly longed *(nichsof nichsafta)* for your father's house."]

And this is the verse: "Moshe finished speaking with them and placed a mask on his face." We need to understand why Moshe Rebbeinu needed to cover his face with a mask. Those who saw his great light and benefited from his radiance, their days were illuminated with the light of the Tzaddik and they didn't need a mask. And those who did not merit seeing his great light saw nothing. If so, why was the mask necessary? According to the words of bbe Nachman we can understand it very well. When a person draws close to the Tzaddik, a mask and a covering are needed to protect his "eyes" from being "blinded" by the abundance of light, because not every time can a person see and understand the light of the Tzaddik. Only when Moshe Rebbeinu would speak with the Jewish people and reveal to them the teachings of Hashem, would they look at the light of his face, and the rays of light would shine on their souls. But, at all other times, Moshe Rebbeinu would cover his face with a mask so that the people would not stumble through the abundance of light. And all of this is due to the power of the *Samech-Mem* (the Satan) that strengthens evil and impurity in the world and causes the wicked and the scoffers to mock and ridicule the Tzaddik's light. For the Tzaddik unites the Next World with This World and brings Hashem's light from all the upper worlds down into This World. And this unification is represented by the combination of the two letters – *Vav* and *Hey* - of Hashem's four-letter name. The *Vav* (numerical value 6) represents the six higher *Sefiros* from *Chessed* to *YeSod*. And the *Hey* is Malchus (Kingship, the last Sefirah), which is the ability to perceive Hashem from within the physicality of This World. And the Tzaddik is constantly involved in bringing both worlds together. Corresponding to this, the *Samech-Mem* is trying to disconnect the two worlds and conceal the light of the Tzaddik. And sometimes he accomplishes this precisely through an over-abundance of light, which seduces a person to look at the Tzaddik and think about his ways with a jaundiced eye, as if he needs to understand all the ways of the Tzaddik despite his deficient knowledge and understanding. And in this way, his "eyes become blind", G-d forbid. Therefore, the Hebrew word for the mask with which Moshe Rebbeinu covered his face is *masveh (Mem-Samech-Vav-Hey)*. It is composed of the two pairs of letters mentioned above: The first two letters – *Mem and Samech* – are the same letters which make up the name of the force of evil in the world (the *Samach-Mem*) and the last two letters are *Vav* and *Hey*, which represent the upper and lower worlds, respectively. So the word *masveh* hints to the fact that the *Samach-Mem* wants to separate the Next World (*Vav*) from

6

This World (*Hey*). And this is why the Tzaddik needs to cover his face with a *masveh*. The masveh gives every person who wants to draw close to the Tzaddik the ability to benefit from the Tzaddik's great light. And Hashem should help us to be close to the true Tzaddikim and to draw upon ourselves their great light until we merit to ascend and be included in Hashem completely, now and forever. *Amen v'amen.*

7

Friday Night, Parshas Vayakhel - Pekuday
Shabbos HaChodesh 5764

Friday night, at the first Shabbos meal, Mohorosh Shlit"a spoke inspiring words based on Lekutei Mohoran, Part II, Lesson 68, which discusses the nature of the Tzaddik and how he is found "above and below".

Rebbe Nachman says: "The essential wholeness of the Tzaddik is that he can be above and below, that he can show the one who is elevated and who thinks he is on a high level, that it is just the opposite. Likewise, for the one who is on the lowest level, literally in the earth, the Tzaddik will be able to show him that, on the contrary, he is near *(samuch)* to Hashem. And this wholeness is necessary for the Tzaddik to have, and without it, he is not a Tzaddik at all." (These are the words of Rebbe Nachman.)

Mohorosh explained that Rebbe Nachman reveals to us in this lesson a very important idea about the nature of the Tzaddik, namely, that the true Tzaddik is "above and below" simultaneously. He is flying in the upper worlds of lofty thoughts and perceptions. He is an expert in the most exalted knowledge. But he is also below in this world. He leads a household with a wife and children. He is an expert of the human condition. And he is able to give people good advice in numerous areas of life. There is no perfection at all in always being bound only to the upper worlds without knowing how to bring oneself down to human beings and how to infuse them with perceptions of G-d. For in this case, he is a "Tzaddik for himself", but not for others. This is not a *Tzaddik Emes* (a true Tzaddik). A *Tzaddik Emes* is one who can bring himself down from all of his lofty spiritual perceptions in order to engage with people down in this world and offer them good advice so that they too can elevate themselves. This was the level of *Moshe Rabbeinu*, about whom it is written (Shemos 19): "And Moshe went down from the mountain unto the people." He was able to bring himself down from his powerful cleaving to Hashem he had achieved on Mt. Sinai – "forty days and forty nights, bread he did not eat, and water he did not drink" – and immediately he was able to reach the most simple among the people, to listen to their concerns and to (Devarim 1) "judge between a man and his brother or his litigant". However, most people cannot comprehend this. It seems to them that a Tzaddik needs to be, for the most part, removed and separated from more "mundane" human activities. And if he does work with people and happens to be an expert in human nature and current events, then this is a sign that he must not be a Tzaddik, as is the custom among some leaders and famous people, that they have very limited dealings with human beings, and their assistants and secretaries do not allow people to make contact with them. And this is wrongly considered by some to be a sign of the Tzaddik's perfection. However, Rebbe Nachman reveals to us in this lesson that this is not so. It is actually just the opposite. The essential perfection of the Tzaddik is measured according to his ability to bring himself down to human beings – to be "above and below" simultaneously, i.e. it is measured by two criteria: a). His ability to make known to those who "dwell above" (those who have achieved and believe they have reached very high levels in the service of Hashem) that they know nothing, and b). His ability to make known to those who "dwell below" (those who believe they are on the lowest level) that Hashem is very close *(samuch)* to them. And only a Tzaddik with these two abilities can be called a "true Tzaddik."

Mohorosh explained that this was the flaw of Korach and his assembly. They could not comprehend how Moshe and Aharon could maintain these two levels simultaneously. For how was it possible for *Moshe Rabbeinu* to be on Mt. Sinai and reach awesome spiritual perceptions, and immediately afterwards come down and judge between people and be deeply involved in their physical needs? And how was it possible for *Aharon HaKohein* to enter the Holy of Holies, burn the incense and perform the other services, and afterwards step outside and immediately engage in making peace between a man and his wife and between a man and his friend, which for the most part required Aharon to lower and disgrace himself to the extreme, all for the sake of making peace between people? And this is the explantion of the verse which speaks about Korach's assembly (Tehillim 106): "The were jealous of Moshe in the camp [and] of Aharon, the holy one of Hashem." The jealousy of Korach's assembly stemmed from Moshe's being "in the camp", i.e. how was it possible that Moshe could be on Mt. Sinai and reach the highest spiritual levels and then immediately come down and be "in the camp" – i.e. (Shemos 19) "from the mountain to the people"? And they were jealous of Aharon for the same reason. For how could the "holy one of Hashem", who performed the service inside the Holy of Holies, immediately involve himself with making peace between a man and his wife and between a man and his fellow? How could these two levels be harmonized? This is very hard for people to understand. But, Rebbe Nachman reveals to us that it is precisely this double quality, two things that are really one, which is the perfection of

2

the Tzaddik and without it, he cannot be called a true Tzaddik at all. Happy is the one who merits to come close to a Tzaddik like this.

Mohorosh connected the above ideas to our Parsha in the following way. Our Parsha records the building of the Tabernacle by Betzalel and Oholiav, as it is written (Shemos 35:30-33): "See, Hashem has called by name, Betzalel son of Uri son of Hur, of the tribe of Yehuda. He filled him with the spirit of G-d, with wisdom, insight and knowledge, and with every craft – to weave designs, to work with gold, silver and copper; stone-cutting for setting, and wood-carving – to perform every craft of design." And immediately afterward it is written (Shemos 35:34-35): "He gave him the ability to teach, him and Oholiav, son of *Achi-samach* of the tribe of Dan (once again the word *samach,* which has a few meanings: to support, to lay one's hands on, or to be near; and "Ahi" means "my brother"); He filled them with a wise heart, etc." First, Hashem commanded it should be made by Betzalel son of Uri son of Hur, of the tribe of Yehuda, and the Torah recounts his praises in great detail ("He filled him with the spirit of G-d, etc"). The very next verse after Betzalel was commanded to build the Tabernacle says that Oholiav should join him, as it is written: "He gave him the ability to teach, him and Oholiav, son of *Achi-samach*, of the tribe of Dan; He filled them with a wise heart, etc." Rashi has already explained this verse (Shemos 35:34): "He [Oholiav] was of the tribe of Dan, of one of the lowest of the tribes, of the sons of the handmaids and yet the Omnipresent equated him with Betzalel with respect to building the Tabernacle even though Betzalel's tribe, Yehuda, was among the greatest of all the tribes, in order to fulfill what is says in the verse (Iyov 34): "He regarded not the rich more than the poor." We need to understand why Hashem commanded that the Tabernacle should be built in this fashion. In other words, why was it necessary to join Oholiav to Betzalel in the building of the Tabernacle? According to the words of Rebbe Nachman we can understand it very well. The perfection of the Tzaddik is precisely when he is "above and below" with the power to connect the greatest one in Israel to the smallest one. And this is exactly the idea of erecting the Tabernacle. It was in order to prepare a place for the *Shechinah* (Divine Presence) to reside near each and every Jew, from the greatest of the great to the smallest of the small. Therefore, at the very beginning of the construction of the Tabernacle, we find the command to Betzalel to build the Tabernacle; Betzalel, one of the elite of Israel, of the tribe of Yehuda, one of the greatest of the tribes, who was called Betzalel because he was so close to Hashem that Moshe said to him (Talmud Berachot 55a), "You must have been in G-d's shadow *(b'tzel el)*," and of whom it is said, "He [Hashem] filled him with the spirit of G-d."

3

And immediately after appointing Betzalel there was the command to join to him Oholiav son of Ahisamach of the tribe of Dan, one of the lowest of the tribes, to teach that it was necessary at that very time to be "above and below" as well as to bring near all those who were still below "in the earth". These people are in the category of the camp of Dan, who is called (Bamidbar 10): "The rear guard [literally, the gatherer] of all the camps," who were partly composed of those who were ejected by the cloud (see the Baal Haturim on Bamidbar 10:25). For the completeness of the "Tabernacle of the Tzaddik" is built upon these two categories and one alone is no perfection at all. For the Tzaddik needs to teach the most elite that they are just "b'tzel el (in the shadow of G-d)", that they still have room to go higher and higher; and to teach those who are on the bottom floor and who think they are far from Hashem, that "**li av** ('I have a Father', from Oho-**li-av**), that Hashem is the Av Harachaman (the Father of Compassion), and that He is **samuch** (next to) and very close to them, and He is ready to support them (li'**smoch** – to support) in all of their falls. And this is *Oholiav* son of *Ahisamach*. Therefore, through building the Tabernacle in this fashion there will be space for each and every Jew, on whatever level he may be, to enter within the bounds of holiness, and to attain divine perceptions according to their level and situation. And Hashem should help us be close to the true Tzaddikim and to enter the wondrous Tabernacle that Hashem is building for the souls of Israel, until we merit to return in perfect repentance before Him, to be included in Him completely, now and forever. Amen v'amen.

Seudah Shlishis, Parshas Vayakhel - Pekuday Shabbos HaChodesh 5764

At the third Shabbos meal, Mohorosh Shlit"a spoke inspiring words based on Lekutei Mohoran, Part I, Lesson 155, which discusses the importance of Emunah and patience.

Rebbe Nachman says: "Sadness is very harmful. And a person's not traveling to the Tzaddik is due to sadness and lethargy. Also, his not praying properly comes from sadness and laziness, specifically from a deficit in Emunah. Certainly, if a person has perfect Emunah and believes that Hashem stands over him and listens to every word that comes from his mouth and pays

4

attention to the sound of his prayer, then, surely, there would be no sadness, laziness or lethargy in his prayer and he would certainly pray properly. However, the main confusion in prayer comes from a deficit in Emunah. Therefore, laziness and sadness fall upon him and confound his prayer. For the main cause of sadness and laziness is a lack of Emunah. And this is an aspect of "*erech apayim* (being slow to anger)", that is, not being afraid of anything, and not obsessing over any lack or confusion he may have in his service [of Hashem]. Rather, he only does what he has to do. And one can merit all this through Emunah. (These are the words of Rebbe Nachman).

Mohorosh explained that the root of the foundation of life is Emunah – to believe with clear and pure faith that there is no absolute existence other than Hashem and everything that a person goes through, either for good or the opposite, all is from Him alone. For there is no small movement that is not guided by the providence of Hashem and there is no absolute existence besides Him. And with this knowledge, a person is redeemed from all of his suffering, because Emunah infuses a person with great patience to be able to endure whatever he goes through in life. And it also puts happiness into his heart to give him courage to withstand whatever happens to him. This is not so for the one who has no emunah. He is constantly filled with sadness and laziness, and depression overpowers him due to the tribulations that pass over him. And he has no consolation from all of his suffering, for he eats himself up from all of the troubles he has to endure. He is also angry with Hashem, G-d forbid, because he can't understand why he has so many problems in his life. This is the difference between a *lev nishbar* (broken heart) and *atzvus* (sadness). A broken heart is when a person truly feels the huge chasm between himself and Hashem and so he prays and pleads with Hashem that He should bring him near to His service. And then he is like a child who longs for and constantly strives to see his father, as he feels the pain of being separated from him. All he wants is to be close to his father. This is not the case with sadness. Sadness derives from anger towards Hashem, G-d forbid, when a person has difficult questions in his heart about why he has to go through what he has to go through. And he just cannot make peace between himself and the reality of life and accept that this is the will of Hashem. Therefore, he falls into laziness and sadness and becomes unable to serve Hashem at all, for it seems to him that his prayers are worthless and that Hashem is not interested in hearing him at all. But this is a very grave error, since it is certain that Hashem yearns for the prayer of every creature and He wants to help a person at every moment of his life. But Hashem does examine whether a person will strengthen himself with more Emunah and recognize

5

that his entire hope and salvation is in Hashem's hands alone. And then, as soon as a person strengthens himself with Emunah and has patience no matter what he goes through, then Hashem reveals Himself to him and saves him from all of his suffering. Therefore, happy is the one who strengthens himself with more Emunah and doesn't become downhearted at all from what passes over him in life. Instead, he will bring a powerful happiness and patience into himself and tolerate whatever comes his way. For then he will merit to live a good and sweet life in this world and the next, forever. Happy is he and fortunate is his lot.

Mohorosh connected these ideas to our Parsha in the following way. Our Parsha describes the construction and erection of the Tabernacle, as it is written (Shemos 40:17): "It was in the first month of the second year on the first of the month that the Tabernacle was erected. Moshe erected the Tabernacle; he put down its sockets and emplaced its planks and inserted its bars, and erected its pillars, etc...So Moshe completed the work (verse 33)." But, the very next verse says (verse 34): "The cloud covered the Tent of Meeting, and the glory of Hashem filled the Tabernacle. Moshe could not enter the Tent of Meeting, for the cloud rested upon it, and the glory of Hashem filled the Tabernacle." We need to understand what is the significance of the cloud covering the Tabernacle until even Moshe Rabbeinu was not able to enter the Tent of Meeting. And what does this teach us immediately after the Torah has described in great detail the entire order of the setting up of the Tabernacle? According to the words of Rebbe Nachman we can understand it very well. It is explained in the Holy Zohar (Introduction to the Tikkunim) that the entire anatomy and physiology of the human being is patterned after the structure and composition of the Tabernacle and the Tent of Meeting. The Tabernacle had within it the Holy Ark, the Ark Cover, the Partition that separated between the Holy and the Holy of Holies, the Menorah and the Table. And all of this is reflected in the human being himself, as it is written (Shemos 25): "They shall make a Sanctuary for me, so that I may dwell **b'socham** ('among them', but also means 'within them'). "*B'socho* (within **it**)", it doesn't say, rather "within **them**", which means within each and every Jew, for the Shechinah rests within each one, and with even greater intensity within the Tzaddikim who diligently work on themselves to sanctify and purify all of their limbs and organs until they actually become sanctified with the holiness of the Tabernacle, as it is brought in the words of Rabbi Moshe Kordovero zal that there are Tzaddikim in every generation within whom the Shechinah rests as it was in the Tabernacle and

6

the Temple. And when people travel to them, it is literally like going to the Tabernacle and the Temple.

The life of a person is certainly filled with many tests in terms of what passes over him in life. On the one hand, Hashem reveals Himself to him and the holy Shechinah rests within him. On the other hand, all sorts of difficult and heavy tests pass over him, and Heaven tests him as to where he is holding in his Emunah. Therefore, immediately after Moshe had completed setting up the Tabernacle, the holy Torah reveals to us that the cloud covered the entire Tent of Meeting all around until even Moshe was unable to enter it, for the cloud represents the concepts of "holding back" and hiding. The cloud and thick fog were a form of *"choshech"* (darkness) and *choshech* is the language of "holding back", as it is written (Bereishis 22): "You [Avraham] have not held back *(chasachta)* your son, your only one." But a person who has the "knowledge of Moshe", knows that also within the obstruction and the cloud rests Hashem, as it is written (Shemos 20): "And Moshe approached the thick cloud where G-d was." The person who has this "knowledge of Moshe" approaches the thick cloud, for he knows that Hashem is also there (Lekutei Mohoran, Part I, Lesson 115). And the Tzaddikim know very well that it is precisely when they ascend and draw close to perceptions of G-dliness, that they need a cloud and a covering with which to cover their eyes, that they should not see too much and blind their eyes, G-d forbid. This was the level of Moshe Rabbeinu – the more he rose upwards to higher and higher levels, he was able to find Hashem there (Lekutei Mohoran, Part II, Lesson 82), because he had the very great wisdom to know how to "cover his eyes" in order not to be "blinded", G-d forbid, by the abundance of light, as sadly happened to Elisha ben Abuya - that it was precisely through his ascending all the way up to Heaven and entering the "Spiritual Gardens", that he became confused and fell into heresy (Talmud Chagiga 14b). Because he came too close to the light, his eyes became damaged and blinded, like a person who gazes directly into the sun damages his eyes. Therefore, the cloud and the covering are great benefits for the Tzaddikim, for this protects them from the abundance of light. Therefore, it is brought in the words of Rebbe Nachman (Lekutei Mohoran, Part II, Lesson 5) that the word for cloud - "*anan (Ayin-Nun-Nun)*" are the first letters of the verse (Tehillim 47): "*Nidivei Amim Ne'asafu* (The nobles {converts} among the peoples gathered, {joining} the people of the G-d of Abraham)." For the person who has a giving heart and strengthens his heart with added Emunah, and is careful not to fall into sadness and bitterness, which could shatter his heart, G-d forbid, is the one who is able to enter into the *anan*, i.e. foggy and dimly lit situations where the

7

light of holiness is very weak. And he is blessed with the ability to gather up all the sparks of holiness dispersed among the nations and bring them to faith in Hashem. Therefore, it was precisely after the Tabernacle was erected, which hints to the resting of the Shechinah within each and every Jew, that the holy Torah reveals to us that surrounding the Tabernacle certainly rests a huge cloud, until even Moshe Rebbeinu at first could not enter into the Tabernacle. But in the end it is written (Bamidbar 7): "When Moshe entered the Tent of Meeting," and as Rashi explains on the verse (Shemos 40:35): "And Moshe was not able to come into the Tent of Meeting: 'As long as the cloud rested upon it, he was not able to enter the Tent of Meeting, but as soon as the cloud lifted he entered and spoke with Hashem." For the person who has this "knowledge of Moshe", knows not to run away from the "Tent" because of the "cloud", but he approaches and faces the thick cloud where Hashem is, and he will find Him also within the cloud and the obstruction. And then the cloud will lift and the Shechinah will be revealed to an even greater extent than before. And Hashem should help us merit clear and pure Emunah until we find Him within each and every detail of life, and from this will come the redemption that should be revealed speedily in our days, and then holy emunah will be revealed to all who walk the earth. May Hashem let us see it with our own eyes, speedily in our days. Amen v'amen.

8

Seudah Shlishis, Parshas Vayikra 5764

At the third Shabbos meal, Mohorosh Shlit"a spoke inspiring words based on Lekutei Mohoron, Part I, Lesson 280, which discusses the secret of a Din Torah (a legal dispute that is decided in Jewish court).

Rebbe Nachman says: "Know! The need to appear in court to be judged in a Din Torah is a punishment and reproof that the Torah gives a person. For in truth, doing business is "Torah", just as studying the laws that relate to business is "Torah". For example, learning the laws that apply to trading a donkey for a cow is of course "Torah". All the more so, actually doing business with another person by trading a donkey for a cow is most certainly "Torah", because the latter is actually practicing the Torah. Therefore, when doing business, one needs to connect his thoughts only to the Torah and to the laws that are enclothed in all the details of the business. And he who uproots his business from the Torah – detaching his business from the laws of the Torah - is punished afterwards in that he needs to be judged in a Din Torah. And then he needs to return and bring back all of the facts – all of the thoughts and all of the dealings that he had at the time he did business, from beginning to end – to the laws of the Torah. That is, he needs to go back and recount it all to the judges and they will issue a Psak Din (Torah Judgment) on this. It turns out that Torah has been made from all of his business dealings. And this is the rebuke that the Torah is giving him for uprooting his business from the Torah and for thinking there is no Torah in his business. Therefore, his punishment is that he needs to come before a Din Torah in order to bring back all of the details of his business dealings and make Torah from them. And now they show him that all business is Torah, for everything has now become a Din Torah (These are the words of Rebbe Nachman.)"

Mohorosh explained that in this lesson Rebbe Nachman reveals to us the secret of a Din Torah. People think that the purpose of a Din Torah is only to settle a monetary dispute or the like between two people, where one claims his fellow owes him such and such, and his friend claims it is not so, and the judge needs to decide who is right. In truth, there is in a Din Torah much more than this. There is an inner secret in a Din Torah, for Hashem's G-dliness is treasured up within each and every detail of creation. The root of the life-force of the inanimate, plant, animal and human worlds, of absolutely everything, is the G-dliness that is enclothed in them. And the main service of a person is to find the G-dliness in each thing and to connect his thoughts to Hashem through each thing. And this is the subject of learning Halacha (Torah law) and Shulchan Aruch (Code of Jewish Law), which teach a person how to find the G-dliness within all of the details of life. The Shulchan Aruch reveals to us how there is Torah and Halacha in inanimate objects. For example, it is forbidden to dig a pit in the ground in a public area and say that it is not your responsibility if someone were to accidentally fall into it. For the Torah reveals to us that a pit dug in a public area becomes yours and you are responsible for any damages that it causes. We also have all of the laws of plant life, such as kilaim (the prohibition against mixing and planting together different species of plants), orlah (the prohibition against using fruit from the first three years of a tree), trumos (crop tithes to the priestly class) and maaseros (various other crop tithes). With regard to animals, there are all of the laws of both domesticated and wild animals – which are kosher and which are not. And with regard to human beings, there are all of the laws between man and his fellow man. We find that the Shulchan Aruch is the life-force of the Jew, as the Chazon Ish zt"l once said that the Shulchan Aruch is the *"Urim v'Tumim"* of the Jew, for it calls out and reveals to each Jew how the will of Hashem is treasured up within each detail of creation. (Note: The *Urim v'Tumim* is a piece of parchment containing G-d's Ineffable Name that was placed inside the High Priest's Breastplate; it would cause the letters on the Breastplate to glow; by combining the letters in the correct order, the High Priest would know G-d's answers to important national questions.)

When a person is involved in any kind of business but forgets to search for Hashem's glory in it, then the Torah will rebuke him and force him to go back and connect his thoughts to the Torah. And this is done by the Torah summoning him to come before the judges to be judged in a Din Torah. Then he needs to bring all of the deeds, words and thoughts that he had at the time he did business to the Din Torah. And the judges make Torah and Halacha from all of them. We find that the person revisits all that transpired and begins to understand how there is Torah and Halacha in all of his interests and business dealings. And in this way, the blemish he created by tearing himself away from the Torah at the time he did business is rectified. Through a Din Torah it is all rectified, for the judges show him how there is Torah in every detail. We see that in addition to the judges settling a dispute by having the money return to its rightful owner, a second aspect of the business transaction is rectified – the blemish of forgetting that Hashem's G-dliness is within his business dealings. And now he goes back and finds the Torah that exists in

2

every detail, which is truly the main purpose of creation. Therefore, happy is the one who merits to find Hashem's G-dliness within all of the details of life, for then it will be a life of Torah and true attachment to Hashem. Happy is he and fortunate is his portion.

Mohorosh connected these ideas to our Parsha in the following way. It is written (Vayikra 5): "If a person sins and wrongfully deviates from Hashem and denies to his friend the possession of a keepsake placed in his trust or, a deposit [regarding money that was loaned or in partnership,] or theft [claiming that something was stolen,] or, oppressed [he withheld wages from] his friend." Let's try to understand the connection between the beginning of the verse – 'If a person sins and wrongfully deviates from Hashem" and the end of the verse – "and denies to his friend"? This verse deals with the laws between man and his fellow man. If so, then why does the verse begin, "If a person sins and wrongfully deviates from Hashem", which seems to be speaking about laws between man and G-d? But according to the words of Rebbe Nachman we can understand it very well. The entire matter of a Din Torah and the monetary disputes between people both originate in a person's forgetting that Hashem's glory is within his business. And so the Torah rebukes him by forcing him to retrace his thoughts through the Torah. We find that it is indeed a matter of "If a person sins and wrongfully deviates from Hashem," as he forgot to search for and find His glory within his business dealings and as a result he came to a Din Torah. "And denies to his friend the possession of a keepsake placed in his trust," for all of the laws between man and his fellow man go hand in hand with the laws between man and G-d and it is forbidden to separate them at all, for it is impossible to be a truly sincere and upright person unless the two are harmonized. If a person is a brilliant scholar and a treasure chest of knowledge, and is precise in his performance of all of the mitzvos between man and G-d with great precision, but with regard to the laws between man and his fellow man he is very careless and negligent; and he speaks badly about others and is careless with their money and possessions, then what is his brilliance and expertise worth? Therefore, happy is the one who does not mislead himself at all, who searches for and finds Hashem's glory within each and every detail of the days of his life, in every place and in every time. For then, he will fulfill the ultimate purpose of creation. And Hashem should help us attach ourselves to Him in truth and simplicity and we will merit to return in perfect repentance before Him until we are included in Him completely, now and forever. Amen v'amen.

3

Friday Night, Parshas Tzav, Shabbos HaGadol 5764

Friday night, at the first Shabbos meal, Mohorosh Shlit"a spoke inspiring words based on *Lekutei Mohoran*, Part II, Lesson 77, which speaks about sweetening harsh judgments through the holiness of eating.

Rebbe Nachman says: "Through eating with holiness and fear of Heaven, the pain that passes over a person everyday is sweetened. For every Jew, even a great Tzaddik, must have some pain everyday. But through eating with holiness and fear of Heaven a sweetening is accomplished, so that the pain should not grow too strong, G-d forbid. For through eating with holiness, the mouth enters the category of 'the stature of *Adam* (the first Man)', which is an aspect of (*Shemos* 4): 'Who gave *adam* (man) a mouth'. For one whose eating is not done with holiness, G-d forbid, his mouth is literally like an animal. But, when he eats with holiness, his mouth causes him to enter the category of 'the stature of *Adam*', and in this way the judgments are sweetened." (These are the words of Rebbe Nachman.)

Mohorosh explained that Rebbe Nachman reveals to us in this lesson the great power of eating with holiness and with awe of Heaven. For when a person eats with holiness and in a dignified manner, he takes on the stature of "*Adam*", which is the category of (*Shemos* 4): "Who gave man a mouth", since it is the mouth that makes him an "*adam*". And then he receives a holy mind which enables him to sweeten the pain and suffering that could pass over him, G-d forbid. Against one's will, some pain and suffering pass over a person everyday. For due to a person's freewill as well as having to go through tests in life, Hashem sends every person every day some pain and suffering in order to arouse him to repent and to correct his deeds. And when he eats with holiness and in a dignified manner, he draws upon himself a holy mind and he sweetens his pain and suffering so that he is not harmed by them, G-d forbid. But, if a person does not eat with holiness and dignity, he takes on the form of an "animal" that has no knowledge, that pounces, tears and eats, and then much pain and suffering are drawn upon him, G-d forbid. Therefore, one needs to be very careful to eat with the proper holiness, and then all of the pain and suffering will be sweetened for him completely.

The first requirement of eating with holiness is to be very careful about the *kashrus* of the food. There should be absolutely no doubts about its *kashrus*, for through eating forbidden foods, G-d forbid, a person's mind is badly damaged, and he becomes like an animal. So this is the first requirement. Next, even when he eats perfectly kosher food, he needs to eat with holiness and with great dignity, and he should picture in his mind that an important person is sitting at the table and watching him eat. As Rebbe Nachman one said (*Chayei Mohoran* #515): "Regarding the holiness of eating, it is necessary for a person to imagine that an important person is sitting at the table, for then he will certainly be very careful to eat in a very dignified way." And when a person eats slowly, with deliberation and with dignity, he draws upon himself a holy mind that can extinguish all kinds of pain and suffering. And then, he can also merit to be illuminated by the greatest desire, which is to yearn for Hashem with a very powerful longing (*Lekutei Mohoran*, II, Lesson 7). It is precisely through eating that he will merit to ascend and cleave to Him in truth. Therefore, happy is the one who merits to eat with the proper holiness and with great dignity, for all types of pain and suffering will be sweetened for him and he will merit to cleave to Hashem with a true and eternal attachment. Happy is he and fortunate is his lot.

Mohorosh connected these ideas to our Parsha in the following way. It is written (*Vayikra* 6): "*A permanent fire shall remain aflame on the altar; it shall not be extinguished.*" We can say that perhaps the words of Rebbe Nachman are hinted to in this verse. Our holy Sages have said (*Talmud Menachos* 97a): "A person's table is like the *mizbe'ach* (the Altar in the Holy Temple). When the *Beis Hamikdash* (Holy Temple) was standing, the *mizbe'ach* would atone for him. And now that the *Beis Hamikdash* is not standing, a person's table atones for him." But this is only when he eats with the proper holiness and purity. And this is the verse "**A permanent fire shall remain aflame on the altar**"; that is, a person will always kindle a holy fire in his heart when he sits down to eat at his table which is compared to the *mizbe'ach*. In this way, all of the *klipos* (negative spiritual forces) will be burnt and consumed and all of the harsh judgments will be sweetened for him. "**It shall not be extinguished**" from the Altar - through not extinguishing the holy fire (the holiness and dignity) on the *mizbe'ach* (a person's table), that is, by always eating with the proper holiness and purity, he will draw upon himself all types of blessings. Moreover, through eating with holiness, he becomes illuminated with the greatest desire, i.e. the powerful yearning for Hashem. We find that the "fire of the *mizbe'ach*", which is eating with holiness, helps to ensure that the fire of holiness in our hearts will "not be extinguished". Instead, it will always burn for Hashem with tremendous enthusiasm. May Hashem help us attain the proper holiness in our eating and

2

may He sweeten for us all of our pain and suffering until we merit to cleave to Him in truth and simplicity all the days of our lives, now and forever. Amen v'amen.

3

Seudah Shlishis, Parshas Tzav, Shabbos HaGadol 5766

At the third Shabbos meal, Mohorosh Shlit"a spoke inspiring words on the significance of the Shabbos before Pesach which is known as *Shabbos Hagadol* ("The Great Shabbos"). He also spoke about Elijah the prophet based on Lekutei Mohoran, Part I, Lesson 117.

It is written in this week's *Haftarah* (Malachi 3): "Behold! I am sending to you Elijah the prophet before the coming of the great *(Hagadol)* and awesome day of Hashem." Our rabbis give many reasons for why we call the Shabbos before Pesach *"Shabbos Hagadol"*. One of the reasons is that it is named after the word *Hagadol* in this verse, since during the entire month of Nissan and especially around Pesach time we feel a special yearning for the coming of Elijah the prophet who will announce the redemption, as our holy Sages have said (Talmud Rosh Hashanah 11a): "In the month of Nissan our forefathers in Egypt were redeemed and in Nissan we will be redeemed in the future." And a verse that shows the connection between the Exodus and the future redemption is (Micha 7): "As in the days of your coming out of the land of Egypt I will show him (Israel) wonders."

Let's now try to understand the idea behind the tradition that Elijah will come before Moshiach; in particular, how will Elijah prepare the world to greet Moshiach? It is explained in the words of Rebbe Nachman (Lekutei Mohoran, Part I, Lesson 117) that Elijah comes to push away falsehood and to bring near the truth, as our holy Sages have said in a Mishnah which speaks about truth (Tractate Aid'yos 8:7):

"Rebbi Yehoshua said: '...Elijah only comes to push away those who are close and to bring near those who are far away...' [The Sages are speaking here about distancing people from falsehood and bringing them close to the truth, as our Sages explain in Talmud Shabbos 104, that falsehood is called 'close' because in this world it is always near, readily available and easy to swallow; but truth is harder to come by and less likely to be accepted, and in this sense it is 'far'] Rebbi Yehuda said: 'To bring near but not to push away.' Rebbi Shimon said: 'To straighten out disputes.' [Elijah will come to nullify hatred and controversy and to make Shalom in the world, as it is stated in the continuation of this Mishnah]: And the majority of the Sages say: 'Not to push away and not to bring near, but to make Shalom in the world,' as it is written: 'Behold! I am sending to you Elijah the prophet, before the great and awesome day of Hashem. He shall return the heart of the fathers to the children and the heart of the children to their fathers..."'

In this Mishnah, it seems as though the rabbis are arguing over what Elijah is coming to do. But they are not really arguing, because as soon as Elijah has made Shalom in the world (the majority opinion), falsehood will flee by itself and the truth will be brought near, and there will be no room at all to lie. For the main strength of falsehood is when there is controversy. And when there is controversy, one of the sides is bound to lie. But as soon as there is Shalom in the world, everybody will acknowledge the truth and admit it to their fellow and then the world will be rectified, as it is explained in the words of Rebbe Nachman (Lekutei Mohoran, Part I, Lesson 27): "When there is Shalom in the generation, it is possible to draw the whole world to the service of Hashem, to serve Him with one consent." For when Shalom exists between people, they are able to search for the truth together and to find it and explain it to each other. In this way, everyone will throw away their false idols of silver and gold and they will bring themselves close to the truth.

When Rebbe Nachman was in the city of Tiberias in Israel, the Tzaddikim there made a great festive meal for him in his honor. At the meal, someone posed the following question to all of the Tzaddikim there: In the Talmud, when our Sages are unable to determine what the law is in a given case they say, "Let it rest until Elijah comes." The law of the Torah is that one witness is not allowed to testify in monetary cases. In such cases, a minimum of two witnesses is required before testimony can be given. But, we find that the Sages give the answer "Let it rest until Elijah comes" even in cases of monetary disputes when they are unable to determine which, if any, of the two parties is responsible for damages. So how can the Sages say "Let it rest until Elijah comes" in monetary cases when Elijah is only one witness, and the testimony of one witness is not accepted in monetary cases! Nobody had an answer until the question was posed to Rebbe Nachman. He answered them as follows: "Is it not explained in the words of our holy Sages that Elijah will push away falsehood and bring near the truth and that he will make Shalom in the world? If so, then when Elijah comes, the one in the wrong will automatically come and admit to the truth. And as we know the law is that when a person admits his own guilt in court, even though it is only the testimony of one witness, we accept it like the testimony of one hundred witnesses." And they all rejoiced when they heard Rebbe Nachman's answer.

2

We see that Elijah is all about uprooting falsehood and hatred from the world. And when this wondrous Shalom will exist in the world, all creatures will be ready to receive Moshiach as one man with one heart. For when there is hatred and controversy, it is impossible to reconcile people's wildly different opinions, and therefore it is also impossible to accept Moshiach, since each person says, "If Moshiach is not from my group, then I am not prepared to accept him as king." And let us not forget that the main cause of the Egyptian exile was that there were provocateurs and slanderers amongst the people (see Rashi on Shemos 2:14). But, as soon as there is Shalom in the world, and everybody is busy only seeking Hashem, for He is the essence of truth, as it is written (Jeremiah 10), "And Hashem G-d is truth", then all of the divisiveness and controversies will be nullified and everybody will be of one consent, like one man with one heart, and they will accept Moshiach upon themselves as king to take them out of *galus* (exile). Therefore it is simply understood why we need Elijah to come before Moshiach, for by means of the Shalom that Elijah will make in the world, people will be ready to accept Moshiach as king, and they will all join hands to serve Hashem in truth. And may Hashem let us see the coming of Elijah the prophet and the revelation of our righteous Moshiach, swiftly in our days. Amen v'amen.

3

Friday Night, Parshas Shmini 5766

Friday night, at the first Shabbos meal, Mohorosh Shlit"a spoke inspiring words based on Lekutei Mohoran, Part I, Lesson 51, which discusses the subject of *Emes* (truth) and *Sheker* (falsehood).

Rebbe Nachman says: "The emergence of *Sheker*, which is evil, which is impurity, is made possible through being distant from 'one', for *Emes* is one. An analogy: When it is said of a silver vessel that it is a silver vessel, this is the *Emes*. But, when it is said that it is a gold vessel, it is *Sheker*. We find that *Emes* is one, since it is possible to say the *Emes* in only one way, i.e. by saying it is a silver vessel and nothing but a silver vessel. However, *Sheker* is many, for it is possible to say it is a gold vessel or a brass vessel, or any other type of vessel. We find that *Sheker* is an aspect of the verse (*Koheles*, ch. 7): 'They have sought many calculations.' Before creation, when the creation was in a potential state, so to speak, before Hashem brought it into actuality, it was all one, all *Emes*, all good, all Holiness; even the word *Tahor* (pure) was irrelevant and meaningless to say, for it is only meaningful when there is such a thing as *Tumah* (impurity), as it is written (*Yechezkel*, ch. 36): 'And you shall be purified (**tahar**-tem) from all your impurities (**tumo**-seichem).' But, when all is one, there is no category of 'many calculations', which is the root of evil and *Tumah*. *Taharah* (purity) is an 'intermediary' between *Kodesh* (Holiness) and *Tumah*, since it is through *Taharah* that *Tumah* is rectified, as it is written: 'And you shall be purified (**tahar**-tem) from all your impurities (**tumo**-seichem).' And *Taharah* is the category of *Bechirah* (free choice), which is an intermediary between two things. *Bechirah* was not applicable before creation when all was one, because with regard to 'one', *Bechirah* is irrelevant. And *Bechirah* is an aspect of *Taharah*. And when the Holy One Blessed is He brought the creation from potential to actual, the category of *Taharah* immediately came into being, for now there are two things: 1) The category of 'the one', and 2) The creation; and then *Bechirah* became relevant – *Bechirah*, which is the category of *Taharah*, which is the intermediary between "one" and creation. *Taharah* is close to 'one', but it has not yet reached 'many calculations', which is evil and *Tumah*. However, *Taharah* is a trace and a sign of the orderly unfolding of creation – the creation that can develop and reach the point where there will be evil and *Tumah*. We find that *Tumah* gets its main foothold from *Taharah*, which is the category of *Bechirah*, as mentioned before. (These are the words of Rebbe Nachman.)

Mohorosh explained that Rebbe Nachman reveals to us in this lesson the secret of *Emes* and *Sheker* – the secret that *Emes* is only one and that all that is connected and attached to Hashem is *Emes*, for Hashem is the essence of *Emes*, as it is written (*Yirmiyahu*, ch. 10): "And Hashem G-d is *Emes*." And *Emes* is called "one" because before creation there was only one thing, namely, the Being and Self-revelation of Hashem's G-dliness, as we say in our morning prayers: "It was You before the world was created." And all that is connected and attached to Hashem is "one", as we continue to say in the same prayer: "It is You since the world was created." Therefore, through attaching 'after the creation" to "before the creation" and by recognizing that all that was created was and continues to be emanated from His G-dliness, the entire creation becomes one - one unit of G-dliness, and as our holy Sages have said (*Talmud Berachos* 6): "You [Israel] have made Me one entity in the world as it is said: 'Hear, O Israel: Hashem is Our G-d, Hashem, the One and Only.' And I [Hashem] will make you [Israel] one entity in the world as it is said: 'And who is like Your people Israel, one nation in the Land.' " When the souls of Israel say 'Hear, O Israel, etc.' and they accept Hashem's kingship upon themselves, they reveal that the entire creation is one unit of G-dliness. And the more a person reveals Hashem's G-dliness from within every detail of creation, the more the entire creation returns to its original state. And the entire creation becomes one for this person and there is nothing for him but the reality of the life force of Hashem's G-dliness. However, there is still the principle of *Bechirah*. Since it is already after the creation, and there is a physical world which appears to our eyes to be far from "one", the power of *Bechirah* can now come into being - the *Bechirah* to perceive the *Emes*, which is Hashem's G-dliness, in and through everything, and to attach oneself to Hashem by means of the G-dliness in everything; **or** the *Bechirah* to stray after *Sheker*, which is the physicality and materialism in everything, and to use everything to tear oneself away from being attached to Hashem, G-d forbid. When things are open and revealed to us, when we can clearly see the good and the evil in them, then it is very easy to make the correct *Bechirah* choices between good and evil, between *Kodesh* and *Tumah*, and there is not such a great danger of going astray after the evil and *Sheker*. However, the main *Bechirah* and *Nisayon* (test) take place in more subtle and delicate situations, in which the good and evil are to a large degree covered and hidden. Through a slight turning away from the *Emes*, one can begin to stumble on *Sheker,* thereby causing oneself to break away from being

2

attached to Hashem. Therefore, happy is the one who does not mislead himself, who toils and strives to always contemplate the spirituality and the inwardness of everything, and in this way, he will once again attach "after the creation" to "before the creation", thus making the entire creation one.

All of the above ideas are actually the true definition and the essence of *Taharah*, as *Taharah* only applies once there is the possibility *Tumah*, which in turn is only possible after the creation, when *Sheker* and *Tumah* have come into being. When a person rises up from the valley of *Sheker* and *Tumah*, and contemplates only the *Emes*, he then merits *Taharah*. The attainment of *Taharah* would have been impossible if Hashem had only allowed us to attain the knowledge of "before the creation", where all is *Emes* and all is "one", and where the concepts of *Tumah* and *Taharah* do not apply at all; since *Tumah* has not yet developed through the unfolding of creation, there is also no *Taharah*. We find that now "after the creation", the main service of Man is to discern and separate between *Tumah* and *Taharah* and to attach himself to *Emes*, which is the G-dliness within everything. And then he will merit to truly ascend from *Tumah* to *Taharah*, to cleave to the Life of life, may He be Blessed, which is the life of the World to Come in this world. Happy is the one who merits this. Happy is he and fortunate is his lot.

Mohorosh tied these ideas to our Parsha in the following way. It is written in the very last verse of the Parsha (*Yayikra*, ch. 11): "To distinguish between the *Tamei* (impure) and the *Tahor*, and between the creature that may be eaten and the creature that may not be eaten." In our Parsha all of the laws of kosher and non-kosher creatures are presented in the Torah for the first time. We can ask why, after all of the laws of kosher and non-kosher creatures have already been presented, the Torah repeats itself in the very last verse of the Parsha and says: "To distinguish between the *Tamei* and the *Tahor*, and between the creature that may be eaten and the creature that may not be eaten." Apparently, before we come to the last verse in the Parsha, the creatures have already been separated into kosher and non-kosher, *Tamei* and *Tahor*, as Rashi explains, "Is it necessary to say [that one should understand to distinguish between a non-kosher] donkey and a [kosher] cow? Have they not already been closely defined [as to their distinguishing characteristics]? But the meaning is: [that you should thoroughly understand to distinguish] between what is *Tameiah* for you and what is *Tahorah* for you – between the case of an animal only half of whose wind-pipe has been cut through by the knife, and the case when the greater part has been cut through (in the former case the animal is forbidden, in the latter it is permitted as food)." Perhaps we

3

can say that all of the words of Rebbe Nachman are hinted to here. The root of all of the mitzvos of the Torah is to bring a person to understand how to separate between the *Tamei* and the *Tahor*, that is, between *Sheker* and *Emes*. Before creation all was one and all was *Emes*, and there was no concept of *Tamei* and *Tahor* at all. But after the creation, when there was already (*Vayikra*, ch. 11) "the law of the animal, the bird, every living creature..." the main thing is to be able to recognize and separate between *Tamei* and *Tahor*, i.e. between *Sheker* and *Emes,* and to attach the entire creation to Hashem through keeping the mitzvos of the Torah. And the primary *Bechirah* and *Nisayon* concerns things that are subtle and delicate, where we cannot see in an open and clear way the *Tumah* and the *Taharah*. To distinguish between the non-kosher donkey and the kosher cow is not such a *Nisayon*. But to be able to distinguish the fraction of an inch that separates a kosher slaughter, which is *Tahor* for us, from a non-kosher slaughter, which is *Tamei* for us, is a very subtle and delicate matter, and great skill is needed in order to discern between the two. Likewise, with all of the details of one's life, one needs extra wisdom to be able to distinguish between the *Emes* and the *Sheker* within everything and to attach oneself to Hashem from everything. Happy is the one who merits this in truth. And may Hashem help us merit the light of Truth that is in everything and to attach ourselves to Him, until we merit to ascend and be included in Him completely, now and forever. Amen v'amen.

4

Seudah Shlishis, Parshas Tazria – Metzora 5766

At the third Shabbos meal, Mohorosh Shlit"a spoke inspiring words based on Lekutei Mohoran, Part II, Lesson 25, which discusses the importance of *Hisbodedus*.

Rebbe Nachman says: "The level of *Hisbodedus* is higher and greater than everything. In *Hisbodedus*, a person sets aside an hour or so to be by himself in a room or in a field, to speak out everything that is on his heart between himself and his Maker. He should put forth all sorts of logical arguments and excuses using graceful, charming, and appeasing words. And he should ask and beg Hashem that He should bring him close to Him to serve Him in truth. And this prayer and conversation should be in one's everyday language [e.g. English]." (These are the words of Rebbe Nachman.)

Mohorosh explained that Rebbe Nachman reveals to us in this teaching that there is nothing higher than prayer and *Hisbodedus* – which is actually prayer in your own language – and that they are the gate and the entrance through which we come to Hashem (*Lekutei Mohoran*, Part II, Lesson 84). Certainly, we are all yearning to come close to Hashem and to attach ourselves to Him totally. But the main source of our distress is that we don't know the path and the gate that leads to Him. In truth, the path and the gate are prayer and *Hisbodedus*, about which it is said (*Tehillim* 118): "This is the gate of Hashem; the righteous shall enter through it." And the mouth is referred to as a doorway, as it is written (*Micha*, ch. 7): "Guard the doors of your mouth." And through this doorway we come to Hashem. The more a person talks to Hashem and speaks out before Him everything that is in his heart with complete honesty and simplicity – as he would speak to a friend and as a child would speak to his parent – the more will *Emunah* (faith) become established and fixed in his heart. And then he will merit to feel the truth of Hashem's existence, which hovers over and shields him always. Everyone can reach this level through increasing in prayer and *Hisbodedus* until eventually one's entire being becomes prayer, as King Dovid wrote (*Tehillim* 109): "But I (*ani*) am [all] prayer." And what part of a person is referred to as "I (*ani*)"? It is a person's *neshama* (*Lekutei Mohoran*, Part I, Lesson 22). And when a person is deeply engaged in prayer, his "I" (*ani*; *aleph-nun-yud;* i.e. his ego) is changed into "Nothing (*ain*; *aleph-yud-nun*)", which means that he ascends and cleaves to Hashem's endless light. However, the Satan attempts to weaken the light of *emunah* by discouraging a person from praying to Hashem. And then it is fulfilled in this person the verse (*Yechezkel*, ch. 1): "I was among the exiles," for his *neshama* is in a very bitter and dark exile where Hashem's endless light is hidden from him. If a person would know with a full heart that (*Yeshaya*, ch. 6): "The whole earth is full of His glory", and that Hashem stands over him when he prays, listening to every word coming from his mouth, then he would certainly pray with great enthusiasm and be very careful to think about every word of his prayer (*Lekutei Mohoran*, Part I, Lesson 62); and there would certainly be no sadness, laziness and heaviness in his prayer and he would truly pray as he should. However, the main cause of confusion in prayer comes from a lack of *emunah* (*Lekutei Mohoran*, Part I, Lesson 155). Therefore, the primary service of a person is to work on strengthening his power of *emunah* and to increase in prayer and *Hisbodedus* to Hashem at all times, for then, he will merit to ascend and cleave to the Supreme Light and he will taste the World to Come in this world. Happy is he and fortunate is his lot.

Mohorosh connected these ideas to our *parsha* in the following way. We find in our *parsha* the laws of the afflictions that come upon a person through forbidden speech. Instead of using his faculty of speech for prayer and *Hisbodedus* to Hashem, he speaks *loshon harah* (lit., evil talk; information which is derogatory or potentially harmful even if the information is true), *rechilus* (information that potentially can cause ill will between Jews) and other forms of forbidden speech, and as a result he is punished with *tzaraas* (leprosy - a physical affliction which is a manifestation of a spiritual illness; the primary cause is slander, but it is also a punishment for other types of anti-social behavior such as bloodshed, false oaths, immorality, pride, robbery and selfishness). At first, the afflictions only affect the walls of his house, to remind him to do *teshuvah* (to repent and return to the proper way); and the verse is fulfilled in him (Chavakuk, ch. 2): "For the stone shall cry out of the wall," as the very stones of his house call out to him to do *teshuvah,* to elevate and repair his speech, to begin to engage in prayer and *Hisbodedus* the way he should. Even the stones and beams of one's house bear witness to all of a person's deeds, as our holy Sages have said (*Talmud Taanis* 11a): "Who testifies against a person? The stones and beams of his house testify against him." Even in our time when there is no *tzaraas*, if a person's home has been damaged in some way, for example, a water pipe breaks or the ceiling leaks from the rain, it is proper for him to contemplate that from Heaven they are reminding him to do *teshuvah* and Hashem is having compassion on him by

2

first striking the structure of his house instead of his body. If a person does not take these hints from Heaven, then the afflictions will begin to affect his clothing; his clothing being much closer to his body than the walls of his house. And again, Heaven is trying to arouse him to do *teshuvah*. And even today, when some mishap occurs to one's clothing, for example a garment suddenly rips or becomes soiled, it is proper to contemplate that this is similar to the *tzaraas* that can affect a person's clothing, as described in our *parsha*, and that once again Heaven is hinting to him to do *teshuvah* and to fix his speech through prayer and *Hisbodedus*. If after all this, he has still failed to do *teshuvah*, then the afflictions finally come upon his body and life becomes very bitter and dark for him, for in the Aramaic translation of the Torah the *metzora* (the person afflicted with *tzaraas*) is referred to as a "*sagirah*" (one who is closed off or shut in). And this corresponds to the Zohar (Parshas Tazria 49b) which describes the *metzora* as one who is: "*sagiro d'nerhora ilaah*", that is, one who is closed off from the Supreme Light – the light of the *Shechinah*. And then life is very difficult for him, for the doorway to holiness has been blocked off; and this doorway is prayer, as mentioned before. And he is left in a state of exile, which is an aspect of the verse (*Yechezkel*, ch. 1): "I was among the exiles". His main rectification is through the *Kohein* – the Tzaddik – who, as described in our *parsha*, must ostracize the *metzora* from all other Jews by sending him to live alone outside the city, as it is written (*Parshas Tazria*, ch. 13): "He shall dwell alone; his dwelling shall be outside the camp." And the main purpose of his isolation and solitude is that he should contemplate well his ways and be alone with Hashem and begin to fix his faculty of speech that he blemished through using destructive words that damaged people's relationships; that ruined friendships, marriages and people's livelihoods. For through solitude he can return to using his speech for prayer and *Hisbodedus* to Hashem and then he will be healed from his *tzaraas*.

The purification of the *metzora* is dependent upon his immersion in water, as it is written (*Parshas Metzora*, ch. 14): "He shall immerse his flesh in water and become pure." Immersing in a *mikvah* helps for all kinds of spiritual contamination. Rebbe Nachman spoke much about the great virtue of regularly immersing in a *mikvah* and Breslover Chassidim traditionally do so every day. Water also hints to prayer, as it is written (*Eichah*, ch. 2): "Pour out your heart like water in the Presence of Hashem." For the main rectification of the *metzora* is to pour out his speech and prayer before Hashem like water, and then the Kohein will show him the path of return to Hashem. The purification process of the *metzora* also includes two live

3

kosher birds – one is slaughtered and the other is set free into an open field. It is explained in the holy *Zohar* (*Parshas Metzora* 53b; also mentioned in *Lekutei Mohoran*, Part I, Lesson 3) that the two live kosher birds correspond to the *sefiros* of *Binah* (Understanding) and *Malchus* (Kingship). The bird that corresponds to the *sefirah* of *Binah* comes to rectify what he blemished with his thoughts. Because he did not contemplate Hashem's G-dliness that shines throughout the entire creation but instead entertained evil and negative thoughts about people, he eventually came to speak *loshon harah* and *rechilus* about them. And the bird that corresponds to the *sefirah* of *Malchus* comes to rectify the blemish of speech, for the main way we accept Hashem's kingship upon ourselves is through speech, which is prayer and *Hisbodedus*. And when one has blemished his speech, his acceptance of Hashem's kingship has been undermined. The bird that corresponds to *Malchus* is slaughtered in order to correct his damaged speech, of which it is said (*Yirmiyahu*, ch. 9): "Their tongue is a sharpened arrow; it speaks deceit," for it is necessary to completely put an end to evil speech. After the first bird has been slaughtered, the second bird that corresponds to the *sefirah* of *Binah* is set free and released upon the open field, for as soon as we have rectified speech, then *Binah,* which is the mind, has also been set free - free to take off and fly; free to contemplate Hashem's G-dliness once again. And may Hashem help us to purify our minds from all kinds of impurities and we will use our speech only for holy words of Torah and prayer until we merit to ascend and be included in Him completely, now and forever. Amen v'amen.

.

4

Friday Night, Parshas Achrai – Kdoshim 5764

Friday night, at the first Shabbos meal, Mohorosh Shlit"a spoke inspiring words based on Lekutei Mohoran, Part I, Lesson 52, which discusses Hashem's purpose in creating the world.

Rebbe Nachman says: "There are heretics that say that the world [i.e. matter and energy] must exist [and has always existed] and everyone parrots back what they say. The truth is that the existence of the world and everything in it is only a possible existence, for it is only Hashem alone Whose existence is intrinsic, independent and eternal, for He created them all from nothing. And with His power and ability to do anything, He could have created them or not created them. Therefore, the whole world and everything in it is certainly only a possible existence. However, where does the error come from that people can go wrong, G-d forbid, and say that the world has independent existence and that it must have always existed, G-d forbid? Know, that this comes about because, in truth, now that the souls of Israel have been created and drawn down into the world, the world is now indeed in the category of a necessary existence [as opposed to a possible existence], for the whole world and everything in it – everything – was only created for the sake of Israel. Therefore, certainly now after the souls of Israel have been created, Hashem is obligated, so to speak, to create and sustain the world, since for this purpose he created the souls of Israel - in order to create, for their sake, all of the worlds. And the primary intention in Hashem's creating the whole world for the sake of Israel was so that Israel would do His will and return and cleave to their Root, that is, they will return and be included in Hashem, Who is the Necessary Existence. And for this reason, everything was created. Therefore, the more the people of Israel carry out Hashem's will and include themselves in their Root, Who is the Necessary Existence, the more the whole world, which was created for their sake, is included in the Necessary Existence." (These are the words of Rebbe Nachman.)

Mohorosh explained that Rebbe Nachman reveals to us in this lesson an amazing secret of the secrets of creation, namely, the origin of the atheists' error that they can say that the world has always existed and that its existence is independent and necessary, as if there *must* be a world; also, how it's possible that they can not acknowledge that it is Hashem Who created the entire world and everything in it from nothing, out of His desire to do good and that it is only Hashem Whose existence is necessary, there being no other existence independent of His existence. And Rebbe Nachman reveals to us that this error stems only from after the time that the souls of Israel were created. For after there are Jewish souls in the world who yearn to do His will and who strive to return and be included in their Root, from this time onward the entire world does indeed have a necessary existence, for now the creation must exist for the sake of the souls of Israel who can return and be included in their Root. Therefore, when the atheists see the creation as it is now, that is, after there are Jewish souls in the world who do His will, it seems to them that the world must exist, for certainly now it is necessary that there is a world for the sake of the souls of Israel. We find that every Jew, when he merits to do Hashem's will in truth and to cleave to his Root, is thus sustaining the entire creation and the entire creation is included in the Necessary Existence in his merit. Happy is the one who merits to reach such a level.

Mohorosh connected these ideas to our parsha in the following way. It is written (*Vayikra*, ch. 19): "Speak to the entire congregation of the children of Israel and say to them, 'you shall be holy, because I, Hashem your G-d, am holy." Let us try to understand the reason Hashem is giving us for why we must be holy? The reason given in the verse is: 'because I, Hashem your G-d, am holy.' And what is the deeper meaning of this reason? According to the words of Rebbe Nachman we can understand it very well. The verse reveals to us that the souls of Israel must be holy, that is, they must do the will of Hashem and return and be included in their Root *because* "I, Hashem your G-d, am holy." Hashem is telling us "I created all of the worlds for your sake, so that you should return and be included in your Root. Therefore now, you must be holy and separated from immorality so that all of the worlds can exist for your sake." And this is the verse: "Speak to the entire congregation (*adas*) of the children of Israel". The letters that make up the word *adas* (*ayin-dalet-sav*) are the same letters that comprise the word for knowledge – *daas* (*dalet-ayin-sav*). For the Tzaddik, who is an aspect of Moshe, needs to bring this knowledge to the souls of Israel – the knowledge that they should recognize well that the entire creation was created for their sakes; for the sake that they would return and cleave to their Root. We can now understand the reason Hashem gives us in this verse for why we must be holy. And the reason is "because I, Hashem your G-d, am holy". Hashem is telling us, "The truth is that only My existence is independent, unconditional and necessary, but I have created the worlds for your sakes. Therefore, in order for the worlds to have existence 'you shall be holy' – i.e., you *must* be holy and then, the

2

existence of the entire creation will be sustained in your merit, and the entire creation will return and be included in the Necessary Existence. And may Hashem help us to be holy and bound to Him in truth until we merit to elevate and repair the entire creation, to bring it to its Root and to see the redemption of Israel swiftly in our days. *Amen v'amen.*

Seudah Shlishis, Parshas Achrai – Kdoshim 5764

At the third Shabbos meal, Mohorosh Shlit"a spoke inspiring words on the topic of one's obligation to correct and improve his speech, based on *Lekutei Mohoran*, Part I, Lesson 29.

Rebbe Nachman says: "Not all speech is called speech. For speech which isn't heard or accepted is not called speech. And this is an aspect of the verse (*Tehillim*, ch. 19): 'There is no speech and no words without their voice being heard." And the main thing which causes a word to be accepted is the good that is in it, for everybody desires what is good. Therefore, when there is good in a word, then the word is heard and accepted. But, when there is no good in a word, it is not accepted. And how can we put goodness into a word? We do this through drawing the word from wisdom (*daas*), and then there is good in it. But, when the word is without wisdom, then there is no good in it. And wisdom becomes established, elevated and exalted through speaking about the virtues of the Tzaddikim." (These are the words of Rebbe Nachman.)

Mohorosh explained that speech only has value when there is good in it, because everybody desires to hear a good word. And what is a good word? It is a word of encouragement and strengthening. Each and every one of us is very thirsty to hear a word of encouragement that will strengthen us in our service of Hashem. Many, if not most, people feel they are very broken. Therefore, they don't need someone to come along and give them rebuke or criticism which will only break them even more, as in this episode from Rebbe Nachman's life (*Chayei Mohoran*, #91): "Once a man who had already passed away revealed himself to Rebbe Nachman and began to rebuke him with such words as, 'How could you have done this, that and the other thing?!' And Rebbe Nachman boldly said to him, 'I thought you were going to comfort me and speak to my heart. But you have only come to break me. Go away....'" Rebbe Nachman understood that such words cannot be from the

3

side of holiness. Only a word that has good in it – a word that can strengthen and encourage a person - is a word that will be heard and accepted. And these kinds of words everyone longs to hear, from the greatest of the great to the smallest of the small, as Rebbe Nachman himself said (*Lekutei Mohoran*, Part II, Lesson 58): "We have heard from a true Tzaddik who said [and this is Rebbe Nachman himself as is known] that if someone – anyone at all – had told him when he first began serving Hashem – 'My brother, be strong and get a grip on yourself!', he would have run to serve Hashem with great zeal. He [the Tzaddik] experienced trials and tribulations but he never heard one word of encouragement from anybody." Therefore, speech only has value when it contains good and has the power to strengthen a person. This is not the case with a word which breaks and puts a person down; such a word has no value at all since people do not want to hear it! Therefore, happy is the one who always puts goodness into his words and speaks words of *emunah* and encouragement with everyone he knows.

Rebbe Nachman reveals to us how to put goodness into our speech. And this is done through taking and drawing our speech from wisdom. The essence of wisdom (d*aas*) is only to recognize Hashem, as it is written (*Devarim*, ch. 4): "You have been shown that you might know (*la'daas*) that Hashem, He is G-d; there is no [power] other than He." And as soon as we connect our speech to Hashem, and speak about Hashem, automatically there is good in our speech, for Hashem is the ultimate good, as it is written (*Tehillim*, ch. 145): "Hashem is good for everything [or 'good to all']". He wants only what is good for a person. And He desires the repentance of the wicked and not their death. Therefore, when we speak about Hashem and the power of His kindness and compassion, immediately, a "light at the end of the tunnel" and hope appear and enter the heart of the listener as he hears that there is a remedy for him in this world, and that the situation is not as bad as he had thought. And this is the power of the one who speaks words of encouragement with others, speaking to their hearts and showing them that they can return in *teshuva* to Hashem. For this is the greatest *tzeddaka* that exists, as Rebbe Nachman says (*Lekutei Mohoran*, Part I, Lesson 106) on the verse (*Tehillim*, ch. 32): " 'Happy is the one who deals intelligently with the poor.' Happy is the one who puts wisdom and knowledge into the 'pauper' who lacks it, because this is worth more than all the riches in the world." A person who is broken and standing on the brink of despair could care less about all the money in the world. And if you were to give him all the money in the world, he would throw it back in your face because it means nothing to him at all. However, if you would speak to his heart and offer him a word of

4

encouragement and bring him out of his depression and bitterness, this would be worth more to him than anything, and there is no way he could repay you for literally saving his life. Therefore, our main service is to always be mindful to put wisdom into our words through speaking about Hashem and the awesome power of His compassion and love, and then our speech will be heard and accepted and we will merit to do much *tzeddaka* and kindness with all people.

Rebbe Nachman says that the way to establish and elevate wisdom is through speaking about the virtues of the Tzaddikim. For through speaking about their virtues and awesome self-sacrifice in serving Hashem, we thus reveal the way each and every one of us can return and bind himself to Hashem, which is the main purpose of creation. Therefore, we find that praising the Tzaddikim causes wisdom to enter the hearts of Israel. And this wisdom will inspire us to yearn and long to go in the footsteps of the Tzaddikim and to attach ourselves to Hashem.

There is no perfection to merely speak about the miracles and wonders the Tzaddikim have performed and then to conclude by saying, "*Zechusam yagein aleinu!* (may their merits shield us). Oy! In the earlier generations there were holy Tzaddikim who worked all of these miracles, but today, in our very low and dark generation we don't have them." This is the exact opposite of the purpose of telling stories about the Tzaddikim! The main value in telling stories about them is to show that even today there are holy Tzaddikim who bind themselves to Hashem. Stories about the divine service of the Tzaddikim and how they serve Hashem with complete dedication and self-sacrifice encourage and strengthen all Jewish souls to go in their footsteps and to emulate their deeds. So, the value of speaking about the Tzaddikim comes not just from discussing the signs and wonders they have performed, as we see in the following episode from the life of the Baal Shem Tov: Once, the holy Baal Shem Tov came to his students who were sitting and discussing the many wonders their master had performed. And he said to them, "Why are you speaking about my miracles, but you are not speaking about my self-sacrifice?" Due to our many sins, people are very much in the habit of speaking about the miracles of the Tzaddikim of the earlier generations and then lamenting that there are no Tzaddikim left like this. But in truth, it is heresy to say such a thing. For just as Hashem is found in each and every generation, there are certainly holy Tzaddikim in each and every generation (*Sichos HaRan*, #192). And as the author of the book *"Tiferes Shlomo"* explained the blessing recited after reading the *Haftarah*: "*Tzur col*

5

olamim, Tzaddik b'chol hadoros (Rock of all the worlds, Tzaddik in all the generations": Just like Hashem is the Rock of all the worlds, so there is a "Tzaddik in every generation" who resembles his Maker and it is proper to draw close to him and to speak about his greatness. For in speaking about them, a powerful yearning to go in their ways and to cleave to Hashem will enter our hearts. Therefore, the main way to elevate and exalt wisdom is through speaking about the Tzaddikim. Happy is the one who always speaks about the greatness of the Tzaddikim and their awesome self-sacrifice in serving Hashem. For in this way, mighty encouragement and inspiration will enter the hearts of all who are listening to the storyteller and the merit of the entire congregation will be attributed to him. Happy is he and fortunate is his lot.

Mohorosh connected these ideas to our parsha in the following way. It is written (*Vayikra*, ch. 10): "You shall not go around as a gossipmonger among your people. You shall not stand idly by while your fellow's blood is shed. I am Hashem." Let's try to understand the connection between the two parts of the verse: 1). "You shall not go around as a gossipmonger" and 2). "You shall not stand idly by." According to the words of Rebbe Nachman we can understand the connection very well (as explained by Rebbe Nachman himself in *Lekutei Mohoran*, Part I, Lesson 29, par. 7). The prohibition of "You shall not go around as a gossipmonger" is a warning against corrupting our speech through speaking *rechilus* and *lashon hara*. And this is the opposite of speech that contains good, as discussed above. It is the opposite of finding the good points and the merits in people, as a gossipmonger searches for the defects and the deficiencies in everyone. Therefore, through the mitzvah of "You shall not go around as a gossipmonger" and by only seeking out the good points and the merits in people, and by speaking much about the virtues, deeds and character traits of the Tzaddikim, revealing to everyone the power of their divine service and their great self-sacrifice, then automatically, "You shall not stand idly by while **your fellow's** blood is shed" – that is, you will not damage your mind and cause it to fall spiritually through speaking *rechilus* and *loshon hara*, G-d forbid, for "**your fellow**" represents the mind, specifically the two intellectual faculties *chochma* (wisdom) and *bina* (understanding), as the Zohar (*Vayikra* 4b) refers to *chochma* and *bina* as being "two **fellows** that are inseparable". Just like an excess flow of blood to the physical brain can cause a person to pass out and fall down, G-d forbid; likewise, speaking and listening to evil speech can also cause us to collapse – it can damage the holy intellectual powers of our minds and cause a terrible spiritual fall, G-d forbid. And this is the meaning of the end of the verse "I am

6

Hashem" – Who is the ultimate **good** – which is the category of (*Tehillim*, ch. 145): "Hashem is **good** for everything [or **good** to all]". That is, the main way to repair our speech is to find only the **good** in every person and to speak only praises of the Tzaddikim and of their total dedication and self-sacrifice in serving Hashem. And in this way, we will merit to truly be bound to Hashem. And may Hashem help us to correct our speech and our minds and will merit to ascend and cleave to Him in truth and simplicity for now and evermore. Amen v'amen.

7

Seudah Shlishis, Parshas Emor 5764

At the third Shabbos meal, Mohorosh Shlit"a spoke inspiring words on the subject of when things go "according to plan vs. not according to plan", based on Lekutei Mohoran, Part II, Lesson 82.

Rebbe Nachman says: "There is a concept of 'according to plan and not according to plan', which is an aspect of Adam and Chava…and this is what we see, that sometimes things do not go according to plan for a person and this is caused by his feelings of self-importance and by his arrogating to himself the kingship, saying, "I will rule." But when he has humility, which is true wisdom (*chochma*; *chaf-ches-mem-hey*), which is an aspect of *chaf-ches* [*co'ach* – strength or power] *mem-hey* [*mah* – what], then things go smoothly and 'according to plan' for him."

Mohorosh explained that we learn from this teaching that the phenomenon of things going "according to plan" for a person depends on his attaining a perception of G-dliness from all of the details of creation. For such was the ultimate plan of creating the world – that we should merit to find Him in each and every detail of creation and we should utilize whatever we go through in life as a means to bring ourselves closer to Hashem. And this skill itself is called "according to plan", for it was the plan of creation that we should acquire this skill. However, due to the materialism and physicality of creation, every person suffers from confusion and from all kinds of trials and tribulations that seem to be "not according to plan." But the truth is that the plan of creation was that we should find Hashem's G-dliness also in those things which are "not according to plan." And when we merit to find it, we reconnect the "not according to plan" to the "according to plan", thus fulfilling the ultimate goal of creation.

This is also the concept of Adam and Chava. Adam is an aspect of "according to plan", because the plan and purpose of his being created was only that he should be bound to Hashem. The same is true of Chava, but she also has another aspect to her. Hashem saw that (*Bereishis*, ch. 2) "It is not good that man be alone; I will make him a **helper corresponding to him**" – an "**eizer k'negdo** (a helper 'corresponding to' or literally, 'against' him). That is, the aspect of *k'negdo* (being 'against' him, so to speak) will help (*eizer*) him to draw closer to Hashem. Therefore, He created Chava. And through her being an aspect of *k'negdo* and "not according to plan" (i.e., not always according to Adam's plan, but certainly according to Hashem's plan), she would become a partner to Adam in helping him bind himself to Hashem. And then automatically, Adam and Chava would be able to attach themselves to each other in shalom – the *k'negdo* having been transformed into *eizer*. And the "not according to plan" would also be converted into "according to plan." And this is precisely the purpose of things not going according to plan.

A person is not in this world to be totally free from suffering and confusion. However, the main virtue of a Jew is to hold himself strong no matter what he goes through and this means having the skill to find Hashem's G-dliness also within the "not according to plan". And as soon as he finds it there, the entire situation transforms into "according to plan." For when he sees how it was Hashem's intention only to bring him closer to His service, he realizes that it was precisely what he went through that was the true "according to plan." Therefore, let a person not think that the Tzaddikim reached their levels through living lives of quietude and serenity and that troubles and afflictions did not pass over them. On the contrary, the Tzaddikim and people of integrity are the ones who go through more than anyone. But their overriding virtue is that they hold themselves strong no matter what they go through and they run to Hashem despite and by means of their troubles and suffering. They know very well that the hand of Hashem is hidden and treasured away in everything they go through. And through holding their ground in any situation they achieved what they achieved. Happy are they!

Rebbe Nachman says in this lesson that the main cause of things going "not according to plan" is a person's own feelings of greatness and his usurping the kingship from Hashem, saying "I will rule." This means that due to his arrogance and desire to be "seen" combined with the delusion that he needs to understand everything that happens in the world with the bit of wisdom and intelligence he has, it is certain that things will go against his will and not "according to plan." And his life becomes very bitter, because it is impossible to truly understand, in any way whatsoever, Hashem's ways of running the world. The ultimate goal of knowledge is to know that "we do not know," which means that we know that we know nothing, as Rebbe Nachman once swore, on one of the last Shabbos' of his life in Uman, that he knew nothing (Chayei Mohoran ?). It also once happened that people heard him crying loudly, "How does one merit to be a Jew?!" When Reb Nosson heard this he

2

was dumbfounded. Only a little earlier, Rebbe Nachman had revealed very awesome and wondrous teachings. So how can he now say that he knows nothing and also cry, "How does one merit to be a Jew"? However, Rebbe Nachman explained to him that, "Before, I did not know there were perceptions and levels like these. This means there are certainly more perceptions and levels that I have not yet merited to know and reach. It turns out that I know nothing."

The more a person continues to grow and progress and the higher he goes, the more he should understand that he really knows nothing, unlike Elisha ben Abuya who was called Acher ("Other" - because after he lost his faith, he became like another person who nobody recognized). Elisha ben Abuya ascended to the Heavens and it was precisely there that he lost his faith and became a heretic, may G-d save us. He did not have the proper amount of self-nullification when he attempted to get closer to Hashem. And from the abundance of light he was totally blinded, just as one who gazes into the sun can become blinded. Coming close to Hashem needs to be with total nullification. What does total nullification mean? Does it mean that you should feel that you are worthless and a nobody? Does it mean that you should lose your sense of who you are? No. It means that you should know that no matter how high one goes, one still knows nothing about the true nature and essence of creation and how Hashem runs the world. And this was the level of Rebbi Akiva, who also ascended to the Heavens, but in his case, he entered in shalom and came out in shalom, because he had the wisdom to know that he knew nothing. And when a person has this wisdom – the wisdom to recognize that he has nothing but Hashem, then he has attained the most essential wisdom (*chochma*) whose letters are *chaf-ches* (*co'ach* – strength) *mem-hey* (*mah* – what) – *mah chocheinu; mah gevrusoseinu!?* (What is our strength, what is our might!?) [from the morning prayers]. He knows that we have no strength and might besides Hashem and this knowledge itself is perfect fear of Hashem, which is an aspect of the verse (*Tehillim*, ch. 96): "*Chilu mipanav col ha'aretz* ("Tremble before Him everyone on earth"); the first letters of each word spells *chochma*. And then everything goes "according to plan" for him, because he knows that whatever he goes through, down to the minutest detail, it all happens with Hashem's personal Providence. And Hashem's personal Providence is the greatest "according to plan" there is!

The concept of "entering in shalom" and "coming out in shalom" is an aspect of the statement in the Zohar (*Vayakel* 113b): "Fortunate is the person who

3

can go in and come out," referring to perceptions of G-dliness. Happy is the one who knows how to ascend to perceptions of G-dliness and also how to come down again. That is, he knows how to find Hashem's G-dliness when everything is going "according to plan" and how to find Him in times of trouble and suffering, may G-d save us. And even when he is engaged in the mundane affairs of this world, he will not forget Hashem for a moment. And this is the concept of "entering in shalom" and "coming out in shalom." When a person is humble and unassuming, he is at peace with all people and he is able to hold himself strong in any situation, which is not true for the person who is conceited and who arrogates the kingship to himself, saying "I will rule." It is impossible for him to be at peace with everyone. And this is the main cause of his downfall. This was the flaw of Rebbi Akiva's students. They did not properly absorb this teaching and as a result, failed to show the proper level of honor to each other. They all died between Pesach and Shavuos, as the days of the Omer are special days for focusing on our character traits in order to improve them one trait at a time. On Pesach night, Hashem shines on us a tremendous light, but starting from the day after Pesach, this light is concealed and each of the forty-nine days leading up to Shavuos are days of constriction of the light, days on which we focus the light of our own intellects on our individual character traits, a different trait on each of the forty-nine days, to improve them and to make them shine. And these forty-nine days are an especially conducive time to realize that in each and every Jew there is a special talent that doesn't exist in any other Jew. Therefore, I need to honor him for his special point. And this is the essence of humility. But when one arrogates to himself the kingship and says, "I will rule", and "only my special point is important", this is the essence of his failure in life. And then everything goes "not according to plan" for him. We find that our main service is to strive to merit true wisdom; i.e. to know "what is our strength and what is our might", which is true humility. And then everything will go "according to plan". And we will find Hashem's G-dliness in everything that we go through and live a good life in this world and the next.

Mohorosh connected these ideas to our parsha in the following way. In the beginning of the parsha we find the special laws for the Kohanim, which forbid them to contaminate themselves from the dead with the exception of a few close relatives (*Vayikra*, ch. 21): "And to his virgin sister who is close to him, who has had no husband, to her shall he contaminate (**yi'tamah**) himself" (i.e. he is required to participate in her funeral). Perhaps we can say that Rebbe Nachman's ideas discussed above regarding the attainment of holy

4

wisdom are hinted to in this verse. We know that holy wisdom is referred to as one's "sister", as it is written (Proverbs, ch. 7): "Say to wisdom, you are my sister." And the Kohein who performs the divine service is in the category of the Tzaddik who ascends to lofty perceptions of G-dliness and who longs to bind himself to Hashem. Therefore, his ascending needs to be in the category of "according to plan and not according to plan", as mentioned above. That is, it must be in the category of (Zohar, *Vayakel* 113b): "Fortunate is the person who can go in and come out." which means that he will enter in shalom and come out in shalom. And he will find Hashem's G-dliness in each and every detail, whether that detail is "according to plan" and understandable or "not according to plan" and incomprehensible. Moreover, not once will he think that he understands all there is to know; rather, he will hold himself strong with the trait humility, as if he were totally **tamei** and has not yet merited to enter the gates of holiness at all. And this is the verse, "And to his virgin sister" – the attainment of holy wisdom - an aspect of "Say to wisdom, you are my sister." "*La yi'tama*" – to her – to holy wisdom - shall he "contaminate" himself. That is, he should consider himself in the category of being completely *tamei* and far away as one who still comprehends nothing. For the essence of wisdom is to know that he knows nothing. Yet, in this way, he will merit to enter the Tabernacle and the Holy Temple and to perform the divine service. And his coming closer to Hashem will not harm him at all since he is a master of "going in and coming out" as in the saying of the Zohar: "Fortunate is the person who can go in and come out". He will enter in shalom and come out in shalom. And he will accomplish all he needs to accomplish. May Hashem help us to be close to the true Tzaddikim and they will place these truths within us and will live by them with all our hearts. And we will merit to be attached to Hashem in truth for now and evermore. Amen v'amen.

5

Friday Night, Parshas Bhar - Bechukosai 5764

Friday night, at the first Shabbos meal, Mohorosh shlit"a spoke inspiring words on the topics of *emunah* (faith) and how we can comprehend knowledge that is beyond our ability to grasp, based on *Lekutei Mohoran*, Part II, Lesson 5.

Rebbe Nachman says: "In perceiving G-dliness there are concepts which are 'internal' and concepts which 'surround'. What a person is able to understand and reach with his intellect is in the category of 'internal', for his intellect has brought the concept within itself. But what he is unable to bring within his intellect, that is, what is impossible for him to understand, is in the category of 'surrounding', for it surrounds and is above his mind and it is impossible for him to bring it within. But through engaging in conversation with others in order to impart to them wisdom and fear of Heaven, the 'surrounding' lights are brought inside. That is, he merits to understand and to know what he had been unable to understand until now. For when he engages people in conversation and places wisdom into them, what occurs is that his mind is emptied of the intellect and wisdom that he had, and place is made for the surrounding intellect to enter within. As a result of his intellect being, so to speak, emptied out and transferred to his friend, the 'surrounding' intellect finds room to come inside and he merits to understand what he could not understand before." (These are the words of Rebbe Nachman).

Mohorosh explained that we learn from this lesson that the aspiration and striving of a person all the days of his life should be to rise from level to level by understanding new concepts which had previously been inaccessible to him. Each person, according to his level, has what is 'internal' and what is 'surrounding'. The 'internal' is what is within his intellect and what he understands well. And the 'surrounding' is what still surrounds his intellect and has not yet entered within it. He might have only an inkling of what it is, as he sees it from a distance. But it has not yet entered the inwardness of his mind and therefore it is in the category of *emunah* (faith) - because he sees it and believes in it - but is has not reached *daas* (knowledge) as he does not yet understand it clearly. When a person is a positive influence on others, placing within them his own intellect and wisdom, every time he speaks with them he merits to receive a new 'inside' and a new 'surrounding'. Through emptying his intellect while speaking with his friend, what had previously been for him in the category of 'surrounding' has now entered within. And then he immediately receives a new 'surrounding'. Thus, he progresses and rises from level to level. Therefore, Rebbi Yehuda HaNassi said (*Talmud Makkos* 10a): "And from my students I have learned the most [even more than he learned from his teachers and colleagues]." For while a person is learning with his students, his intellect is constantly being emptied out. Therefore, he is also constantly receiving a new 'inside' and a new 'surrounding'. And this is how he rises from level to level. Happy is he!

Rebbe Nachman explains (*Lekutei Mohoran*, Part I, Lesson 106) that the greatest *tzedakah* (charity) is to give wisdom and intelligence to the one who lacks it, which is an aspect of the verse (*Tehillim*, ch. 32): "Happy is the one who deals intelligently with the poor person." That is, he puts wisdom into the one who lacks it. In this way, the giver's mind is also expanded. For every time a person speaks with his friend in order to give him wisdom and intelligence, automatically, a new 'inside' enters him and a new 'surrounding' takes its place and his mind keeps expanding. And it is written regarding the mitzvah of *tzedakah* (*Devarim*, ch. 15): "Continually open your hand to him and continually lend him according to what he lacks." By opening his hand to the poor person, he opens a new door for himself. For when a person gives *tzedakah* and does *chesed* (kindness) with others, it seems that his own resources are being emptied out. But then measure-for-measure he receives in return a completely new blessing. And this is alluded to in the verse describing Hashem's challenge to us in our giving of tithes (*Malachi*, ch. 3): "Bring the entire tithe into the storehouse, that there may be food in My house, and test me now in this, says the Lord of Hosts, if I will not open for you the windows of Heaven and pour out a blessing for you that will be more than sufficient." That is, all who do *tzedakah* and *chesed* with others, whether the kindness is physical or spiritual, receive many, many times over in return, and all of their lacks are filled. Therefore, happy is the one who merits to always be involved in *tzedakah*, specifically the *tzedakah* of speaking words of *emunah* and fear of Heaven with others. For then, he will draw down upon himself new and holy wisdom every time he speaks with them and he will ascend and cleave to Hashem in truth. Happy is he and fortunate is his lot.

Mohorosh connected these ideas to our parsha in the following way. It is written in our parsha, among the blessings bestowed on those who keep the Torah (*Vayikra*, ch. 26): "You will eat very old [stored crops] and will have to

2

take out the old [stores] because of the new." We can ask why is this blessing disguised in the form of moving out "old because of new" and not simply described as an overabundance of food. Perhaps we can say that this verse hints to the above teaching of Rebbe Nachman. Because of the blessing that a person "takes out" for others, whether this kindness is something physical or spiritual, this blessing becomes emptied out for the giver, but then a new blessing comes in to take its place. And this is an aspect of "You will have to take out the old because of the new," as the giver will gain a new "inside" and a new "surrounding" and he will continually rise from level to level. And this is how the Aramaic translation of the Torah translates the verse: "You will eat *atika d'atik* (lit., 'old of old')..." The phrase "*atika d'atik*" hints to the highest levels of G-dly perceptions and wisdom. For *atik* is an aspect of the illumination of *kesser (the Crown)* – the revelation of the highest surrounding wisdom as is mentioned many places in the holy Zohar (see introduction to Zohar 4b). Just like a crown surrounds the head and adorns it, so will the Heavenly Crown surround your mind and envelop it. And this is the meaning of "You will eat "*atika d'atik*", that is, you will merit to comprehend the supernal crown (*kesser*), and you will perceive totally new conceptions every time you give of your wisdom to others. May Hashem help us to always be involved in *tzedakah* and *chesed* and we will draw down upon ourselves the illumination of Hashem's G-dliness from the highest level until we merit to be included in Him completely, for now and evermore. *Amen v'amen.*

3

Seuda Shlishis, Parshas Bamidbar, 5766

At the third Shabbos meal, Mohorosh Shlit"a spoke inspiring words on the subject of "elevating fear to its root", what it means and how we can do it, based on *Lekutei Mohoran*, Part I, Lesson 15.

Rebbe Nachman says: "If you want to have a taste of the hidden light, that is, the secrets of the Torah that are destined to be revealed when Moshiach comes, then you must elevate fear to its root. And with what do you elevate the trait of fear? You do so with judgment. This means that you judge yourself with regard to all of your deeds and activities. By doing this, you will free yourself from all fears. And then pure and refined fear will prevail, and the only remaining fear will be the fear of Hashem. When a person does not judge himself, then he will be judged from Heaven, for 'If there is no judgment below, then there is judgment Above [*Sifri Parshas Shoftim*]. And when a person is judged from Heaven, the judgment clothes and disguises itself in all things. And all things become messengers of the Omnipresent to carry out against a person the written judgment, as our Sages have said [*Talmud Nedarim 41a*]: 'When one is judged by Heaven then everything becomes a messenger and servant to carry out the verdict against him.' But when one judges himself and there is judgment below, then there is no judgment Above and fear will not clothe itself in any object in order to wake a person up [to teshuvah], for the person wakes himself up. When a person is afraid of something, whether the source of the fear is some person in a position of authority, or a dangerous criminal, etc., this comes about because fear has clothed itself in one of these objects. For if fear had not clothed itself in the object, then it would have had no power to cause a person to be afraid......The root of fear is knowledge – for one must *know* from whom to fear – and when one attains knowledge, he merits to comprehend the Torah as it is written (*Mishlei*, ch. 8): 'I, wisdom, am neighbor to shrewdness', that is, the Torah is a neighbor of the man of wisdom, as it is written (*Daniel*, ch. 2): 'He gives wisdom to the wise.' But there are two aspects to the Torah: the revealed aspect and the concealed aspect. A person will not merit the hidden aspect except in the future world. Nevertheless, even in this world, one can merit the hidden aspect through total dedication and devotion in prayer. And one merits prayer through the revealed Torah, for the revealed Torah is an aspect of Sinai, as our Sages have said (*Talmud Brachos* 64a): "*Sinai* is a name given to a Torah scholar with vast knowledge". And the concept of *Sinai* is the aspect of smallness and humility as our Sages have said (*Talmud Sota* 5a) that Hashem turned down all of the other mountains and only gave the Torah on Mt. Sinai. And the Sages say (ibid 5b) that the prayer of the one who is small in his own eyes is not despised as it is written (*Tehillim*, ch 51): 'A broken and humbled heart, G-d, You will not despise." And through prayer with devotion where one nullifies all of one's materialism with no boundary or limit as to what should be nullified - and when there is no boundary, then one can comprehend the Torah of the future world, which is unbounded and which can never be circumscribed by any boundary." (These are the words of Rebbe Nachman.)

Mohorosh explained that in this lesson Rebbe Nachman reveals to us how a person can merit even today the revelation of the secrets of the Torah of the future world. This Torah is called the "Torah of the Ancient Hidden One (*Lekutei Mohoran*, Part I, Lesson 33)", that is, the teachings of "*Atik* (ancient)" which are the first three *Sefiros* of the *Sefira of Kesser*. The Sefira of Kesser is divided into three parts, the first three are called "*Atik*" and the lower seven are called "*Arich* (long)". And the revelation of *Atik* is the revelation of G-dliness in an open and very exalted way where a person sees only complete G-dliness from each and every detail of creation. And this is the category of the revelation of *Yechida of Yechida* (Oneness of Oneness), where a person totally nullifies himself within the Infinite Light, and he sees before his eyes only the essence of the revelation of Hashem's G-dliness. But this matter will only be revealed some time in the future with the coming of our righteous Moshiach. For Moshiach will reveal wondrous teachings like these until everyone will merit a clear perception of G-dliness. However, even today, to the degree that a person elevates the trait of fear to its root, the more he will be able to taste the hidden light, that is, he will taste the secrets of the Torah that will be revealed in the future, and he will draw down upon himself a sweet and wondrous light, literally a taste of the world to come.

The matter of elevating fear to its root involves refining and purifying the trait of fear until no external fear remains at all. This means he will not be afraid of any person, whether he is a powerful ruler or a criminal, nor of any dangerous animal. Because he has only pure fear of Hashem, he will fear nothing but the splendor of His glory since He is the master and ruler of all the worlds. However, it is impossible to acquire this higher fear except through the trait of judgment. And this is part of the service of *hisbodedus* that Rebbe Nachman has taught us - that a person should judge himself every day as to whether or not his actions are proper and in accordance with the will of Hashem. People can live their entire lives without any *cheshbon hanefesh* (an accounting of one's soul). All of their ways seem straight and proper in their eyes. And they will not permit the threatening thought to enter their heads that there may be much to fix in their lives. But when a person makes an accounting every day between himself and his Maker with prayer and *hisbodedus*, reflecting deeply on all of his deeds, he will start to see what he has damaged and what he needs to repair. In this way, he exempts himself from all types of judgments from Above, as our holy Sages have said (*Sifri Parshas Shoftim*) "When there is judgment below there is no judgment Above". This means that if a person passes judgment on himself below with regard to all of his deeds, then the trait of Heavenly judgment does not need to judge him from Above. Also, fear no longer needs to clothe itself in any powerful ruler or judge or dangerous animal or criminal, because the person has already awoken *himself* to the trait of holy fear. But when there is no judgment below, there is judgment Above as the trait of fear clothes itself in everything to frighten him and to wake him up to the trait of holy fear and *teshuvah*. And then all types of trials and tribulations pass over him from the side of Heavenly judgment. Therefore, happy is the one who judges himself every day, for in this way, he frees himself from all types of external fears and merits to raise up the pure and clear fear of Hashem.

When one merits to acquire the trait of elevated fear, he thereby merits the revelation of knowledge. For the essence of knowledge is to know and recognize Hashem, as it is written (*Devarim*, ch. 4): "You have been shown that you might know that Hashem, He is the G-d, there is no [power] other than He." And this knowledge is of one piece with the trait of fear. Fear is in the heart as our holy Sages have said (*Talmud Kiddushin* 32b): "Regarding something that is hidden in the heart the Torah always says 'and you shall fear your G-d.' " And knowledge is also in the heart as it is written (*Devarim*, ch. 29): "And He has not given you a heart to know." For the main thing is to *know* what to fear. And that is the splendor of Hashem's glory and nothing else. Therefore, fear and knowledge are closely related and one depends on the other.

When one merits the revelation of knowledge, he merits the ability to comprehend the Torah. For in order to comprehend the Torah one needs knowledge as it is written (*Daniel*, ch. 2): "He gives wisdom to the wise." But there are two general levels of comprehending the Torah, namely, the revealed level and the hidden level. Everyone can merit to acquire the revealed part of the Torah through diligent study. But few people merit to understand the hidden aspects of the Torah, since it is in the category of the "Torah of the Ancient Hidden One" that is destined to be revealed only in the future world. These are the secrets of the Torah which uncover the inwardness of Hashem's G-dliness concealed in all of the details of creation, and not every mind can withstand these revelations. Nevertheless, by nullifying one's selfishness while praying with devotion, a person can merit, even today, the revelation of the Torah of the future world. For as soon as one prays with devotion, nullifying one's materialistic desires without any limits or boundaries as to what should be nullified, he becomes capable of comprehending the Torah of the future world, which is also without limits or boundaries. Therefore, one should start with learning the revealed parts of the Torah. For through learning the revealed Torah for its own sake, the precious trait of humility enters a person. And humility is an aspect of Mt. Sinai, as our holy Sages have said (*Talmud Sota* 5b): "Hashem turned down all of the mountains and only gave the Torah on Mt. Sinai because it made itself small." And as soon as humility enters a person, his prayer takes on tremendous power and significance, as our holy Sages have said (ibid): "The prayer of the low one is not despised as it is written (*Tehillim*, ch. 51): 'A broken and humbled heart, G-d, You will not despise.' " And then a person becomes capable of praying with total devotion and of nullifying completely his feelings of greatness and self-importance. Next, he merits the revelation of the hidden aspects of the Torah, which is the "Torah of the Ancient Hidden One". We find that all of these ideas are connected with one another: the revealed Torah emplaces humility within a person, which allows him to pray with total devotion, which in turn enables him to merit the hidden wisdom of the Torah, the revelation of the Torah of the world to come. Happy is the one who truly merits all of this!

The matter of praying with total devotion and nullifying all of one's feelings of self-importance and materialism, is also explained in the above section of the Talmud on the verse *(*Isaiah, ch. 26): " 'My dead bodies shall arise. Wake up and sing those who dwell in the dust.' This is the one who makes himself a neighbor to the dust in his life." For the main perfection of a person is that he merits to such a true self-nullification that it will seem in his own eyes that he is already neighbors with the dust and that he is lying down within it. It is a great service for a person to picture the day of his death and how they will bury him and how he will lay in the grave alone (*Sichos HaRan* # 109). At that time he will have nothing left but his attachment to Hashem's blessed light. However, to reflect upon these thoughts sometimes requires more than a little self-sacrifice since it is a very great fear, as Reb Nosson related about Rebbe Nachman (*Sichos HaRan* #57): "In his youth he was very afraid of death. But he would still picture the day of death and this was an act of self-sacrifice for him." When a person accustoms himself to think of his final and eternal destination, and how his body will have to lay in the grave and nothing will remain for him but the attachment of his soul to Hashem's blessed light, then true humility will enter him and he will merit the revelation of the secrets of the Torah even in his lifetime. Therefore, happy is the one who internalizes these ideas and thinks well about his final and eternal end, for then he will taste the World to Come in his lifetime and he will merit to be attached to Hashem with a true and eternal attachment in this world and the next forever and ever. Happy is he and fortunate is his lot.

Mohorosh connected these ideas to our parsha in the following way. We find that the book of *Bamidbar* (In the Desert) begins with the verse: **"Hashem spoke to Moshe in the Sinai desert (***b'Midbar Sinai***)."** The book of Vayikra ends with the verse (*Vayikra*, ch 27): **"These are the mitzvos that Hashem commanded Moshe to the Children of Israel at Mt. Sinai."** It is brought in the Torah commentaries (see *Baal HaTurim* and the commentary of the *Shach* on this verse) that the juxtaposition of these two verses comes to teach us that if a person does not make himself like a desert, he will not be able to know the Torah and the commandments. This is precisely the message of Rebbe Nachman here. That by starting with learning the revealed parts of the Torah, which is the verse **"These are the mitzvos that Hashem commanded Moshe to the Children of Israel"**, one comes to the category of **"at Mt. Sinai"**, which is the trait of humility. And then one can come to the level of being able to pray with total devotion, which leads to being able to comprehend the inside and hidden parts of the Torah. And this is the beginning of the book of *Bamidbar* – **"Hashem spoke to Moshe"** – which is the revelation of the inwardness of His G-dliness from all of creation and this is accomplished through the category of **"in the Sinai desert"**, which is prayer with total devotion when a person makes himself like a desert which is available and free to everyone, and with the utmost humility like Sinai, like one who literally dwells in the dust, and then the secrets of the Torah of the future world will be revealed to him - the "Torah of the Ancient Hidden One". Therefore, we always read parshas Bamidbar before Shavuos to hint to us that the main way to acquire the inwardness of the Torah is through the category of *"Bamidbar"* which is prayer with total devotion through which one nullifies himself without limit. And then he will truly merit to acquire the Torah. And may Hashem help us to receive upon ourselves the holiness of these days, and to receive the Torah literally as new, until we merit to return in perfect *teshuvah* before him, to be included in him completely, now and forever. *Amen v'amen.*

Seuda Shlishis, Parshas Nossoh, 5766

At the third Shabbos meal, Mohorosh Shlit"a spoke inspiring words on the topic of why some people oppose, disgrace and insult pious Jews, based on *Lekutei Mohoran*, Part I, Lesson 28.

Rebbe Nachman says: "People who oppose, disgrace and insult pious Jews, do so because they have received their Torah knowledge from Jewish 'demon' Torah scholars. For Jewish 'demon' Torah scholars receive their Torah knowledge from the demons that have a fallen Torah from fallen *alephs*. Regarding these *alephs* it is written (*Melachim* I, ch. 5): 'And he [King Solomon] spoke three thousand (*alaph-im*; the plural of *aleph*) proverbs and his songs were five and a thousand (*aleph*).' For Shlomo merited this wisdom through holiness. Jewish 'demon' Torah scholars receive their knowledge from these *alephs* but through spiritually impure means. As a result, all of their words are said in the form of proverbs, metaphors and brilliant logic, for the root of their words is from the above mentioned *alephs*." (These are the words of Rebbe Nachman.)

Mohorosh explained that Rebbe Nachman reveals to us in this lesson the root of the opposition against the truly G-d-fearing Jews. It would seem only natural and proper for people to feel much shame and humility in the presence of truly G-d fearing Jews. As a result, they would honor them and hold them in very high esteem. For when they would take an honest look at their own spiritual and moral standing and how they are very far from true attachment to Hashem compared to the moral level and attachment of G-d- fearing Jews, they would naturally feel it only proper to honor and love the truly pious Jews very much. But the reason why they turn into adversaries who only know how to disgrace and insult is because they receive their Torah knowledge from Jewish 'demons', that is, from Torah scholars who themselves receive their Torah from the demons. And demons are creatures that damage the world, their only desire and aim being to harm people, G-d forbid. And because these Torah scholars receive their Torah from the demons, the only thing they can accomplish with their Torah knowledge is to harm people and to inspire them to disgrace and insult G-d-fearing

Jews. Their teachings stem from the fallen *alephs* alluded to in the five *alephs* which comprise the first letters of the words (*Shemos*, ch. 15): "*Amar oyeiv erdof asig achaleik shallal (The enemy said, 'I will pursue, overtake, divide the spoil')*." From the side of holiness these five *alephs* allude to the *Aluf* of the world (The *Master* of the world) who is found everywhere, even in the words of the enemy who says, "I will purse, overtake, etc." Hashem is also found there, as it is brought in the name of the holy Baal Shem Tov in the book *Toldos Yakov Yosef*. But from the side of spiritual impurity, they are words of the evil inclination and the demons – a person's main enemies – which say, "I will pursue, overtake, divide the spoils, etc." They pursue the Tzaddikim and the G-d-fearing Jews with the aim to disgrace and insult them.

The Torah has two powers. It has the power to be a potion of life or a potion of death. One who learns Torah in order to strengthen and encourage himself and others, in order to teach each and every person that there is hope for them to fix their deeds and to return in perfect *teshuvah* to Hashem, such a person receives his Torah from the *alephs* of holiness. And he finds hints everywhere in the Torah for how to bring people closer to Hashem. In such a person's hands, the Torah is a potion of life. This is not the case for one who learns Torah for the sake of showing off his knowledge or in order to insult and disgrace people with his learning. The talks he gives to people are full of insults and ridicule and his listeners are made to feel there is no hope for them because of the multitude of their evil deeds. They are also made to believe that their judgment is already sealed for punishment in *gehinnom*. A teacher like this receives his Torah knowledge from the fallen *alephs*, that is, from the demons whose function is to damage the world. He goes after Jewish souls in order to weaken and destroy their hope and strength. And he goes after the truly G-d-fearing people in order to insult and disgrace them. In such a person's hands, the Torah turns into a potion of death and he actually performs the deeds of the demons that seek to harm people. As a result, this is what he does with his Torah knowledge: He brings proofs from the whole breadth and depth of the Torah to make people's knees buckle and to distance them from the possibility of doing *teshuvah*. He is imitating the heretics who also bring 'proofs' from the Torah for their defiled views. Therefore, one needs to guard himself very much from such Torah scholars and he should beg Hashem to save him from them and their followers.

Distinguishing between true Torah scholars and Jewish 'demon' Torah scholars is without a doubt a very difficult test for people. For both of them externally look the same. They both wear the garb of Torah scholars. And they both fill their lectures with parables, metaphors and brilliant logic. So how is it possible to tell them apart? There are two main ways to make the distinction. 1). Are his words built and established on the strong foundations of the holy Torah; not on his own fantasies and visions, which happens to be very popular in our times? There are people who dress themselves up in the garb of Torah scholars and in the garb of kabbalists, and then proceed to give over lectures of falsehood, based on what they claim to have seen in the upper worlds or in a dream or in a vision. But it is all emptiness and an evil spirit because their words have no source or foundation in Torah; rather, it is all from their hearts, in accordance with their own vain imaginings. 2). Are his words of Torah said in order to strengthen and encourage people, to inspire them to the service of Hashem or are they said to weaken and break their spirits with harsh rebuke. As soon as people hear from the mouth of a talented speaker that a certain person or type of person has no hope or way to fix himself, they should know that this man's Torah comes from the fallen *alephs* and from the Jewish 'demons'; and they need to distance themselves from him as much as possible.

It once happened that two young Torah scholars came to Reb Nosson and related to him that they had just listened to a Torah class given by a certain famous *maggid* (speaker). They told Reb Nosson that when the *maggid* noticed they weren't moved or inspired by his words, he interrupted his speech, turned to them and said, "Let me give you an analogy. A *maggid* such as myself is like a blacksmith who takes the bellows and pumps air onto a tiny spark of fire that was already there until he fans it into a roaring blaze. But if there is no spark, there is nothing to fan. It is the same with the two of you. There is no spark in you. Therefore, there is nothing with which to inspire you." So these two young scholars were left very discouraged and depressed from the *maggid's* words. They came and related to Reb Nosson what he said. Reb Nosson answered these young men that what this *maggid* said to them is just not so; every Jew has a spark – no matter who he is – it is just that not everyone is qualified to fan it into a flame. And he said in Yiddish, referring to the *maggid*, "You are not my blacksmith." For not everyone who has the talent to create parables and dazzle people with his brilliant logic receives his Torah from the *alephs* of holiness. And not everyone knows how to fan Jewish souls into a roaring fire. There are people who receive their Torah from the demons. Therefore, there is no need to be bothered by the speech of anyone who 'proves' from the Torah that a Jew doesn't have a spark of holiness, for it is just not so. Every Jew has a spark. One only needs to know how to inspire it and how to ignite it. Therefore, happy is the one who merits to be close to a true Rebbe and Tzaddik, whose every word of Torah is geared to inspire and lift up Jewish souls from their falls. And from such a teacher, one will receive the hope and optimism that will enable him to return to Hashem in truth and to attach himself to the Life of life. Happy is he and fortunate is his lot.

Mohorosh connected these ideas of Rebbe Nachman to our parsha in the following way. It is written at the end of the parsha (*Bamidbar*, ch. 7): "When Moshe came to the Tent of Meeting to speak with Him, he heard the Voice speaking to him from atop the Ark Cover that is upon the Ark of the Testimony, from between the two Cherubs, and He spoke to him." Rashi explains on this verse that when there are two verses which seem to contradict each other there comes a third verse to reconcile them and our verse is a case in point. One verse says (*Vayikra*, ch. 1): "And Hashem called to Moshe and spoke to him out of the Tent of Meeting", which was outside of the curtain separating the Holy of Holies from the Holy. And another verse says (*Shemos*, ch. 28): "I will speak to you from above the Ark Cover [i.e., within the curtain]." Our verse in our parsha comes and reconciles them: Moshe entered the Tent of Meeting and there he heard the Voice coming from atop the Ark Cover from between the two Cherubs. The Voice would go out from Heaven to the space between the two Cherubs and from there it would go out to the Tent of Meeting where it was heard by

Moshe (These are the words of Rashi). Perhaps this Rashi alludes to the above teachings of Rebbe Nachman. The difficulty in discerning between a true Torah scholar and a Jewish 'demon' Torah scholar can be compared to two verses which contradict each other and we do not know how to reconcile them. This one says that he receives his teachings from heaven and this one says he receives his teachings from heaven. How can we know who is telling the truth? But then comes a third verse which decides between the two. This is what is written: **"When Moshe came to the Tent of Meeting to speak with Him, he heard the Voice speaking to him from atop the Ark Cover that is upon the Ark of the Testimony, from between the two Cherubs, and He spoke to him"** - the true Torah scholar who is an aspect of Moshe receives his words "from atop the Ark Cover **that is upon the Ark of the Testimony**" - the Ark of the Testimony which is where the Torah rests. The first condition is that all of the scholar's words must be built and established on the strong foundations of the Holy Torah and not on vague imaginings and visions of falsehood. And the second condition is "**he heard the Voice speaking to him**" – all of the words said to him were in order to inspire and strengthen him in the ways of holiness and not to distance him and weaken him, G-d forbid. This is how we know that the Voice from above has clothed itself in the words of the Torah scholar – the voice of the holy angels and not of the demons and the evil spirits, G-d forbid. And this is how the Baal Haturim explains the verse: "from between the two Cherubs (**m**i'bein **s**hnei **h**akeruvim)" – the first letters spell 'Moshe' to teach us that he is considered as a Cherub from above. For the holy angels clothe themselves in the voices of the true Torah scholars who are an aspect of Moshe. And these scholars wake up and inspire Jewish souls to a supreme cleaving to Hashem. And may Hashem help us to be close to the true Tzaddikim and to always hear their holy voices until we merit to return in perfect *teshuvah* before Him, to be included in Him completely for now and evermore. *Amen v'amen.*

Seuda Shlishis, Parshas Bhaloscha, 5766

At the third Shabbos meal, Mohorosh Shlit"a spoke inspiring words about the great benefits that come from *limud haTorah* (the mitzvah of learning Torah), based on *Lekutei Mohoran*, Part I, Lesson 1.

Rebbe Nachman says: "Know, that through the Torah all the prayers which we pray and all the requests that we make are accepted; and Israel's charm, grace and importance are enhanced and exalted before all those who Israel needs – whether the need is spiritual or physical. Now unfortunately, due to our many sins, Israel's true charm, grace and importance have fallen. For at the present time, the main importance and charm is found with the other nations. But through the Torah, Israel's charm and importance will be enhanced, for the Torah is called (*Mishlei*, ch. 5): 'A loving hind and a graceful doe [*Ayeles ahavim v'ya'alas chein*; a graceful doe – *ya'alas chein* – also means "to confer charm and grace"], because it bestows charm and grace upon those who learn her (*Talmud Eiruvin*, 54b). And when one has charm and grace, all his prayers and requests are accepted." (These are the words of Rebbe Nachman.)

Mohorosh explained that we learn in this lesson that the main charm and grace of the Jewish nation in general, and of the individual Jew in particular, comes through the holy Torah. For the Torah bestows grace and importance upon all who occupy themselves with it. And the one who cleaves to the holy Torah shines brightly with a very great light and exudes a special charm which we can't find anywhere else. Even though we see today that people's estimation of Israel's true grace and importance has fallen greatly; and we also find that the greatest charm and importance is ascribed to the other nations and to those who are distant from the Torah; despite all of this, the charm and importance possessed by those who have forsaken the Torah and mitzvos are not real charm and importance at all. For without Torah a person has nothing and his life is similar to that of an animal and at times like that of a dangerous beast. Such a life is even inferior to the animals in the sense that animals live exactly according to the nature that Hashem has implanted within them. But a human being with no Torah is always in great danger of going way beyond the bounds assigned to him by Hashem: by committing murder and theft and by harming people to a much greater extent than wild animals are capable of. As we have seen throughout the generations, the nations of the world who did not accept the Noachide Laws of Hashem and disparaged and ridiculed the Torah, have pursued and afflicted the Jewish people with the harshest suffering – afflictions which are impossible to fully describe. And to our great shame, even some of our own brethren, who have forsaken and despised the Torah, have harbored great hatred for those who are dedicated to *limud haTorah* and the performance of mitzvos. They too have pursued and embittered the lives of faithful Jews, as our holy Sages have said (*Talmud Pesachim*, 49b): "Greater is the hatred of those who are ignorant of Torah for Torah scholars than the hatred of the nations of the world for Israel." For without the Torah, a person has nothing. He lives with no real purpose, and this makes his life very bitter. So, although it appears as if he has a certain charm and importance due to his wealth, material prosperity and the honor that people show him, it is all vanity and emptiness, absolutely devoid of any permanence. For true charm, grace and importance are only possessed by those who are occupied with the Torah – those who toil to find Hashem in every detail of the days of their lives and strive to fulfill the purpose of their lives. And this purpose is to recognize and know Hashem, as it is written in the Zohar (*Parshas Bo*, 42a): "The entire creation was brought into being in order that we recognize Hashem." This is what brings true charm and grace to a person and causes the light of his soul to shine with a very great radiance until he is elevated above the natural order of the world.

The main reason why people are distant from the Torah is because the Torah seems to be a tremendous burden to them. They see that there is so much to learn, so they end up learning nothing, as it is brought in the Midrash (*Devarim Rabbah* Ch. 8): "The fool enters the house of learning and sees a profusion of Torah: Tractate Shabbos with 24 chapters, Tractate *Keilim* with 30 chapters, etc.. He says to himself, 'When will I learn all this?' So he learns nothing. But the wise person says, 'Who said we have to learn it all in one day. Today, I will learn one *halacha*, and tomorrow one *halacha* until I will have learned the entire Torah.'" And so our holy Sages have said (*Tanchumah Pinchas* Ch. 11): "Why is the Torah compared to a fig tree? Just as the fruit of a fig tree does not all ripen at the same time, but today one fig ripens here and tomorrow another fig there, so too are the words of Torah: they are not all learned in one day, but only little by little, a set amount each day." This is the idea behind the system of learning that Rebbe Nachman has taught us (*Sichos HaRan*, #76): Every man should make a schedule for himself to learn a fixed amount in different areas of the Torah each day. And he should begin learning from the very beginning of a book, such as the *Tanach*, all the way through to

2

the end and he should not go back to earlier sections until he has gone through the entire *Tanach*. The same rule applies to learning *Mishnah* and *Gemara* as well as to all of the other holy books of the Torah. One should make a fixed schedule to learn a little bit every day, sticking to the order of the plan no matter what. And even when one encounters areas in his learning that he doesn't yet understand, he should not skip them; but he should read the words verbatim and continue following his daily schedule until he has completed the entire book from beginning to end. For through a gradual accumulation of learning and by finishing what one has started, unknowingly a great amount of Torah will be acquired and then one can return to the beginning of the book and learn everything another time. And the second time one learns any subject, one already understands more than he understood the first time around. And the third time through, one will understand even more, until he will be very well versed in the subject. This is an awesome and wonderful way to acquire Torah but it is only understood by those who have followed it. Those who do not deceive themselves but follow Rebbe Nachman's learning method with total sincerity and simplicity will merit to traverse most areas of the Torah and become well versed in them. And the Torah will bestow true charm and esteem upon him. This is not true for those who are wise in their own eyes and do not want to accept the words of Rebbe Nachman at face value. Instead, they fool themselves and say, "Rebbe Nachman couldn't have meant this literally. What he really meant was this..." Sadly, these people remain the same ignoramuses they were from the start, and true charm and grace will not be found with them, for without Torah a person ends up being idle and idleness has very serious negative effects on one's mental health. Our holy Sages have already said (*Talmud Kesubos*, 59b): "Idleness leads to psychosis and to lewdness." Without Torah a person is liable to commit all of the evils in the world, for the spirit of folly within him seduces him to sin, as our holy Sages have said (*Talmud Sotah* 2a): "A person does not commit a sin unless a spirit of folly enters him." But the holy Torah shields a person from all of this, for it graces him with true charm and importance until the spirit of folly flees from him. And he merits to feel a wonderful sweetness and pleasantness in his life, as it is written (*Mishlei*, 3): "Its ways are ways of pleasantness and all its paths are peace." For there is true pleasantness in the Torah and the goal is to merit to feel this pleasantness (*Lekutei Mohoran*, Part II, Lesson 71). And when one feels it, he will desire nothing else but the Torah itself and live a truly good life.

It is essential to always remember what Rebbe Nachman once said to Reb Nosson: "A little bit is also good." And Reb Nosson declared that this saying

3

emplaced within him true diligence in learning Torah. For when a person wants to learn, the *yetzer hara* comes to him and says, "See, you don't have much time to learn now, and your mind isn't settled properly. So, just put off your learning for a different time." But when one knows the rule – "a little is also good" – then every bit of learning he can grab will be important and precious in his eyes, even without complete comprehension. In this way, he will learn another bit, and then another bit, until he has learned many pages. This is awesome advice for one who understands it, truly worth more than its weight in gold. Therefore, happy is the one who spends his days and years learning Torah, for in so doing, true charm, grace and importance will rest on him, and his soul will shine with a very great light until it can well be said of him that the entire world exists for his sake alone. And he will merit a glimpse of the World to Come in his lifetime. Happy is he and praiseworthy is his lot.

Mohorosh connected these teachings to our *parshah* in the following way. It is written (*Bamidbar*, ch. 8): "Speak to Aaron and say to him: 'When you kindle the lamps (*beha'aloscha es haneiros*, lit. 'when you elevate the lamps') towards the face of the menorah the seven lamps shall give light." Perhaps we can say that this verse can teach us about the great benefits of *limud haTorah*. The menorah represents the wisdom of the Torah as our holy Sages have said (*Talmud Baba Basra 25b*): "He who wants to become wise should pray towards the south (we actually pray facing east but the Sages mean to turn *slightly* towards the south as explained there in the *Gemara*). And your sign for this is the menorah which was situated in the south side of the Holy Temple." And the verse reveals to us – "**When you kindle the lamps**" – when you want to kindle and elevate Jewish souls who are likened to a lamp, as it is written (*Mishlei*, 20): "The lamp of Hashem is the soul of *Adam*", they must be "**towards the face of the menorah**" – that is, when they are facing the Torah their souls will shine, for the Torah will draw upon them a supernal grace and charm that will shine throughout the entire world. And then the entire creation will be humbled towards them, which is – "**the seven lamps**" – as it is brought in the *Baal HaTurim* that the seven lamps of the menorah correspond to the seven constellations. In other words, all of the constellations, through which the laws of nature are channeled, will shine and conduct themselves according to the will of the holy people who are occupied with learning and performing the will of Hashem, which is the holy Torah. For the Torah elevates them above the world. May Hashem help us to always be occupied in the Torah with mighty diligence and perseverance, and we will merit to draw down upon ourselves a supernal charm and grace, until we

4

ascend to be included in Him completely for now and evermore. Amen v'amen.

5

Seuda Shlishis, Parshas Shlach, 5760

At the third Shabbos meal, Mohorosh Shlit"a spoke inspiring words about the holiness of the Land of Israel and of the Tzaddik, based on *Lekutei Mohoran*, Part I, Lesson 129.

We find in our parsha the failure of the spies that were sent to Eretz Yisroel and how they spoke *loshon hara* about the Land. In reality, everything they saw in the Land was truly for their good, for everything Hashem does with a person is only for the good. However, the spies did not have the proper level of *hisch`azkus* (moral and spiritual self-fortification); so they turned everything upside down and saw bad where they should have seen good. Rebbe Nachman poses the following question (*Lekutei Mohoran*, Part I, Lesson 47): It is true that the spies spoke evil about the Land of Israel, but how can their lie be written in the Torah which is the Torah of Truth? We must say that there must be a certain amount of good hidden within their words; it was only that they did not know how to interpret and explain it correctly. And this is what Rebbe Nachman reveals in this lesson: How the words of the spies, when they said that the Land of Israel is "A land that devours its inhabitants", actually contain a great secret about serving Hashem and how we can derive from it a profound lesson. The spies said these words when they saw – everywhere they went in the Land – the Canaanites burying their dead (*Bamidbar Rabbah*, ch. 16:24). They did not understand that Hashem caused this to happen for their own good, i.e. that the Canaanites should be so involved with their mourning that they would pay no attention to the spies.

And Rebbe Nachman says: **"When one comes close to a Tzaddik, even though he receives nothing from the Tzaddik at all, the mere coming close is also very good. The *emunah* alone – that he believes in the Tzaddik – helps in his service of Hashem. And the secret of this is as follows: The nature of eating is that the nourishment is transformed into the one who is nourished by it. For example, when an animal eats vegetation, such as grass, the grass turns into the animal when it enters the animal's innards and is digested. Likewise, from an animal to a human being – when the human being eats the animal, the animal turns into a person. And to every part of the body to which the food is sent – as** it is distributed to all parts of the body – it literally becomes transformed there into the essence and nature of that part of the body. For example, a component of the nourishment that enters the brain is turned into the brain. The part that enters the heart becomes a heart; and so too, with respect to all other parts of the body.

And this is the meaning of: "A Land that devours its inhabitants". 'Land' represents the concept of *emunah* (faith), as it is written (*Tehillim*, ch. 37): 'Dwell in the Land and be nourished by *emunah*." 'A Land that devours its inhabitants' teaches us that when one enters the Land, he becomes 'devoured' by the Land. That is, he is transformed and turned into the Land's essence and nature which is faith. Therefore, our Sages have said (*Talmud Kesubos* 111): 'All who dwell in the Land of Israel dwell without sin, as it says (*Isaiah*, ch. 33).: 'The people that dwell in it, their sin is forgiven', for it is 'A Land that devours its inhabitants', as the one who lives there is 'devoured' by it and thus converted into its holy essence and nature. Therefore, even one who 'walks four cubits in the Land of Israel is assured of a place in the world to come', as our Sages have said (ibid).

The same thing happens when one is attached to and believes in the Tzaddik. The Tzaddik also represents the concept of *emunah* because he teaches *emunah* to all his followers. When one comes close to the Tzaddik he is 'devoured' by the Tzaddik and is literally transformed into the essence of the Tzaddik.

This concept of spirituality 'devouring' physicality is also explained in another place in *Lekutei Mohoran* (Part I, Lesson 101) regarding the verse (*Tehillim*, ch. 27) 'When *mereiyim* approach me to devour my flesh'. *Mereiyim* literally means 'evildoers', but can also mean 'friends'. The 'friends' referred to here are the two intellectual faculties of *chochmah* (wisdom) and *binah* (understanding) that are like two inseparable friends. When I want these 'two friends' to come together [and together they teach a person *daas* (knowledge)], then I need to eat my own flesh, that is, I must subdue physicality through spirituality. This is called 'to eat my flesh' because it is the intellectual faculty of the soul that is eating the body and converting it into its very essence. And this is the concept of eating: food becoming converted into the essence of the one who eats it. This is what happens in the Land of Israel and at the court of the Tzaddik. You become devoured by their spirituality and

2

become part of them. **But every thing depends on a persons will. If one has a very strong will to come close to Hashem and to serve Him, but it is difficult for him to break the lusts of his body, then through coming close to the Tzaddik, and through coming to Eretz Yisroel, he enters the category of 'eating', and he will be 'eaten' by the Tzaddik, and by the Land of Israel and he will be converted into their very essence and character. However, if it is not his will to serve Hashem, then coming to the Tzaddik or to Eretz Yisroel will not help him, and he enters the category of food which is not able to be digested. If one eats a certain food which he cannot tolerate, then it will not be digested and converted into the person. Instead, the body will vomit it out. The same thing applies to the situation where the person is not 'eaten' by the Tzaddik or by Eretz Yisroel. Since the Tzaddik or the Land cannot tolerate him, they must disgorge him. This alluded to in the verse which speaks about the Land of Israel (*Vayikra*, ch. 18): "And the Land shall not vomit you as it vomited out the nations before you". The Land cannot tolerate people that do not want its holy essence. So it disgorges them."** (These are the words of Rebbe Nachman.)

Mohorosh explained that the very act of coming close to anything of holiness, even though one does not feel that anything has been gained from it, is nonetheless very good. And *emunah* alone – that one believes in the Tzaddik or in the object of holiness – helps very much in one's service of Hashem. And in the end, one will merit to be converted to the very essence of the thing he believes in. Rebbe Nachman gives an example of this: When an animal eats a plant, the plant is literally converted within the animal to the essence of the animal itself. Likewise, when a human being eats an animal, the animal is transformed within the human being into the human being himself, for the nourishment is transformed into the one who is nourished by it. The same thing applies to drawing close to anything of holiness. When one brings himself close to something holy, for example, a Tzaddik or the Land of Israel, and one believes in their holiness, then, little by little, one is 'eaten' by the Tzaddik or by the Land of Israel and is transformed into their essence and character. And this is the meaning of: "A Land which devours its inhabitants", that is, the Land of Israel 'eats' the one who lives there and converts him into its essence. For the essence of the Land of Israel is *emunah*, as it is written (*Tehillim*, ch. 37): "Dwell in the Land and be nourished by *emunah*", for in the Land of Israel Hashem's divine Providence is revealed to a greater degree than anywhere else in the world, as it is written (*Devarim*, ch. 11): "The eyes of Hashem your G-d are always on it [the Land], from the

3

beginning of the year until year end." Therefore, when one lives in the Land of Israel in order to recognize and find Hashem's Providence there, one will be 'eaten' and converted to the essence of the Land – and that essence is *emunah*.

It is the same with regard to coming close to the Tzaddik. The entire essence of the Tzaddik is only about revealing *emunah* in the world. His entire will and desire all the days of his life is to reveal and publicize Hashem's G-dliness to all the earth's inhabitants, until everyone, from the greatest to the smallest, will recognize Him. Therefore, the closer one brings himself to the Tzaddik and the more one believes in him – even though he does not feel he has benefited from the Tzaddik in any way – little by little, he will be 'eaten' by the Tzaddik and become transformed into the essence of the Tzaddik. Through the sheer abundance of speech that he hears from the Tzaddik, and from the open G-dliness that surrounds the Tzaddik, the Tzaddik's great light will be engraved within him, and he will also begin to radiate the holy light of *emunah*.

And this is how Rebbe Nachman concludes this lesson: Everything depends on the will. If a person wants to come close to Hashem through some holy means, for example, through the guidance of a Tzaddik or through the Land of Israel, then these things will certainly help him get close to Hashem. But, if it is not a person's will to come close to Hashem, and he comes to the Tzaddik in order to mock him, or he comes to the Land of Israel to do whatever he wants there, throwing off from himself the yoke of Torah and mitzvos, G-d forbid, then the opposite effect will occur – the Tzaddik and the Land of Israel will disgorge him and he will be thrown out, as it is written (*Vayikra*, ch. 18): "So that the Land not vomit you out when you defile it." For exactly as in the analogy of a person that eats something which isn't fit for consumption and how his body will vomit it out; so too, the Tzaddik and the Land of Israel will disgorge him and he will be expelled.

If we find a person who had originally been close to a Tzaddik but afterwards distanced himself from him, we should know that his initial coming close to the Tzaddik was not sincere (*Sefer HaMiddos*, ch. Tzaddik). One needs *mesirus nefesh* (self-sacrifice) to be able to remain close to the Tzaddik and not distance himself from him. And with respect to the Land of Israel, one should not think that he will be free from the *yetzer hara* and not need to do battle with it there. Just the opposite! In the Land of Israel there is more of a battle against the *yetzer hara*, since in the Land the *yetzer hara* is extremely

4

strong and it clothes itself in things which appear to be mitzvos but are actually not; and it uses this ploy to a much greater extent than it does outside the Land. As the holy Rebbe Rabbi Mendel Vitebsker once remarked when he moved to the Land of Israel, that when he was living outside the Land he always thought that the *Satan* (*yetzer hara*) was found outside the Land and only the Satan's emissaries were in the Land. But when he began living in the Land of Israel, it became apparent to him that the *Satan* is found in the Land and his emissaries are outside the Land. For the holier something is, the lower it falls. And the Land of Israel is precisely where the *klippos* (impurities) are the strongest. Therefore, one needs to come to the Land of Israel with a strong will to come close to Hashem and then the essence of the Land will help him truly come close to Him. But if one's will to come close to Hashem is not strong, in the end the Land of Israel will disgorge him. We see with our own eyes how many people flee from the Land of Israel and go to other lands because they are unable to find a place for themselves there. The same dynamic applies with coming close to the Tzaddik. If one does not come with the sincere intent to come close to Hashem through the guidance of the Tzaddik, then the Tzaddik will disgorge him and he will no longer be able to remain with the Tzaddik. Therefore, happy is the one who does not deceive himself, but dedicates himself totally to come close to every holy thing. And in good time, a very awesome holiness will be drawn upon him and he will merit to come close to Hashem in truth.

Mohorosh said that according to the words of Rebbe Nachman an awesome and wonderful secret is hidden in the words of the spies – "A Land which devours its inhabitants". And the secret is that by living in the Land of Israel, each and every person's essence is transformed into the essence of the Land itself. If such a wonderful teaching is hidden in the spies' words, then in what way did they fail? And why should we even begin to look at their words in a negative way? But the matter is as explained at the end of Rebbe Nachman's lesson above: It all depends on a person's will. If a person has the will to sincerely come close to Hashem and he also has the proper *hischazkus* to strengthen himself no matter what he goes through in life, even in situations which appear bad to him, then in the end he will be included within the light of holy *emunah* and see with his own eyes how everything turns into good. But if he does not have a sincere desire to come close to Hashem and lacks the proper *hischazkus*, then as soon as things start not going his way, he will become very broken and he will flee from holiness. And this is what happened to the spies. They saw "a Land which devours its inhabitants": In its simple meaning, many of the Canaanites, the inhabitants of the Land, had

5

160

died. But if they had had a strong will and true *hischazkus*, they would have believed that it was all for their good. And in the end, they would have understood how Hashem did them a wonderful favor by causing the Canaanites to be distracted and preoccupied with burying their dead. But, because they didn't have the proper *hischazkus*, they imagined that Hashem had decreed evil against them. So they thought, "Why do we need to enter the Land of Israel only to die?" But Yehoshua and Kalev, who both had a different spirit, were equipped with true *hischazkus* which they constantly received from Moshe Rabbeinu. They were therefore able to nullify themselves totally, feeling no need to ask difficult questions about what lay before them. In this way, they merited what they merited: Yehoshua brought the Jewish people into the Land of Israel and Kalev received a beautiful inheritance – the city of Chevron. Everything depends on a person's will and *hischazkus*!

And this is how Rabbi Efraim'l from Peshedborzh zat'zal, author of the book "*Oneg Shabbos*", explains what we find in our parsha regarding the spies bringing back with them some of the fruit of the Land, whereas Yehoshua and Kalev brought nothing back. It seems to be difficult to understand how Yehoshua and Kalev fulfilled the words of Moshe Rebbeinu who commanded all twelve of the spies: "Strengthen yourselves and take from the fruit of the Land." Rabbi Efraim'l explains that the spies merely fulfilled the second part of Moshe Rabbeinu's command, namely, "take from the fruit of the Land." But they forgot completely about the "Strengthen yourselves" part. But this was the main part! The main thing was that they should have true *hischazkus*, to know what was before them and to bring back a positive report that would strengthen the Jewish nation. On the other hand, Yehoshua and Kalev fulfilled the essence of "Strengthen yourselves" entirely because they had true *hischazkus* in understanding that all that Hashem does is for the good. And how did they fulfill "take from the fruit of the Land"? By having the proper *hischazkus*, they automatically took from the fruit of the Land because they took the essence of the spiritual illumination of the Land which is the illumination of holy *emunah*. What more beautiful fruit than that can be found anywhere! And in this way, they merited what they merited.

Mohorosh said that this is a profound teaching for everyone in every generation: How one needs true *hischazkus* in everything he goes through. For a person does not know what awaits him in life. And when the groom stands under the *chuppah* he can't dream of what will be in the coming days. But when he prepares himself with true *hischazkus*, that is, in everything he

6

goes through in life he will run to Hashem in prayer and believe that the hand of Hashem is treasured away in everything, then it will be a good and sweet life and he will merit to cleave to Hashem with a true attachment. This is not the case for one who believes that everything in life should go according to his will. For as soon as things do not go as planned, he becomes completely broken. A person like this will be so broken and weak that he will not be able to hold his ground in life.

The essential level of a person is measured only according to his *hischazkus*, as once expressed by Rebbe Nachman when he said: "The main thing is what we call '*derhaltin zich* (holding oneself strong)." And Reb Nosson once gave an amazing talk on *hischazkus* in which he related that all the Tzaddikim reached their levels only through the trait of *hischazkus* and he said, "How did Moshe Rebbeinu reach his level? Only through his having the trait of *hischazkus*. How did Rebbi Shimon bar Yochai reach his level? Only through his having the trait of *hischazkus*. How did the Arizal reach his level? Only through his having the trait of *hischazkus*. How did Rebbe Nachman reach his level? Only through his having the trait of *hischazkus*. And he concluded, How did I come to what I have come to? Only through my having the trait of *hischazkus*." For over all of the Tzaddikim passed suffering and afflictions, disputes and controversy within their own homes and without. But through holding their ground and not complaining about the ways of Hashem, G-d forbid, and by strengthening themselves and accepting everything with love, they came to what they came to. But if a person complains and speaks harshly about Hashem's ways, G-d forbid, in the end he was suffer a great fall, as we find regarding Levi (*Talmud Sotah* 53a) that he spoke harshly against heaven and as a result became lame in one leg. For although his intentions were good in praying for rain, he did not pray for it in the proper way, i.e. in the form of supplication and begging for compassion. Instead he said to Hashem, "Have you gone up to the heavens and forgotten Your children?" As a result he was punished by falling to the ground and becoming lame. For a person always needs to beg for compassion before Hashem and afterwards to believe that everything Hashem does is for the good. And then he will have true *hischazkus* and be very successful all the days of his life. May Hashem help us to acquire the trait of true *hischazkus* and to hold our ground no matter what, until we merit to see the redemption and salvation of Israel with the coming of our righteous Moshiach swiftly in our days. *Amen v'amen.*

7

Seuda Shlishis, Parshas Korach, 5765

At the third Shabbos meal, Mohorosh Shlit"a spoke inspiring words on the topics of *yishuv hadaas* (having a calm, clear and settled mind) and *simcha*, based on *Lekutei Mohoran*, Part II, Lesson 10.

Rebbe Nachman says: "The reason why the people of the world are distant from Hashem and why they do not bring themselves closer to Him, is only because they do not have *yishuv hadaas* and they do not think clearly about and come to terms with the question: 'Of what real purpose and ultimate benefit are all of the lusts and all of the matters of this world; both the bodily lusts and the emotional and mental lusts, such as the lust for honor?' Once they have reconciled themselves to the answer, they will certainly return to Hashem. But you should know, that due to sadness and bitterness it is impossible to have control over one's mind and it is difficult to calm and settle the mind in order to think clearly. Only through *simcha* can one have control over and be able to calm and settle the mind. For *simcha* is the 'world of freedom', an aspect of the verse (Isaiah, Ch. 55): 'For you shall go out with *simcha*.' For through *simcha*, one becomes a freeman and leaves *galus* (exile). Therefore, when one attaches *simcha* to the mind, the mind becomes a 'freeman' and is no longer in the category of *galus*. And then one is able to direct the mind at will and calm and settle the mind, as the mind is now free and no longer in *golus*. For as a result of being in *golus* the mind isn't settled, as our Sages have explained (*Talmud Megillah* 12b) regarding the Children of Ammon and Moav that they had *yishuv hadaas* because they had not gone into exile, as it says (Jeremiah, Ch. 48): 'Moav has been at ease from its youth, and he has settled on its dregs [like wine in a vat], and has not been emptied out from vessel to vessel, neither has he gone into exile: therefore, his taste remained in him and his aroma is not changed.' Coming to *simcha* is accomplished through finding at least some good point in oneself, as explained on the verse (*Lekutei Mohoran*, Part I, Lesson 282): 'I will make music to my G-d while I yet exist [lit., with my 'little bit more'].' At the very least, one can be happy that he merited to be from the seed of Israel, 'that He did not make me a heathen', as we say: 'Blessed is He, our G-d, Who created us for His glory and separated us from those who stray and gave us a Torah of truth...' From all this and from similar things, it is fitting for a person to derive *simcha* to bring joy to his mind. And this is the category of (*Talmud*

Shabbos, 77b): '*b'dicha daatei* (being in a very good mood)', which is a great thing; that is, one attaches *simcha* to one's mind, and then the mind is set free, granting one *yishuv hadaas*. And also in the upper worlds a great unification is made from this through *b'dicha daatei*." (These are the words of Rebbe Nachman.)

Mohorosh explained that Rebbe Nachman reveals to us that it is clear that the essential reason that causes a person to distance himself from Hashem is only a lack of *yishuv hadaas*. For if a person had *yishuv hadaas*, he would recognize clearly that it is impossible to distance himself from Hashem at all. For who moves within a person? It is only Hashem. And who breathes within a person? Only Hashem. If so, how is it possible to distance oneself from Hashem when He is found in a person's each and every movement? A person has no existence without Hashem. We find that the essential cause of being distant from Hashem is a lack of *yishuv hadaas*. And this lack makes one feel that everything is only nature, chance and luck, which in turn causes one to fall into a state of sadness and despondency. And then one feels far from Hashem, as far from Him as a person can get. However, when he has *yishuv hadaas* and brings the trait of *simcha* into himself, he has the freedom of mind to see the truth. And then he is very close to Hashem. And he goes out of *galus* completely, which is an aspect of the verse (Isaiah, Ch. 55): 'For you shall go out with *simcha*', i.e. through *simcha* one leaves *golus*. For the main *golus* is the *golus* of the mind and soul. But when one has *simcha* and revives himself with the knowledge of the truth of Hashem's existence, he is literally a freeman and lacks nothing at all.

The advice for coming to a state of *simcha* is basically that a person should revive himself with every good point he has, even if it is the smallest thing. For as soon as one recognizes the level and the greatness of what it means to be a Jew, and how every mitzvah is very important and precious in the eyes of Hashem, one will certainly rejoice greatly beyond all bounds because he merited to be created from the seed of Israel and to fulfill His *mitzvos*. And this will give him *yishuv hadaas*, until he recognizes clearly that he is very close to Hashem and that there is no absolute existence at all besides Hashem. Sadly, this is not the case for the person who is stuck in a state of constricted consciousness and sadness, not being able to revive himself with the good points he merited to grab in this world. How will he ever have *simcha* and *nachas ruach* in his life as long as he feels far from Hashem? And all the money and wealth in the world will not make him happy, for "one who has a hundred wants two hundred" and is therefore always lacking very much. We

2

find that there is no other advice in the world but to always gladden oneself with the good point of his Jewishness: that he merited to be a Jew and to fulfill the will of Hashem. Then, through this *simcha*, he will come to true *yishuv hadaas* and feel his closeness to Hashem. And it will be a good and sweet life. Happy is he and fortunate is his lot.

Mohorosh connected these ideas to our parsha in the following way. We find in our parsha the failure of Korach, his dispute with Moshe Rebbeinu and his consequent downfall. We need to understand what Korach was lacking that he felt compelled to instigate a dispute with Moshe and Aaron. After all, he was one of the people who were privileged to carry the Holy Ark and also one of the wealthiest people in the world, as our holy Sages have said (*Talmud Pesachim* 119a): "Three hundred white mules carried the keys to his treasure chests." If so, what did he lack that he needed to contend with Moshe and Aaron and to seek even more greatness and honor? According to the words of Rebbe Nachman we can understand it very well. Korach lacked *yishuv hadaas* and this was his downfall. Because he distanced himself from Moshe Rebbeinu who was the "*daas* (wisdom)" of the Jewish nation, Korach found himself in a state of lacking *yishuv hadaas*. Therefore, he did not know how to revive himself with all his good points. As a result he came to mock and scoff at the *mitzvos* of *tzitzis* and *mezuzah* and he said, "If one thread of *techeilis* makes an all-white *talis* permitted to be worn, then why should a *talis* that is made entirely of *techeilis* need a thread of techeilis tzitzis in order to be worn?. And if the two small chapters of '*Shema Yisrael*' and '*Vehaya im shamoah*' attached to the doorpost of one's house permits the home to be lived in, then why should a house full of holy books need a mezuzah in order to be lived in?"

But this was his mistake. For Hashem desires specifically the small points of the Jewish people, e.g. that one thread of *techeilis* can permit a garment to be worn; and a small *mezuzah* containing two small chapters of the Torah permits a house to be lived in. From these *mitzvos* and similar ones, we receive the *yishuv hadaas* to know how to enliven and gladden ourselves with every small point we have. But if one wants only a whole thing, something that is complete and perfect, like a *talis* that is 100% *techeilis*, or a house that is filled with holy books, then he will never be able to be happy and revive himself with what he has. For he will always be lacking very much. And all of the wealth in the world will not make him happy, for "one who has a hundred wants two hundred" and thus he will always lack half. Therefore, all of Korach's honor and wealth did not satisfy him, since he only wanted a

3

whole thing. It wasn't enough for him to be one of the carriers of the Holy Ark, which is absolutely the closest one can come to Hashem in this world. It did not suffice because he lacked *yishuv hadaas* and desired only to be the *Kohein Gadol*; i.e. he desired only a whole and perfect leadership role. Therefore all of his riches did not satisfy him, for he needed more and more. And the lack of *yishuv hadaas* is what seduced him to contend with Moshe and to lust after what he did not have. And in the end, he also lost what he did have and was left lacking and empty of everything. Therefore, it is an essential part of one's service of Hashem to always search for one's good points and to give oneself life with all one possesses. And then one will live a truly good life.

We find regarding Moshe Rebbeinu that he was the antithesis of Korach in terms of *yishuv hadaas*, as Moshe said (*Bamidbar*, Ch. 16): "I have not taken one donkey from them, nor have I hurt one of them." Moshe Rebbeinu could boast that he had no need for what others had, for he gave himself life with what he did have, and he did not desire any greatness or honor. And this was the "*daas* of Moshe", the wisdom of true *yishuv hadaas*, which means that he gave himself life with every good point he possessed and he had no need to derive any benefit from others. So too, Shmuel *HaNavi* could boast in our *Haftarah* (*Shmuel* I, Ch. 12): "Whose ox have I taken? Or whose donkey have I taken? Or whom have I robbed? Whom have I coerced?" For Shmuel *HaNavi* was a true leader who had the "*daas* of Moshe" - true *yishuv hadaas*. Therefore, it is written about him (*Shmuel* I, Ch. 7): "And his return was to Ramah, for there was his house." And our holy Sages have commented on this verse (*Talmud Berachos* 10b): "Wherever he went, his home was with him." For because of the greatness of his *yishuv hadaas*, he always had all he needed and therefore felt no need to benefit from what others had. He was a true leader who would place this *yishuv hadaas* into the Jewish people, so they too would know how to give themselves life with every good point they possessed, whether the good point was something spiritual or material. And it was this *daas* that allowed them and us to have a truly good life. May Hashem help us to attain true *yishuv hadaas* and we will draw down upon ourselves the light of the *daas* of the Tzaddikim until we merit to ascend and cleave to Hashem in truth and simplicity all the days of our lives. *Amen v'amen.*

4

Seuda Shlishis, Parshas Chukas, 5765

At the third Shabbos meal, Mohorosh Shlit"a spoke inspiring words on the meaning of the verse (*Tehillim*, Ch. 4): "When I was in distress, You opened a wide expanse for me", based on *Lekutei Mohoran*, Part I, Lesson 195.

Rebbe Nachman says: "It is written: 'When I was in distress, You opened a wide expanse for me.' This means that even from within the distress itself, Hashem opens a wide expanse for us. For if one would contemplate the loving kindnesses of Hashem, one would see that even when Hashem challenges a person with difficulties, from within the very difficulty itself, Hashem also opens a wide expanse for him and increases His loving kindness towards him. Aside from our hope that Hashem should save us soon from all troubles and do much good with us, still, even in the very midst of the hardship itself, He widens the straits we are in." (These are the words of Rebbe Nachman.)

Mohorosh explained that in this lesson Rebbe Nachman offers us awesome advice and encouragement for all the days of our lives, namely, that one should always look for the wide openings that Hashem opens up for him in the very midst of his troubles. For although a person may go through quite a lot (and there is no one who is free from troubles and suffering), nevertheless, if he would just take a good look at his life, he would understand that the entire purpose of the troubles and suffering is only to bring him closer to Hashem and closer to his true self. And if he thought deeply about it he would realize that from all of the troubles that have befallen him great benefits have also come out, as our holy Sages have commented (Talmud *Yerushalmi Taanis* 11a) on the verse "In a time of distress, You have opened a wide expanse for me": "Dovid said before Hashem: 'Master of the universe, every hardship I have gone through, you have widened it for me. I went through the ordeal with Bas Sheva and you gave me Shlomo. I went through the crises and hardships of Israel and you gave me the *Beis Hamikdosh*." For Dovid *HaMelech* had this skill, and he was an expert in it – the skill to find Hashem in all of his sorrows, and in this way he wrote the book of Psalms which is filled with praises to His Name. Even though many troubles and afflictions befell him from childhood through old age, he did not forsake his way of praying to Hashem and singing and offering praises before Him. He constantly searched for the expanses that Hashem opened up for him within the hardships and he praised His Name for them. And this is what he said in the verse mentioned before (*Tehillim*, Ch. 4): "Answer me when I call, oh G-d of my righteousness, When I was in distress You opened an expanse for me; Be gracious to me and hear my prayer": "You, my G-d, Who does righteousness with me, behold, my entire life, whenever I was in distress, You have widened things for me, for I have found the expanses that You have opened up for me within the troubles. And for this I am begging: Be gracious to me and hear my prayer that I should merit to come out completely from all the troubles." For when a person merits to find Hashem's G-dliness within everything that befalls him, not forsaking his way of praying to him for every detail of his life, then in the end, Hashem will save him from all his troubles and he will merit to find great expansiveness, relief and blessing in every matter.

This ability to find Hashem within the troubles and not to flee from Him no matter what is a special strength that the Jewish nation has above all the nations of the world, for Israel are "those who are carried [by Hashem] from the womb (Isaiah, Ch. 46)" and they are called children of Hashem who accept upon themselves with love the decrees of their Father in heaven and are, in the root of their souls, unable to separate themselves from Him at all. The nations of the world do not have this skill. As soon as some trouble or suffering comes upon them, they curse the object they perceive to be the source of their pain and even curse their gods, because they do not have this skill of "When I was in distress, You opened a wide expanse for me". Therefore, we find in the Talmud (*Avoda Zara* 3a): "In time to come, when the nations of the world seek reward from Hashem like that of Israel, Hashem will say to them, 'I have an easy mitzvah called *sukkah*, go and do it. Right away, each one goes and builds himself a *sukkah* atop his roof and Hashem causes the hot sun to beat down upon them as if it were the middle of summer and [not being able to tolerate the heat for the sake of the mitzvah] each one gives his *sukkah* a good kick as he walks out of it." For with regard to the nations of the world, there is no concept like this of holding one's ground within the pain and suffering; rather as soon as some bitterness befalls them, they run, unlike the Jewish people who, even if they need to leave the *sukkah* because of the heat or rain, leave with submissiveness and shame and they long to be able to return as soon as possible. Therefore, the distinction here is made specifically through the mitzvah of *sukkah*, for the *sukkah* is called the 'shadow of faith' (source?), and the mitzvah of *sukkah* reveals the eminent level of Israel with respect to their strong faith in Hashem - how even when

2

pain and afflictions befall them, they accept it all with love and know that Hashem is opening a wide expanse for them within their troubles; and in the end, He will widen things for them completely.

Therefore, converts will not be accepted in the days of Moshiach (Talmud *Yevamos* 24b), but only before Moshiach comes. For in an unredeemed world, who would want to live with the Jewish people in their suffering and afflictions? - Only those who have the strength to bear the yoke of Hashem even in times of pain and hardship. *They* will have permission to come close. In this world, the G-d fearing and upright people suffer much from the wicked and base people who pursue and afflict them. But in time to come, their level will be revealed to everyone, as Rebbe Nachman has said (*Lekutei Mohoran*, Part I, Lesson 66): "Our main greatness and splendor will be revealed in time to come, for then everyone will see the greatness and splendor of the Tzaddikim and the upright. Happy are they. Praiseworthy is their lot." Therefore, happy is the one who always goes with the teaching of "When I was in distress, You opened a wide expanse for me", finding the expanses of Hashem in all the details of his life. For then, he will live a truly good and sweet life. And in the end, he will merit complete expansiveness in every matter. Happy is he and fortunate is his lot.

Mohorosh connected these teachings to our parsha in the following way. It is written (*Bamidbar*, Ch. 20): "Moshe sent emissaries from Kadeish to the King of Edom: 'So said **your brother** Israel: You know all the hardship that has befallen us. Our forefathers descended to Egypt...We cried out to Hashem and He heard our voice....Please let us pass through your land." We need to understand why Moshe Rebbeinu needed to tell the King of Edom these things – "...all the hardship that has befallen us ... We cried out to Hashem and He heard our voice." Why would this make a difference to the King of Edom - that troubles have passed over Israel from then until now? But according to the words of Rebbe Nachman we can understand it very well. Moshe *Rebbeinu* revealed to the King of Edom the greatness of Israel's strength, namely, that they have the power to strengthen themselves in any situation and they accomplish this through the advice mentioned above of "When I was in distress, You opened a wide expanse for me". They are always finding the openings and the expansiveness that Hashem creates for them within their troubles. And this is: "**You know all the hardship that has befallen us...We cried out to Hashem and He heard our voice**" – we are always crying out to Hashem from the midst of our troubles and He hears our voice and widens the straits we are in. Therefore, you should permit us to pass through your land on our way to the Land of Israel, for we have paid the debt

3

that had been placed upon us, and you have no right to lay claim to the Land of Israel as an inheritance, as Rashi explains (verse 14): "We are **brothers**, sons of Abraham, to whom it was said (*Bereishis*, Ch. 13): 'Know for sure that your seed shall be a stranger [in a land not theirs], and upon both of us [being of Abraham's seed] was the obligation of paying that debt. **'You know all the hardship that has befallen us'** – it was for this reason that your father [Esav] separated himself from our father, as it is said (Bereishis, Ch. 6): 'And he [Esav] went to another land on account of Yaakov, **his brother'** – on account of the debt which was upon both of them and he cast [the whole debt] upon Yaakov…. Just as you have not paid the debt, you also have no right to lay claim to the land of Israel as an inheritance. Give us therefore a little assistance [by permitting us] to pass through your land. (These are the words of Rashi.)" It is only the nation of Israel who accepted upon themselves to pay off the debt of "Your seed shall be a stranger in a land not theirs", for they can always find the wide openings that Hashem makes for them in difficult times and they know that it is worth tolerating everything in order to reach their desired goal. "But, you," says Moshe, "who did not accept upon yourselves to pay the debt, in the way of the nations who cannot tolerate pain and bitterness, you have no right to lay claim to this inheritance because you have no relationship to it. Only permit us to reach the land that Hashem has promised us, since from everything we went through, in the end, we will undoubtedly merit to reach our goal." Now it is very clear why Moshe *Rebbeinu* related all of these things to the King of Edom. May Hashem help us to see very soon the salvation of Israel, and He will open wide for us the straits, troubles and afflictions, spiritually and physically and we will greet our righteous Moshiach speedily in our days. *Amen v'amen.*

4

Friday Night, Parshas Balak, 5765

Friday night, at the first Shabbos meal, Mohorosh *Shlit"a* spoke inspiring words about "the sword of prayer" and the rectification of the *Bris* (Covenant), based on *Lekutei Mohoran*, Part I, Lesson 2.

Rebbi Nachman says: "The main weapon of Mashiach is prayer…and this weapon needs to be received through the concept of 'Yosef', that is, through *shmiras habris* (guarding of the Holy Covenant)…And Yosef received this specifically through Yaakov, as it is written (*Bereishis*, Ch. 48): 'And as for me, I [Yisrael/Yaakov] have given you one portion more than your brothers, which I took from the hand of the Emorite with my sword and with my bow.' (And Rashi explains that sword and bow refer to prayer and supplication), for Yisrael represents the concept of *Bris*." (These are the words of Rebbe Nachman.)

Mohorosh explained that in this lesson Rebbe Nachman reveals to us that the main weapon of the King *Mashiach*, and of each and every Jew, is prayer. This means that there is power in his mouth to request and pray to Hashem for everything he needs, spiritually and materially. For with the power of prayer we can win all of our battles and merit to accomplish whatever we need to accomplish in our lives. And when a person is strong in his prayer, there is no level in the world he can't reach.

However, the power of prayer needs to be received through the concept of 'Yosef HaTzaddik', who represents the concept of *shmiras habris*. For *shmiras habris* is the sanctity of thought. And *shmiras habris* actually begins with the sanctity of our thoughts, that one should not blemish his mind with foreign and evil thoughts, G-d forbid. And when a person has a clear and pure mind, he can pray with great vitality and attachment to Hashem and accomplish everything he needs to accomplish, spiritually and materially. However, when a person lacks *shmiras habris*, G-d forbid, and has blemished his mind with foreign and evil thoughts, clouds gather and cover his eyes and prevent him from praying properly, as thoughts of despair and discouragement begin to enter his mind: "Is Hashem really listening to my prayers?" "Does Hashem really need me?" These thoughts hold him back from praying properly. Therefore, a person needs to gird himself with might to sanctify his mind and thoughts. And he should actually pray for this itself, i.e. that he should merit a clean and pure mind which will enable him to perceive Hashem's G-dliness from everything in creation. And then he will receive, in the proper measure, the "sword of prayer" and he will win all the battles he needs to win.

Yaakov Avinu merited the "sword of prayer" in the most complete way, because he was holy to the highest degree, as our Sages have commented on the verse (*Bereishis*, Ch. 49): "[Reuven, you are] my initial vigor", that he had never experienced a night time emission in his life (*Talmud Yevamos* 76a; Rashi on this verse). Therefore, Yaakov *Avinu* tells Yosef (ibid, Ch. 48): "…which I took from the hand of the Emorite with my sword and with my bow", that is, he won the battle against the Emorites with the sword and bow of prayer, as our holy Sages have said (*Talmud Bava Basra* 123b): "Did he really take [from the hand of the Emorites] with his sword and bow? Behold, it is written (*Tehillim*, Ch. 44): 'For I will not trust in my bow; nor will my sword deliver me.' Rather, 'my sword' is prayer and 'my bow' is supplication." We find that Yaakov merited the 'sword of prayer" to its fullest extent and passed it down to Yosef HaTzaddik. For Yosef also attained true *shmiras habris,* having withstood the test with Potifar's wife (*Bereishis*, Ch. 39). And at the crucial moments of the test, it was precisely the image of his father Yaakov that he saw in his mind's eye and this is what saved him from the sin, because his father was the one who transmitted this holiness to him. Therefore, the power of prayer was also passed down to him, as it is written (*Bereishis*, Ch. 45): "And as for me, I have given you one portion more than your brothers, which I took from the hand of the Emorite with my sword and with my bow" – it was specifically "**me**" – Yaakov/Yisrael, i.e. *shmiras habris* – **I have given to you** – Yosef – **one portion more than your brothers** – for you will also have this power in an exceedingly great measure - **which I took from the hand of the Emorite with my sword and with my bow.** Therefore, it is an essential service of a Jew to strive to sanctify and purify his mind as much as possible - and this is the matter of *shmiras habris* - and to put all of his strength into the service of prayer until he merits to win all of his battles and he accomplishes everything he needs to accomplish in his life. Praiseworthy is the one who merits this in truth. Happy is he and fortunate is his lot.

Mohorosh connected these ideas to our parsha in the following way. It is written (*Bamidbar*, Ch. 22): "Balak son Tzippor saw all that Israel had done to the Emorite. Moav became very frightened of the people for it was

2

numerous, and Moav was disgusted because of the Children of Israel." Let's analyze the specific wording of these two verses. In the first verse it is written: "Balak son Tzippor" alone, that he saw all that Israel had done to the Emorite. In the next verse it is written: "Moav" became very frightened and "Moav" was disgusted – i.e. Balak's nation. From the wording of these verses it would appear that Balak saw and understood something more than his entire nation of Moav had. Also, why in the first verse is it written: "all **that 'Israel' had done to the Emorite**, whereas in the next verse it says: "Moav was disgusted because of the *'Children of Israel'* and not just because of *'Israel'*? Let us try to answer these questions according to the above teachings of Rebbe Nachman. *'Israel'* written in the first verse alludes to grandfather Israel – Yaakov Avinu – who possessed the perfect "sword of prayer", and about whom it is written: "**which I took from the hand of the Emorite** with my sword and with my bow." And this is what Balak perceived and understood: He understood the great holiness of grandfather Israel and how it was through the great holiness of his *shmiras habris* that he merited the 'sword of prayer'. And this was "all that **Israel** had done to the Emorite." And therefore, "Moav became very frightened of the people for it was numerous" - it was specifically the nation of 'Moav' that became very frightened of the Jewish people, for their nation was called Moav in reference to a lack of *shmiras habris*, as Moav was born from the incestuous act of Lot and his daughter. And she unashamedly and brazenly called his name "Moav" because he was from her father (*me'av* – from father); and this was the blemish and corruption of the mind and chochmah (wisdom), as wisdom is called *Av*, as is known in Kabbalah. Also, the numerical value of Moav is forty-nine, which alludes to the forty-nine gates of impurity that are opened through the defilement of the mind.

As soon as Balak understood the tremendous holiness of the people of Israel, which they had inherited from their grandfather Israel, Moav became very frightened of the people; Moav - those whose minds are defiled - are afraid and terrified that the people of Israel would overpower them through the holiness of their thoughts and the service of their prayer. "And Moav was disgusted because of the Children of Israel" because it is the way of defilement to become disgusted with holiness and to be unable to tolerate it at all, as it is written concerning the Egyptians (*Shemos*, Ch. 1): "And they became disgusted because of the Children of Israel."; for the Egyptians were more immoral and immersed in filth than any other nation in the world, as it is brought in *Tanna D'bei Eliyahu*, Ch. 7. Therefore, when Moav saw the holiness of Israel, they were completely disgusted by them, because

3

defilement and filth cannot tolerate holiness. And this is "Moav was disgusted", that is, those whose minds were corrupted were disgusted "because of the Children of Israel" who possess an inheritance of holiness from their grandfather Yaakov. Therefore, Moav's strategy was to attack the Children of Israel with the spiritual impurity of the wicked Bilaam, whose main advice to them was to defile Israel's minds with sexual immorality, may Hashem save us, as he said (Rashi 24:14): "The G-d of these people hates unchastity", and through this it is possible to nullify their weapon, which is prayer, and then the curse upon them will take effect, G-d forbid. And when Moav saw Israel winning their battles in a supernatural way, they said (Rashi, 22:4): "The Jews are coming with the one [Moshe] whose power lies only in his mouth (in prayer). Then we will also come against them with a man whose power lies in his mouth (Bilaam)" - a man with an impure mouth who will defile them through immorality and corrupt their minds with foreign and evil thoughts, G-d forbid. But Hashem, who guards the souls of Israel, protected them from the curse of the wicked Bilaam and shielded them in the merit of their forefathers. And through this, in the end, they were able to bring Bilaam down and remove him from the world. May Hashem always protect us from all evil and may we merit to sanctify and purify our minds with the utmost degree of holiness and purity, and to always involve ourselves in prayer all the days of our lives until we merit to be victorious in all of our battles and to see the revelation of our righteous *Mashiach* swiftly in our days. *Amen v'amen.*

4

Friday Night, Parshas Pinchas, 5766

Friday night, at the first Shabbos meal, Mohorosh *Shlit"a* spoke inspiring words about the strength of the 'master of prayer' who stands in the 'throat' of the Satan, based on *Lekutei Mohoran*, Part II, Lesson 8.

Rebbe Nachman says: "When there is the blemish of the lust for sexual immorality, G-d forbid, then a person's prayer is [looked upon from Above] with the attribute of judgment [instead of with the attribute of mercy and favor], and the *sitra acharah* [the side of spiritual impurity; the Satan] tries to swallow the prayer [and prevent it from rising to heaven and accomplishing its appropriate mission]. We then need a man of great strength who will offer a prayer that [also] has the attribute of judgment [a forceful prayer, zealous and assertive – a prayer with all of one's strength – as opposed to a submissive and quiet prayer of supplication], as happened during the episode of Zimri, when Pinchas needed to offer a prayer that was in the category of judgment. For when this mighty man offers a prayer that has the attribute of judgment [a bold and assertive prayer], the *sitra achara* wants to swallow it [thinking it is an improper prayer and hoping to draw strength from it], for it always swallows prayers that are in the category of judgment. But when it wants to swallow *this* prayer, it stands in the Satan's throat, forcing the Satan to vomit, that is, the Satan is forced to vomit out and eject all of the holiness he swallowed, which is an aspect of the verse (Job, Ch. 20): 'He has swallowed down riches and he shall vomit them up.' Not only will he vomit and eject all of the holiness he swallowed, but he will also be forced to vomit out and eject the very essence of his life-force." (These are the words of Rebbe Nachman.)

Mohorosh explained that we see from this lesson that the true Tzaddikim in every generation are at war with the *sitra achara* – the force that increases the lust for sexual immorality in the world and that seeks to break the spiritual channel from which Israel draws its strength. This lust destroys the holiness of Israel and steals from them their prayers and their morale. For the one who is held in the grips of this spiritual impurity, G-d forbid, his mind and very being cleave to it, like a mouse stuck in a glue trap from which it is impossible for it to escape. So too, this lust seizes the mind and the very being of a person, making it impossible for him to offer a proper prayer and mixing all of his prayers with foreign and evil thoughts. This is when we need the prayer of the man of strength, the true Tzaddik, who descends into the throat of the *sitra achara* (willing to sacrifice his life and soul and praying with all his strength) and forces it to disgorge the souls of Israel it has swallowed; for the true Tzaddik has awesome teachings for souls that have been seized by the *sitra achara*, and he teaches them that there is never – ever – such a thing as giving up.

Teshuvah helps for every sin and from every fall and descent there is a way to escape and return to holiness, as Rebbe Nachman decreed and said (*Lekutei Mohoran*, Part II, Lesson 112): "If you believe you can destroy, believe you can fix." The main thing is that a person "believes" and has faith, that is, if he will "believe" he can destroy then he will also "believe" he can fix. And this is the great power of the true Tzaddik – that he can go down into the spiritual channel of the Wicked One from which it draws sustenance and destroy the very source of its life-force (*Lekutei Mohoran*, Part I, Lesson 8). And through this, he takes the souls of Israel out from under the Satan's hand. And not only does he make the *sitra achara* disgorge the holy souls he swallowed, but he actually extracts from the *sitra achara* the essence of its life force. For the Tzaddik teaches the souls of Israel such awesome teachings of strength until he heals them completely from the terrible sicknesses that cling to them from the lust for sexual immorality; and he brings them back in complete *teshuvah* until the name of the *sitra achara* is blotted out from the world entirely.

The main way the Tzaddik accomplishes this is through "prayer with strength". He is always offering his prayers with tremendous strength and self-sacrifice. And he is always praying to Hashem that the souls of Israel should be rescued from the blemish of the lust for sexual immorality and that they should not be caught in the evil trap of the *sitra achara*. The Tzaddik is ready to sacrifice his very being in order to raise up and elevate a soul that has fallen and descended into this filth. He teaches this soul wonderful ways to strengthen itself in the service of prayer and how to cry out to Hashem with strength to save him from destruction. And then his prayers stand in the throat of the *sitra achara* and force it to vomit up and eject all of the holiness it had swallowed, which is an aspect of the verse (Job, Ch. 20): "He has swallowed down riches and he shall vomit them up again." And the first letters of the words in this verse spell out the holy name *Ches-Beis"Vav*, a name which is a remedy for restoring the holiness of the *Bris*. Therefore, the main hope a person has is through drawing close to the true Tzaddik, the true man of strength. For through the true Tzaddik, a person will receive the right advice

2

for how to escape from all of his base lusts and how to straighten everything that is twisted. And then he will merit a complete *teshuvah*, to illuminate his days with Hashem's blessed light. Happy is he and fortunate is his lot.

Mohorosh connected these ideas to our parsha in the following way. We find in our parsha Hashem's high praise of Pinchas HaTzaddik who saved the souls of Israel from annihilation, as it is written (*Bamidbar*, Ch. 25:11): "Pinchas the son of Elazar the son of Aharon the Kohen, turned my wrath away from the Children of Israel, when he was zealous for My sake among them and I did not annihilate the Children of Israel in my zealousness", in reward for which (*Bamidbar*, Ch. 25:12) "Therefore say, 'Behold, I am giving him My covenant of shalom (*brisi shalom* – My covenant of peace).' " Let us ask the following questions: First, where do we see the divine principle of measure-for-measure in this, that in reward for Pinchas' zealousness, Hashem declares: "Therefore say, 'Behold, I am giving him My covenant of shalom'"? Secondly, what is meant by Hashem's preface to the declaration of Pinchas' reward, i.e. the words "Therefore say", instead of saying immediately after verse 11: "Behold, I am giving him My covenant of shalom" without the words "Therefore say"? Lastly, what is the meaning of the "broken" letter *vav* in the word 'shalom'? Let's try to answer these questions according to the above teachings of Rebbe Nachman.

In the episode of Zimri, there was a strengthening of the lust for sexual immorality in the world. Pinchas reacted to this with zealotry and descended into the throat of the *sitra achara* in order to break its power and save the souls of Israel from being annihilated. Pinchas' main strength came from "prayer with strength", as our holy Sages have commented (*Talmud Sanhedrin* 44a) on the verse (*Tehillim*, Ch. 106): " 'And Pinchas stood up and wrought judgment (*vaye'pallel* - he judged; also has the connotation of praying - *hispallel*)', this teaches that he worked judgment with his Maker [he acted and prayed with the attribute of strict judgment and served as Israel's defense attorney before his Maker]" – in other words, he offered "prayers with strength"! And he showed all the souls of Israel that they need not be frightened at all by the *sitra achara* and its lusts; rather, they only need to strengthen themselves with the power of prayer and with this they will defeat the *sitra achara* completely. And this was the zealousness that Pinchas had for G-d – it was the prayer with strength that he offered; and with this he stood in the throat of the *sitra achara* and forced it to disgorge the souls of Israel it had swallowed. For Pinchas taught everyone that with the power of prayer we can be victorious in everything. And "when he was zealous for My

3

sake among them (*b'socham* – among them)", that is, he took his zealousness, which was prayer with strength, and placed it "*b'socham* (which also means 'within them')" – within each and every Jew - and he taught them that there is never – ever – such a thing as giving up and that with the power of prayer they can subdue the lust for sexual immorality and break the spiritual channel of the *sitra achara* completely. And this is hinted to in the prefatory words "Therefore say"; that is, in the merit of "saying" and prayer, then measure-for-measure, "Behold, I am giving him My covenant of shalom (*brisi shalom*)" - he will merit perfection (*sheleimus*) of the Covenant – the *Bris*. With the power of prayer we can merit everything. Even where there is a "broken" letter *vav* – symbolizing a break of holiness (in Kabbalah the *vav* represents the *bris*) – and the *sitra achara* wants to swallow the prayers of Israel, nevertheless, the prayers of the true Tzaddik stand in its throat and annihilate its spiritual channel of sustenance. And he elevates the souls of Israel from there in peace, drawing upon them a supernal holiness. May Hashem help us to be close to the true Tzaddikim and to draw down upon ourselves the holiness of the *bris* in the most perfect way, until we merit to ascend and be included in Him completely, now and forevermore. *Amen v'amen*.

4

Friday Night, Parshas Matos Maasay, 5766

Friday night, at the first Shabbos meal, Mohorosh *Shlit"a* spoke inspiring words on the opening verse of parshas Masei: "These are the journeys of the Children of Israel", based on *Lekutei Mohoran*, Part II, Lesson 62.

Rebbe Nachman says: "It is written (*Bamidbar*, Ch. 33): **'These are the journeys of the Children of Israel'**. It is brought in a Midrash that the journeys of the Children of Israel, that is, their travels from place to place, which are referred to in the verse '**These** are the journeys of the Children of Israel', atone for their having said regarding the Golden Calf: '**These**, Israel, are your gods (*Shemos*, Ch. 32)', that is, they atone for the blemish of idolatry. For even when they are not worshipping idols, there is still the blemish of idolatry, for the corruption of *emunah* (faith) is also an aspect of idolatry, as it is brought in the name of the Baal Shem Tov on the verse (*Devarim*, Ch. 11): '[Lest] you turn away and serve other gods' – that as soon as they begin to turn away from Hashem, this is already an aspect of idolatry. But through the journeys of Israel, it is atoned for.'" (These are the words of Rebbe Nachman.)

Mohorosh explained that we see from this lesson that the travels of the Children of Israel from place to place are not a simple thing at all. In fact, many very lofty matters are hidden within them. We see with our own eyes how every Jew is constantly moving around from place to place – this one travels for business, that one to visit someone who is ill, this one on a leisure trip. But where does the sudden inspiration to travel to a certain place come from? The real cause of this desire to travel comes from the need to rectify one's soul. A person needs to travel to a place where he will be able to perfect a certain aspect of his soul. And in that specific place there is something he needs to fix. The fixing sometimes is accomplished through his eating a particular piece of food or by praying a certain prayer, or by performing a certain mitzvah. Hashem leads each and every person, according to the root of his soul, to the place he needs to be in order to fix and perfect his soul. Therefore, Rebbe Nachman says (*Sichos HaRan* 85): "When a person sees a necessity to travel to a certain place, he should not be stubborn and refuse to go, for perhaps he needs to fix something in that place in order to perfect his soul; and if he does not go willingly, he will end up being forced to go there in iron chains, as the Midrash states regarding Yaakov *Avinu* (*Yalkut Shimoni Hoshea* 528) that it was fitting that Yaakov be brought down to Egypt in iron chains, had it not been for the sale of Yosef.'"

No matter where a Jew goes, he is in the process of fixing something and it is essential that he be particularly vigilant to guard himself from transgression when he is traveling. Wherever he is, he recites blessings, prays and fulfills other mitzvos. And through this, he effects rectifications wherever he goes. Sometimes, a person finds himself on a long business trip, and it turns out that the trip was not a financial success; but what he doesn't realize is that the main purpose of his trip was for the sake of rectifying an aspect of his soul, as the Baal Shem Tov explained the verse (*Tehillim*, Ch. 37): "From Hashem the steps of a man are established, and he desires his way." He explained that all of the steps a person takes are prepared and guided by Hashem, where and when he needs to reach every place; but in a person's own eyes – "he desires his way" – it seems to him that he desires to go to a certain place for the sake of some practical need or desire, such as for the sake of his business or for some other rational matter. But in truth, all of his steps are prepared by Hashem. In the same spirit, the Baal Shem Tov explained the verse (*Tehillim*, Ch. 107): "Hungry and thirsty, their soul was wrapped in them". Sometimes a person arrives at a certain place and feels a sudden hunger or thirst and is thus compelled to eat and drink, but he doesn't know the cause of these sudden pangs. But the true cause is "their soul was wrapped in them", that is, with that particular piece of food or drink he wraps his soul with sparks of holiness hidden in the food or drink – sparks that relate to the root of his soul and which he needs in order to perfect his soul. Therefore, Hashem causes him to feel hungry or thirsty at this particular time. So, we find that hidden in all of a person's paths and journeys are great rectifications for the sake of perfecting his soul. Happy is the one who merits to give himself over to Hashem with simple and clear faith and with the intention to fix that which needs to be fixed in every place he finds himself.

Rebbe Nachman says in the name of the Midrash that all of the travels of the Children of Israel, which the Torah refers to as "**These** are the journeys of the Children of Israel", are in their inner essence a rectification for the blemish of "**These**, Israel, are your gods (*Shemos*, Ch. 32)", which is the sin of the Golden Calf. What was the sin of the Golden Calf? It was a weakening and corruption of *emunah*. They wanted to set up the calf as an intermediary between themselves and Hashem and they said (*Shemos*, Ch. 32): "make us a god that will go before us", meaning an intermediary. Even today, most

2

people fall into this error by making the "apparent" causes of things into intermediaries between themselves and Hashem (*Lekutei Mohoran*, Part I, Lesson 62). They believe in Hashem, but they also believe in the power of the intermediary and think that without it they are lost. For example, they believe in Hashem, but they feel that the main cause of their sustenance is their job, as if, G-d forbid, without this specific job, Hashem wouldn't be able to give them a livelihood. And likewise with regard to healing, they feel that the medicine is what is responsible for healing them, as if, G-d forbid, without these specific medicines, Hashem wouldn't be able to heal them. It is just not so. Hashem is the Cause of all causes, and He has no need for any other causes. A person who is involved with one of these causes (e.g. his occupation or medicines) needs to believe in Hashem alone, and not make the "apparent" causes into the real causes. Therefore, when a person is on the road and he gives himself over completely to Hashem, hoping to fix whatever it is he needs to fix in these places, in this way, he automatically fixes all of the blemishes of faith that he caused by making the "apparent" causes into the true causes, as he now gives himself up entirely to Hashem, understanding that He alone is the Cause of all causes. Through this hope and faith in his heart he will merit reaching all of the places he needs to reach in order to fix and perfect his soul. And through this, he will once again be illuminated by the light of Hashem. Therefore, happy is the one who merits to give himself up entirely to Hashem; to have the intention in all of his travels to fulfill the will of Hashem and to straighten out all that is crooked. And through this, he will merit to completely rectify his soul and to illuminate his days with the Light of Life. Happy is he and fortunate is his lot.

Mohorosh connected these ideas to our parsha in the following way. "These are the journeys of the Children of Israel." - Our parsha lists the entire route the Children of Israel followed in the wilderness from the time they left Egypt until they were about to enter the Land of Israel. And it gives the names of each of their encampments – a total of forty-two places. And regarding all of their travels it says (*Bamidbar*, 9:18,20,23): "According to Hashem they encamped and according to Hashem they journeyed." Likewise, it is written in our parsha (*Bamidbar*, Ch. 33): "And Moshe wrote down their goings forth for their journeys 'according to Hashem', and these are their journeys for their goings forth." What is the deeper meaning of the phrase "according to Hashem" that is mentioned in connection with all of the travels of the Children of Israel? Also, what is the meaning of the reversal of words in this verse: First it says "Their goings forth for their journeys" and at the end of the verse the words are reversed to read - "Their journeys for their goings forth"?

3

Let's try to answer these questions according to the above teachings of Rebbe Nachman.

All of the paths and travels of the Children of Israel were exactly "according to Hashem", for in every place they needed to accomplish rectifications which were known only to the "Knower of mysteries", the One who prepares the footsteps of man for each and every journey. And this is: "And Moshe wrote down their goings forth for the journeys according to Hashem" – Moshe *Rebbeinu* wrote down in the Torah the names of each of their encampments to hint to the great rectifications that the souls of Israel accomplished on all of their journeys (see Ramban on this verse). "Their goings forth (*motza-eihem* – also has the connotation of 'their findings' or 'things they brought forth into actuality')" – that is, what they found and accomplished on the way was all "according to Hashem" – for the sake of reaching their eternal rectification. And the places were named after the great rectifications that were effected there (see Sefer Avodas Yisroel of the Magid of Koznitz). "Their goings out (*motza-eihem*) for (or of) their journeys according to Hashem" – first "*motza-eihem*", that is, the rectifications they found and effected in every place were the reason **for** "their journeys", they were the true cause **of** all their travels. But most people travel innocently, only looking at the road before them, unaware of the inner content, i.e. the rectifications they need to accomplish, as the Baal Shem Tov explained the verse "he desires his way" – that a person desires to take a certain path for his own reasons, but in truth, all is caused by the need to fix his soul. And this is "These are their journeys for their goings forth" – First it says "**These** are their journeys" – they traveled for the practical reason of being commanded to travel and it was their desire to obey the command of Hashem to journey forward, but the inner reason of all their travels was because of "**These**, Israel, are your gods" – because they considered the "apparent" cause (the Golden Calf) to be the real cause, not realizing that every detail of their lives is "according to Hashem" - that Hashem is the Only Cause. And this is "And these are their journeys for their *motza-eihem*" – the purpose of their journeys was for them to find and bring out all of the sparks of holiness that were hidden in every place, and to accomplish great rectifications for the perfection of their souls. May Hashem help us attain perfect faith, and we will give ourselves over to Him totally until we merit to ascend and be included in Him completely, now and forevermore. *Amen v'amen.*

4

Friday Night, Parshas Devarim, 5766

Friday night, at the first Shabbos meal, Mohorosh Shlit"a spoke inspiring words about the inspiration a person can receive from specific places, based on Lekutei Mohoran, Part II, Lesson 124.

Reb Nosson says: "I have heard in the name of Rebbe Nachman that sometimes a thought of *teshuvah* and a yearning for Hashem can come to a person suddenly in a certain place. At that very place, a person should strengthen himself with this thought of *teshuvah* and yearning before moving from there. For example, he should speak at that very place some words of prayer and supplication, or words that describe his longing for Hashem without waiting or leaving that place, even though the place is not specifically designated for this, as is a *shul* or *beis medrash*. For if he is to leave this place, it could very well be that his inspiration will cease. We saw this phenomenon occur many times with Rebbe Nachman himself. He would be pacing back and forth in his house and then suddenly remain standing in the middle of the room, whereupon he would start speaking to us amazing words of inspiration and wondrous and beautiful teachings. It was very noticeable that he did not want to move from his place until he had finished what he wanted to say. This happened many times." (These are the words of Reb Nosson.)

Mohorosh explained that it is known (see Lekutei Mohoran, Part I, Lesson 61) that the souls of Israel possess a great power to sanctify the places where they live or merely pass through. When they learn Torah and perform mitzvos in a particular place, a supernal holiness descends upon that place, to the extent that whoever comes there experiences a special enlightenment and a great desire to elevate himself and cleave to Hashem. For a trace of the holiness that was generated in that place enters the visitor and inspires him to get closer to Hashem.

There are many stories about Tzaddikim who came to a certain place and sensed there a special enlightenment and even the smell of *Gan Eden*. And when they looked into the matter, it was revealed to them that in this place a great mitzvah or *Kiddush Hashem* was made which left a trace and an imprint of supernal holiness there. Therefore, Rebbe Nachman revealed to us that if a person is suddenly struck with a thought of *teshuvah* or suddenly feels inspired toward holiness in a certain place, even if it is in the middle of the marketplace, he should not move from there until he has spoken some words of prayer and supplication that express his desire and longing for Hashem. For if he would leave that spot, it is possible that this sudden inspiration will also leave him, because inspiration is literally connected to certain physical locations. Therefore, he should be careful to *daven* or to perform some other act of holiness in the exact spot at which he became inspired.

Likewise, in a place where a certain sin was done, G-d forbid, great darkness and impurity rest there. And when a person comes to that place, he might feel a spirit of darkness descending upon him with no idea of where it is coming from, when in reality it is due to a certain sin that was done there. As a result, the *klippos* (unclean spirits) that were created from the sin now rest in that place.

There are many stories of Tzaddikim who, upon their arrival at a particular place, suddenly became very shaken, whereupon they left as fast as they could. And it became revealed afterwards that at this place certain sins had been committed, as in the following well-known story about the Baal Shem Tov: He once traveled together with his students in a carriage driven by his personal wagon driver, Alexi. At a certain place on the way, the Baal Shem Tov suddenly became very shaken. He ordered his wagon driver to drive on from there as quickly as possible. And so he did. Afterwards, his students asked their holy master why he had suddenly started trembling and why he ordered the wagon driver to leave so quickly. The Baal Shem Tov said that they should ask the wagon driver what entered his mind when they reached that place. At first, the wagon driver was very embarrassed to tell them, but the Baal Shem Tov told him not to be ashamed. So Alexi said to them that it had suddenly entered his mind to stop the wagon, kill them all and take their money. As soon as he drove away from that place, the evil thought also went away. The Baal Shem Tov's students were dumbfounded because Alexi was a very trusted and dedicated servant of the Baal Shem Tov. How could such a perverse and strange thought have entered his mind? The Baal Shem Tov then told them that in that place a Jew was once murdered and the *klippos* that were created from the act were still resting there. Therefore, when they passed through that place, the *klippos* seized the non-Jewish wagon driver and caused him to have these thoughts.

2

184

So we see that a place can be the cause of our thoughts and feelings, sometimes for good and sometimes for bad. And because of this, it was the opinion of many Tzaddikim, among them the holy Satmar Rebbe, Rebbe Yoel of blessed memory, not to visit the city of Auschwitz and its infamous camps for it was a place of tremendous destruction – where millions of our brothers and sisters were murdered, may Hashem avenge their blood – and powerful *klippos* rest there. Therefore, we have no need to enter that place at all. Happy is the one who merits to sanctify every place he reaches by performing some act of holiness or through speaking words of desire and yearning for Hashem. For in this way, a supernal holiness will rest upon these places which will generate holy inspiration and a desire for Hashem for many more souls of Israel who will one day be in those places. And the merit of all these people will be ascribed to him. Happy is he and fortunate is his lot.

Mohorosh connected these ideas to our parsha in the following way. It is written (Devarim, Ch. 1): "These are the words that Moshe spoke to all Israel, on the other side of the Jordan, concerning the Wilderness, concerning the Aravah, opposite the Red Sea, between Paran and Tofel, and Lavan, and Chatzeiros, and Di-Zahav." And Rashi explains: "Because these are words of rebuke, and all of the places where they angered Hashem are enumerated here, therefore, Moshe did not mention the sins explicitly but instead only hinted to them [by the names of the places] for the sake of Israel's honor." Why did Moshe Rebbeinu allude to specific sins with the names of the places where they occurred, instead of using other kinds of hints – hints that allude to the nature of the sins themselves rather than to *where* they occurred? Let's try to answer this question based on the above teachings of Rebbe Nachman.

As we previously explained, it all depends on the place. There are places that inspire a person towards good and holiness and there are places that have the opposite effect. Therefore, on the one hand, Moshe Rebbeinu mentioned all of these places in order to rebuke them in a way that would not embarrass them, but that would rather inspire them to thoughts of *teshuva*, especially as they were on the verge of entering the Holy Land; on the other hand, he mentioned all of these places so that they should be judged favorably before Hashem and to arouse divine mercy toward them, **since it was the places themselves that influenced them to sin**. The Sinai desert was a place of powerful *klippos*, as explained by the Zohar on the verse (Devarim, Ch. 8): "Who led you through the great and dreadful wilderness, snake, fiery serpent, and scorpion, and thirst where there was no water..." These animals – snake, fiery serpent and

3

scorpion – are the names of *klippos* that rested in the desert and that needed a rectification through the divine service of the Children of Israel.

And this is the way of the Tzaddikim when they need to rebuke the Jewish people for their bad deeds: To the people themselves they give words of rebuke but before Hashem they seek to recall the merits of the Jewish people and to arouse divine mercy towards them, as Moshe Rebbeinu had done in the sin of the Golden Calf. To the Jews he said (Shemos, Ch. 32): "You have sinned a great sin…" but to Hashem he said (ibid): "Why, Hashem, are You angry with your people?... (see Lekutei Mohoran, Part I, Lesson 22). Although Moshe's intention in mentioning all of the places where the Jewish people fell short was to rebuke them, at the same time it was also his intention to recall on their behalf all of the good deeds they had done there, as explained in the book *"Igra d'Kalla"* by the holy Rebbe, Rabbi Tzvi Elimelech of Dinov, that Moshe advocated for the Jewish people before Hashem in mentioning the words "On the other side of the Jordan"; with these words he recalled on their behalf what they had done "on the other side of the Jordan", namely, that they nullified through their holiness the *klippah* of Sichon and Og. In the same spirit, the words "concerning the Wilderness" recall how the Jewish people followed Hashem in an unsown land (the Wilderness). "Concerning the Aravah" – in this place, Pinchas risked his life for the holiness of His name, in the episode of Zimri. "Opposite the Red Sea" – this is where Nachshon ben Aminadav sanctified the name of Hashem by leaping into the sea.

This is the way of the Tzaddikim, to advocate for the Jewish people by always mentioning their positive points and their merits. And even when they rebuke the Jewish people, the rebuke is given in a way of love, which enhances their beauty and causes a wonderful fragrance to be poured upon their souls. The rebuke is given in order to strengthen them, as Moshe Rebbeinu rebuked them in our verse. Our holy Sages explain (Talmud Shabbos, 88b) that the verse (Shir HaShirim, Ch. 1): "While the King sat at His table, my spices gave forth their fragrance (*Nirdei nasan reicho* – my spices gave forth their fragrance)" is a reference to the episode of the Golden Calf and specifically to the rebuke given by Moshe Rebbeinu. The Sages explain the verse as follows: "When the King was giving the Torah at Mt. Sinai, my rebels (*nirdei*) gave (*nasan*) their fragrance." The verse should have said "my rebels lost (*azav*) their fragrance i.e. due to the sin, the people lost the pleasing 'fragrance' of their good deeds. However, when Moshe Rebbeinu came down from Mt. Sinai and saw the people worshipping the Golden Calf, instead of saying, "You wicked idol

4

worshippers!" he rebuked them with love and said to them, "Even though you have sinned, Hashem still loves you." And this caused them to do *teshuvah*. So the verse says "My rebels *gave* their fragrance", because by rebuking them with love, Moshe Rebbeinu poured over them a wonderful perfume which inspired them to once again give off their beautiful fragrance." (see Lekutei Mohoran, Part II, Lesson 8).

Moreover, it is explained in other holy books on the verse (Mishlei, Ch. 9): "Do not rebuke a scoffer lest he hate you. Rebuke a wise man and he will love you" as follows: When you rebuke someone do not say to him "You are a scoffer", lest he come to hate you, since by rebuking him this way you will embarrass and offend him. And he will surely hate such rebuke. Rather, say to him: "See, you are a wise man, how could such an act have come to you?" And then he will of himself feel ashamed and do *teshuvah*. And he will also love you. This is the explanation of the verse (Vayikra, Ch. 19): "You shall surely rebuke your fellow Jew and do not bear a sin because of him (can also be read 'do not cause him to carry a sin')" – that even if you rebuke him, see to it not to arouse divine judgment against him as if you were his prosecutor; rather you should judge him favorably and recall his merits at the same time you rebuke him. And in this way, you will surely inspire him to do *teshuvah*. May Hashem help us to be close to the true Tzaddikim, to receive their words with love and awe until we merit to return in perfect *teshuvah* before Hashem, to be included in Him completely for now and evermore. Amen v'amen.

5

Friday Night, Parshas Vaeschanan, 5766

Friday night, at the first Shabbos meal, Mohorosh *Shlit"a* spoke inspiring words about the type of prayer known as *tachanunim* (supplications), based on *Lekutei Mohoran*, Part I, Lesson 196.

Rebbe Nachman says: "It is brought in the *Mishna* (*Pirkei Avos*, Ch. 2): 'When you pray do not make your prayer *keva* (a set routine), but rather [beg with] compassion (*rachamim*) and supplications (*tachanunim*)...' The meaning of this *Mishna* is: It is forbidden for a person to be stubborn and refuse to budge in his prayers regardless of what he is praying for; that is, it is forbidden to be obstinate in one's prayer, feeling that Hashem must do for him exactly what he is asking for, for this is similar to taking something by force or stealing; rather he needs to pray and beseech Hashem in a way of asking for mercy and compassion – if Hashem will give, He will give, if not, not. This is the meaning of the *Mishna*: 'Do not make your prayer *keva*', *keva* connotes stealing, as it is written (*Mishlei*, Ch. 22): '...and rob the life of those who rob them (*v'kava es koveihem nafesh*)', that is to say, whatever one asks for, whether it is a livelihood, or children, or any other need, it is forbidden to be obstinate and refuse to budge in one's prayer, insisting that Hashem should do exactly what one asks for, for this is a *tefillas keva*, since that he takes something by force and by stealing; rather, he should only pray in a way of asking for mercy and compassion." (These are the words of Rebbe Nachman.)

Mohorosh explained that the essence of prayer is the cleaving and self-nullification to Hashem that one experiences during prayer, whereby one cleaves to Hashem to the degree that everything is nullified and included in Him completely. And for this reason, prayer is called "*tefillah*" which has the connotation of cleaving and attachment, as in the verse (*Bereishis*, Ch. 30): "*Naftulei Elokim niftalti*" which the Aramaic translation *Onkelos* renders as "attachment" (*Lekutei Mohoran*, Part II, Lesson 84). Therefore, as soon as a person nullifies himself before Hashem during prayer, he thus becomes ready to give himself over entirely to the will of Hashem, desiring only that things should be exactly as Hashem desires them to be. Therefore, he will certainly not be stubborn in his prayer, expecting that Hashem should do exactly *his* will, since his entire will is only to be in synch with the will of Hashem, as

Rabban Gamliel the son of Rabbi Yehuda *HaNassi* used to say (*Pirkei Avos*, Ch. 2): "Treat His will as if it were your own will, so that He will treat your will as if it were His will." Therefore, if Hashem's will is one way, a person will certainly be pleased and satisfied that this is the way it should be. And a sign that he has reached a state of cleaving in his prayer is when his entire will becomes included in the Supreme Will; that is, he wants things to be only as Hashem wants them to be. And this is the secret of the words from the Kaddish prayer "...in the world that He created according to His will" – which means that a person is satisfied and pleased with the will of Hashem (see *Lekutei Mohoran*, Part I, Lesson 177).

However, this is not the case if a person is obstinate in his prayer, believing that Hashem *must* fulfill his request. This is as if he is taking something by force, against the other's will. Perhaps Hashem's will is one way, and his will is different than Hashem's, G-d forbid. If so, how can he possibly succeed in his way? This is what our holy Sages refer to as the blemish of "*iyun tefilla*" about which they have said (*Talmud Brachos*, 55a): "Three things cause a person's sins to be recalled...*iyun tefilla* [is one of them]." And they have also said (ibid): "Whoever is *m'ayin* in his prayer comes to heartache", as it is said (*Mishlei*, Ch. 13): "Hope deferred makes the heart sick; but desire fulfilled is a tree of life." The definition of "*iyun tefilla*" is when a person stubbornly thinks that Hashem should fulfill his prayer just because he prayed with *kavanah* – focused concentration (ibid, see Rashi there, and in *Tosfos Talmud Shabbos*, 118b, the words beginning "*iyun tefilla*"). This type of praying with *kavanah* is not the ideal of prayer at all, for the essence of prayer is that a person should come to a state of total nullification before Hashem, until he is completely satisfied and pleased only with Hashem's will, with nothing remaining of his own will. Therefore, happy is the one who merits true cleaving in his prayer until his entire prayer is one of supplication, of appealing for compassion before Him, to include himself in the Supreme will. For then, he will surely merit to see the fruits of all the requests he has made of Hashem, and he will be included in Him completely through his prayer. Happy is he and fortunate is his lot.

Mohorosh connected these ideas to our parsha in the following way. Moshe *Rabbeinu* said (*Devarim*, Ch. 3): "I beseeched Hashem at that time saying..." And Rashi explains: "All forms of the word *chinun* [such as *Vaeschanan*] signify a free gift (*matana chinam*). Although the Tzaddikim can rely [in their requests of Hashem] upon [the merits of] their good deeds, yet they only request from Hashem an unearned gift [i.e., not in reward for their good

2

deeds]...Another explanation: This [the language of *chinun*] is one of the ten types of prayer..." Let us ask the question: Why specifically here does Moshe *Rebbeinu* make use of the type of prayer known as *techina* - "*va'eschanan*" - which signifies an unearned gift? Let us try to answer this based on the above teachings of Rebbe Nachman.

Moshe *Rebbeinu* taught us the secret that *tefilla* needs to be done in a way of imploring for mercy and compassion. And this is "*va'eschanan*" – an unearned gift – if Hashem will give, He will give, and if not, not. Moshe *Rebbeinu* himself had prayed 515 prayers (the *gematria* of the word *va'eschanan*) that he should be allowed to enter the Land of Israel. But when Hashem said to him (verse 26), "It is too much for you! Do not continue to speak to me further about this matter", he was stubborn no longer, and instead nullified his will completely before Hashem. And this is the idea of praying for an unearned gift: A person does not rely on his good deeds or on his prayer that he prayed with much *kavanah*, for this is the blemish of *iyun hatefilla* as mentioned before; rather, he gives himself over completely to Hashem and implores like a poor and needy person for a free gift – if Hashem will give, He will give, and if not, not. And this is the true perfection of prayer. Therefore, Moshe *Rebbeinu* used the language of "*va'eschanan*" to teach us the way of prayer – that it needs to be done precisely in the mode of begging for compassion (*rachamim*) and for a free gift (*tachanunim*). And then one will surely accomplish tremendous things with his prayers. For through his prayers he will merit to be included in the Supreme Will, and this is the greatest perfection of all.

And now we can understand what I have heard from my father and master, may his merit protect us, (see the book "*Minchas Zev*", beginning of parshas *Vaeschanan*) concerning the Midrash: " '*Vaeschanan el Hashem* [And I beseeched Hashem – '*el Hashem*' means '*to* Hashem']', do not read '*el Hashem*' but '*al Hashem* [*for* Hashem]." My father and master explained, according to another Midrash (see the book *Parshas Drachim*, *drush* 8), that had Moshe *Rebbeinu* entered the Land of Israel, the *Beis HaMikdosh* would not have been destroyed, and Israel would not have gone into exile. Therefore, Moshe *Rebbeinu's* entire prayer to enter the Land of Israel was for the sake of the *Shechinah* (the Divine presence), that Israel should not go into exile, for the *Shechinah* is with Israel in exile, as it is written (*Tehillim*, Ch. 91): "I am with him in pain". It is also written (Isaiah, Ch. 63) "In all of their pain, He has pain." Moshe *Rebbeinu's* prayer was not for his own benefit at all, as our holy Sages have said (*Talmud Sotah*, 14a): "Moshe surely did not

3

need to enter the Land in order to eat of its fruit…rather, Moshe *Rebbeinu* wanted to enter the Land of Israel so there should be no further exiles nor pain to the *Shechinah*." And this is " '*Vaeschanan el Hashem* (And I beseeched Hashem)', do not read *el* (to), but *al* (for – I beseeched *for* Hashem)", since his entire prayer was for the sake of Hashem and the *Shechinah*, that they should not be exiled. All of the prayers of the Tzaddikim are only about including themselves in the Supreme Will for the sake of the *Shechinah*, and not at all for their own sake. Therefore, they certainly do not become obstinate in their prayers. Instead, they give themselves over completely to Hashem and to the knowledge that everything will be according to His will. May Hashem help us to be occupied with *tefilla* and *tachanunim* always, and we will give ourselves over totally to Hashem until we merit to be included in Him completely for now and evermore. *Amen v'amen.*

Seuda Shlishis, Parshas Vaeschanan, 5766

At the third Shabbos meal, Mohorosh *Shlit"a* spoke inspiring words on the topic of praying with passion and attachment to Hashem, based on *Lekutei Mohoran*, Part I, Lesson 62.

Rebbe Nachman says: "In truth, if a person would know this with his whole heart, that (Isaiah, Ch. 6): 'The whole earth is full of His Glory', and that Hashem stands over him at the time of prayer and listens to his prayer, then he would surely pray with tremendous passion and be very particular about concentrating on all his words [of prayer]. However, because a person does not know this with a full heart, he therefore does not pray with passion and is not so careful [with each word]. And each person according to the degree he lacks this knowledge, thus will his passion and concentration in prayer also be lacking." (These are the words of Rebbe Nachman.)

Mohorosh explained that we see from this lesson that the most important preparation for the service of prayer is in the area of *emunah* – the *emunah* that Hashem stands over him at the time of prayer, listening to every word that leaves his mouth. For when he integrates this *emunah* within himself and fixes this knowledge in his heart, he will then be very particular to concentrate in his prayer, and he will burn with tremendous passion for Hashem when he prays, for he realizes that Hashem is listening to every word

4

and awaits the prayer of every Jew. Therefore it is certainly fitting to devote as much time and effort to prayer as possible.

When a person is not so particular about concentrating on his prayers and feels little passion to pray, he should realize that this is a result of undeveloped *emunah*. This is due to all sorts of questions and doubts that have entered his heart. He thinks to himself, (*Shmos*, Ch. 17) "Is Hashem among us or not?" And he starts questioning whether Hashem truly needs his prayers. Know, that all of this comes from the *klipa* of Amalek (Amalek has the same *gematria* as the word *safeik* – doubt). Amalek causes all of this doubt and confusion, even thoughts of atheism and heresy, G-d forbid, to enter a person's mind. But simple faith is to know that "The whole earth is full of His Glory" and that Hashem wants and desires the prayers of Israel, as we say in "*Ani maamin*" – "I believe with perfect faith, that the Creator, may His Name be blessed, to Him alone is it proper to pray and not to any other." Therefore, the more a person fixes this knowledge in his heart, the greater will be his concentration and passion during prayer. And he will merit to see the fruits of every request of his heart that he made to Him. Happy is the one who merits to occupy himself with prayer always.

Mohorosh connected these ideas to our parsha in the following way. It is written (*Devarim*, Ch. 3): "I beseeched Hashem at that time saying…" The *Baal HaTurim* notes that the words "Hashem your G-d (the last verse of the preceding parsha, parshas *Devarim*)" are juxtaposed with the word "*Vaeschanan*" to teach that (*Tehillim*, Ch. 16) "I have set Hashem before me always." That is, the previous parsha concludes with the verse "Do not fear them, for Hashem your G-d is the One Who fights for you" and the very next verse is "*Vaeschanan*", to say that "I have placed Hashem before me always." What is the Baal HaTurim trying to teach us here? Is it not already written in the verse "*Vaeschanan* **el Hashem**", which automatically puts it in the category of "I have placed Hashem before me always"? Moreover, it is an explicit teaching of our Sages (*Talmud Sanhedrin*, 22a): "One who prays should regard himself as though the *Shechinah*, the Divine Presence, were before him, as it says: 'I have set Hashem before me always.' So what new idea is the *Baal HaTurim* teaching us here? Let's try to answer this question based on the above teachings of Rebbe Nachman.

The essential preparation for the service of prayer is to fix in one's heart the knowledge mentioned above – "The whole earth is full of His Glory" and Hashem stands over a person at the time of prayer, listening to every word

5

that leaves his mouth. So, we see that one who comes to pray needs to regard himself as though the *Shechinah* were before him, for then he will surely feel much passion in his prayer and be very particular to concentrate on his words. However, to be able to do this, one first needs to do battle with all of the confusion and strange thoughts that want to bring him down and conceal this knowledge from him. Generally speaking, all of this confusion and these strange thoughts are referred to as the *klippos* of Amalek and of the other nations of the world that want to prevent the souls of Israel from serving Hashem through prayer and from cleaving to their Maker. Therefore, first it is written in the previous parsha, "**Do not fear them**", that is, do not be afraid at all of any of these *klippos* that want to stop you from praying; instead you should only know that "**Hashem your G-d is the One Who fights for you**" – Hashem will fight for you when He stands over you at the time of prayer, to protect you from all of these evil *klippos*. And with this you will be able to fulfill the verse "I have placed Hashem before me always", and then you will surely fulfill "**I beseeched Hashem** (*Vaeschanan el Hashem*)" – you will be occupied with prayer always, with great concentration and passion. For as soon as you know with a full heart that Hashem stands over you at the time of prayer, you will surely occupy yourself with prayer always. May Hashem help us to be occupied with prayer and *hisbodedus* all our days, until we merit to see the fruits of all of the requests we have made of Hashem and to see the consolation of Zion and Yerushalayim, swiftly in our days. *Amen v'amen.*

6

FRIDAY NIGHT PARSHAS EIKEV 5758

On Friday evening, *Shabbos Kodesh Parshas Eikev*, during the first *Seuda*, *Mohorosh Shlit"a* spoke awesome and wondrous words on the lesson of Rabbi Nachman in *Likutei Mohoron*, part one Chapter 248. He started by saying that according to Rabbi Nachman one must realize that all tales about the Holy Tzadikim (Righteous Men) are very great indeed, for by means of such stories and tales the heart is aroused and excited to a great awakening towards HaShem, and a strong desire for Him. That is because the original impression that a certain Tzadik made by his service to HaShem is the same impression that is awakened when his tale is told, and it creates a great awakening towards HaShem. Such are the words of Rabbi Nachman.

Mohorosh explained that this is an important rule in serving HaShem. The main stimulus a person receives to approach HaShem in truth, and to be engaged in His service through utter innocence and simplicity, is by means of listening to stories and tales of the Tzadikim - how they sacrificed their lives for Him, and how they overcame all kinds of obstacles that had prevented them from serving Him. By hearing such stories a person's heart is aroused to go in the ways of the Holy Tzadikim and to perform deeds similar to theirs. And this in turn was the main stimulus of the Tzadikim themselves to become engaged in the service of HaShem, namely that they heard marvelous stories of other Tzadikim who had preceded them, so that their hearts were excited to perform similar deeds to those of their predecessors. And as Rabbi Nachman himself has told us, all his awakening to HaShem was through hearing stories and tales about the Tzadikim, especially the stories about his grandfather, the Holy Baal Shem Tov, whose disciples were accustomed to come and stay in his parents' house. There they would tell wondrous stories about their master, the Baal Shem Tov, of blessed memory - for the house where Rabbi Nachman was born had been the home of the Baal Shem Tov himself. The mother of Rabbi Nachman, Feige, had inherited it from her mother, Adel, daughter of the Baal Shem Tov. That was because Adel had three children: Rabbi Boruch of Medziboz, Rabbi Ephraim of Sadilkov (author of the "Degel Machne Ephraim"), and Feige the Righteous. Rabbi Boruch and Rabbi Ephraim were not in need of the house because they were leaders of congregations in their cities, so the house was passed on to Feige, and in it Rabbi Nachman was born.

When the Tzadikim would come to prostrate themselves on the grave of their master, the Baal Shem Tov, they were all accustomed to stay in that house and to sit and tell wondrous tales about their holy teacher. Rabbi Nachman, then a little boy, used to wander about the house and hear all those tales, and that is what so aroused his heart to the service of HaShem. Especially when he heard the wonderful story of how the Holy Baal Shem Tov entered into the service of HaShem. His father had summoned him when he was five years old and told him, "*Srulik* (for that is how young Yisroel was called), "Know that I am going the way of all flesh. The time has come for me to depart, but have no fear at all, for you will never be alone; the Holy One, Blessed Be He, is always with you, near you, and in you." With these words he passed away, and from that moment it entered into the little boy's mind that he had no one in this world except the Holy One, Blessed Be He, and wherever he went he attached himself to Him and asked of Him his needs, and in that way achieved all he achieved.

And behold this story entered well into the ears of Rabbi Nachman. Indeed, he said that from it he learned the secret of the Holy Baal Shem Tov's disciples and their success, namely by planting in his mind the truth of HaShem's reality, and that no reality exists without Him, so that whatever a person requires he must ask only of HaShem. From that time, Rabbi Nachman began to engage in prayer and meditation which is called *Hitbodedut*. He would take walks in secluded places, and pour out his heart before HaShem, asking to be brought closer to His service. And in that way he merited to accomplish all that he accomplished, for indeed the essential awakening that a person receives to come closer to HaShem is by means of hearing stories and tales of the Tzadikim so that his heart is greatly aroused to follow their holy ways. For that reason, happy is the person who merits to hear and to read the tales of the Tzadikim, for this will also arouse his heart to follow in their holy ways, and he will merit all that is truly good and eternal in this world and the world to come. Happy is he, and happy is his lot!

And *Mohorosh* connected this matter to the weekly Parsha (*Eikev*, Deut. 7:12 to 11:32), for it is written: "It will be because ("*Eikev*") you listen to these regulations, observing and performing them, HaShem your G-d will keep the gracious covenant that He made on oath with your forefathers." *Mohorosh* explained that in this verse, the word "*Eikev*" (which also has the meaning of "heel") suggests the lower levels of Holiness. Thus even if a person is on the very lowest spiritual level, truly a "heel," and considers himself to be the worst person in the world, nevertheless his main hope is that he "listen to" - namely, that he listen to the tales of the Tzadikim, for from them he will obtain a great awakening to the service of HaShem. Only after that does it state "these regulations," meaning that he will merit to observe all the laws and commandments of the Torah. For in the Holy Torah itself we find that the Holy One, Blessed Be He, first put in the stories and tales of the Patriarchs and of Moses, and so on, before giving us the commandments of the Torah. For that is the same way mentioned above, that stories and tales of Tzadikim arouse the heart to observe the Torah and come closer to HaShem. And that is the meaning of "because ("*Eikev*") you listen," that even if you are as low as a heel, you still can listen, namely to the stories and tales of the Tzadikim. Only after that will you merit to receive "these regulations, observing and performing them." For you will derive a great awakening through these tales, and then by measure for measure "G-d will keep the gracious covenant that He made on oath with your forefathers." When these tales and stories of the Tzadikim are told, their merit and their power are awakened in the Heavens. Then the Holy One Blessed Be He recalls for our sake their covenant and their lovingkindness, and in their merit He is gracious unto us. May HaShem grant us the merit to listen to, to read, and to tell the stories and tales of true Tzadikim so that we may be worthy of awakening to His service, so that we may cling and cleave to Him in truth, now and forever. Amen.

SHABBOS MORNING PARSHAS EIKEV 5758

On Shabbos morning at *Kiddush*, *Mohorosh* spoke very awesome, wondrous words about one of the Tales of Rabbi Nachman, "The Rabbi and His Only Son," story 8.

The Tale begins: "There was a Rabbi who was childless for some time until he was blessed with a son. He raised him lovingly, and when the young man was old enough, found him a proper bride. The son was given an upstairs room so that he could continue his studies undisturbed, as was the custom of the well-to-do in that area. The son was conscientious. He spent his time in study and prayer. But he had the feeling that there was something missing in his life. Sometimes he didn't feel complete devotion when he prayed, or it seemed as if he missed the inner reason in his study. He spoke of this lack to two of his young comrades, and they suggested that he visit a certain Righteous Man, a Tzadik. This young man had already reached the level where he'd become a *small light* in the world, by virtue of his good deeds".

Mohorosh began by saying that Rabbi Nachman tells us of the Rabbi who had been childless, and then had an only son and found him a bride, for that is one of the commandments of a father towards his son - to find him a wife. As our holy sages have said (*Kiddushin*, 29a), "A father is obligated to circumcise his son, to redeem him, and to marry him to a proper bride." The last of these is an extremely important commandment which unfortunately many people today do not take seriously. They do not make every possible effort to have their sons married at an early age. As a result so many youths fall into sins and immorality, G-d forbid, and no one understands what they go through. But if they had been married off while still young they would have been spared all those troubles.

"The son was given an upstairs room so that he could sit and pursue his studies undisturbed, as was the custom of the well-to-do in that area." For the first year of marriage is the best time to sit and constantly study the holy Torah. Afterwards, children and the burdens of life and the need to support his family weigh down the young man so that it becomes very hard to sit and study Torah diligently all day. But if he gets accustomed even from the first days of his married life - to be constant in his Torah studies and to be engaged with great effort in the service of HaShem - then that strength will stay with him all his life. He will merit to grasp much true and eternal good every single day.

"The son was conscientious. He spent his time in study and prayer. But he had the feeling that there was something missing in his life. Sometimes he didn't feel complete devotion when he prayed, or it seemed as if he missed the inner reason in his study." As long as a person is alone and not associated with a true Tzadik, he will surely feel a great lack in his Torah studies and prayers. Although he himself may not be aware of this, the main cure for all imperfections can be obtained only from the true Tzadik of each generation, from whom one draws the vital spirit to perfect whatever is lacking (see *Likutei Mohoran* I:8). As long as a person is not associated with the Tzadik he will surely feel a major imperfection in all his service, but as soon as he merits to be associated with him he will experience a different feeling in every aspect of life.

"He spoke of this lack to two of his young comrades." It is a very great thing for a person to have a good friend with whom he can speak about his service to HaShem and from whom he can receive good counsel for success in life. Rabbi Nachman spoke at length on the matter of friendship (see *Likutei Mohoran*, I:34), saying that it is one of the three main points that every person needs to address. The first point being to acquire a Rabbi, the second to acquire a friend, and the third to find himself. Acquiring a friend is very important, because together with a friend, it is much easier to find the true Tzadik of the generation and to come close to him. With a good friend you can discuss what you heard from the Tzadik, until things become so clear that you really finally find yourself. So in essence, having a good friend is the basis of all three points.

"And they suggested that he visit a Righteous Man, a Tzadik," For through the Tzadik one receives the vital spirit to correct his imperfections, and through him a person receives good counsel to draw nearer to Ha Shem.

"This young man had already reached the level where he'd become a *small light* in the world, by virtue of his good deeds". Mohorosh explained that a person needs to prepare himself very well in order to approach a true Tzadik; that is, he must humble himself completely and recognize his place, that without the Tzadik he is nothing. This way he will merit to receive much good from him and to reflect the light of his countenance. For the Tzadik indeed resembles the sun, the great light that illuminates with huge radiance, and a person must become like the moon, the *small light* that has no radiance of its own except that which it reflects from the sun. And if a person truly humbles himself, he will then receive very much from the Rabbi, the Tzadik of that generation. It is precisely this that the young man felt, that something was missing in his service of HaShem, that he did not feel the inner reason in his Torah studies and his prayers. This in itself caused him to be a *small light*. Most people that study and pray alone become influenced by pride, feeling that there is no one in the whole world who is quite like themselves, as if they have become truly great scholars, supposing they can disregard other people and call them ignorant. Even though such a person prays enthusiastically, pride and conceit enter into him, as if he were praying with the highest intensity, or as if he were a great Tzadik himself. But in truth he has only begun to pray properly, and because of his proud, conceited thoughts he does not merit to become even a *small light*. Never does such a one merit to approach a true Tzadik because he does not feel that anything is missing in himself. However, as soon as a person ceases to delude himself, humbles himself and senses how much truly is lacking in himself, he becomes a small light that is ready to receive from the great light, the Tzadik, much true and eternal good. May HaShem, Blessed Be He, grant that we merit to draw near to the truly Righteous Men, the Tzadikim, and receive within ourselves their holy countenance until we come to cling to HaShem, Blessed Be He, with a true and eternal connection henceforth and forever.

Amen.

Seuda Shlishis, Parshas Eykev, 5766

At the third Shabbos meal, Mohorosh *Shlit"a* spoke inspiring words on the subjects of the Land of Israel and Rosh HaShannah, based on *Lekutei Mohoran*, Part II, Lesson 40.

Rebbe Nachman says: "He who knows the significance of the Land of Israel, and has truly experienced a taste of the Land of Israel, can recognize in another person whether or not he had been together with a Tzaddik on Rosh HaShannah, and whether this was a great Tzaddik or not, or whether he himself is a Tzaddik…The essence of the special sanctity of the Land of Israel is due to Hashem's Providence that is felt there acutely, that is, His constant overseeing of the Land of Israel, as it is written (*Devarim*, Ch. 11): 'The eyes of Hashem your G-d are always upon it [the Land of Israel] from the beginning of the year until year end.' And this [intense Divine Providence] causes the special sanctity of the Land of Israel. And because the eyes of Hashem are always upon the Land of Israel 'the air of the Land of Israel [also] makes one wise (*Talmud Baba Basra*, 158a).'

However, why are 'the eyes of Hashem always upon it [the Land of Israel]'? This is due to the souls of Israel, which Hashem takes pride in, which is an aspect of the verse (Isaiah, Ch. 49): 'Israel, in you, I [Hashem] take pride.' And through Hashem's pride in the souls of Israel, the concept of *tefillin* emerges, as *tefillin* are called 'pride' (Talmud Sukkah, 25). Therefore we find the concept of donning tefillin, so to speak, by Hashem, as our Sages teach us (Talmud Berachot 6a): 'From where do we know that Hashem dons *tefillin*? For it says (Isaiah, Ch. 62) Hashem swore … by His strong hand, referring to the *tefillin* which are called 'strength'. And what is written in the tefillin of Hashem? Who is like Your nation Israel, one nation in the Land.' So we see that the pride of Hashem in Israel is the concept of His tefillin. The Ariza'l explains that *tefillin* represent the concept of intellect, and they penetrate [the intellect and the soul which is in the brain] and cause one's [spiritual] eyes to open. So too, in regards to the *tefillin* of Hashem, for from the pride that Hashem takes in His holy nation – which is His *tefillin* – emerges His unique Providence over them and over the Land He gave them, which gives rise to the special sanctity of the Land of Israel. And therefore it is called the Land of **Israel** because it receives its sanctity from the concept of '**Israel**, in you, I

[Hashem] take pride'. And when a person is able to perceive this pride that Hashem takes in His people Israel, he also receives the concept of 'pride and intellect' and then the concept of *tefillin* emerges for him, penetrating the intellect and the soul which is in his brain and causing his spiritual eyes to open. And then his *own* eyes enter the category of 'the eyes of Hashem' – seeing Divine Providence everywhere – and so, every place he looks upon also enters the category of 'the air of the Land of Israel which makes one wise.'

And who is the one who has the ability to perceive the pride that Hashem takes in Israel? It is he who sees the person who brings people close to the service of Hashem and who is the main factor in the Jewish people's drawing close to their Father in Heaven – and this is the true Tzaddik. It turns out, that the Tzaddik himself is the pride which Hashem takes in His people. For it is through the service of the Tzaddik, that all of Israel's drawing close to Hashem and all of the pride that Hashem takes in them come about. Then, the one who sincerely observes the Tzaddik – particularly at a time when a large number of people gather around the Tzaddik, and especially on Rosh HaShanah when the gathering is very large – receives some of this pride, and the concept of *tefillin* and intellect emerge for him – the concept of 'the eyes of Hashem'. And then every place he looks upon becomes an aspect of the Land of Israel." (These are the words of Rebbe Nachman.)

Mohorosh explained that Rebbe Nachman reveals to us in this lesson wondrous secrets concerning the Land of Israel and concerning the pride that Hashem takes in the souls of Israel. The sanctity of the Land of Israel stems from the pride that Hashem takes in the souls of Israel, the children of Avraham, Yitzchak and Yaakov, who desired His closeness every moment of their lives. And this causes Hashem to take pride in them and to watch over them with "open eyes", that is, with very close personal supervision, and to bestow upon them every manner of blessing and kindness. And because of this, He gave them the Land of Israel, the land He chose from all lands and gave to the people He chose from all peoples. Therefore, regarding the Land of Israel it is written (*Devarim*, Ch. 11): "The eyes of Hashem your G-d are always upon it from the beginning of the year until year end", for there in the Land of Israel, Hashem's Providence is revealed to the greatest extent. And someone who comes to the Land of Israel and truly experiences the taste of the Land will be able to perceive the pride that Hashem takes in the souls of Israel when he sees the wondrous gift Hashem has given them, namely, the Land, and how He has exalted them above all the families of the earth as

2

Hashem's own children and representatives, and therefore, He watches over and personally supervises them down to the minutest detail of their lives, to satisfy all their needs, spiritually and materially.

This process of Hashem taking pride in Israel and the Divine Providence this pride engenders is taking place constantly through the service of the Tzaddikim, for the true Tzaddikim of the generation are always searching and seeking out merits on behalf of the souls of Israel. And they are always taking pride before Hashem in the Children of Israel, mainly over the fact that they are the people that Hashem has brought close and has sanctified to carry the banner of Hashem – to be a kingdom of *kohanim* and a holy nation. And the Tzaddikim know that no matter how far a Jew has fallen away from Hashem and His Torah, it is always fitting to have compassion on him and bring him close in every way.

And he who merits to be in the company of such a Tzaddik receives an amazing illumination from this pride that the Tzaddik takes in the souls of Israel, for the Tzaddik will also look upon *him* with his holy eyes and find in *him* his good points and take pride in him before the Throne of Glory. And this is especially true on Rosh HaShannah when everyone gathers together by the Tzaddik, for then the Tzaddik judges each and every one to the side of merit and intercedes on their behalf before the Throne of Glory, effecting for each one a good and sweet year. For on Rosh HaShannah, the day of awesome judgment, when each and every one is judged as to what will be with him the entire year, one needs a very great lawyer who will advocate expertly on his behalf and bring him out innocent in judgment. Therefore, we go to Tzaddikim on Rosh HaShannah and include ourselves in their holy gathering, for through this we are included in the pride that Hashem takes in His people Israel.

From the above discussion, we find that one who comes to a true Tzaddik on Rosh HaShannah becomes fit to actually feel the sanctity of the Land of Israel, for the Tzaddik transforms the atmosphere of the gathering into the holy air of the Land of Israel, for he draws down to this place the pride that Hashem takes in the souls of Israel and this pride draws down Hashem's Providence, and it is the special Divine Providence which is the essence of the sanctity of the Land of Israel, as mentioned before. Therefore, in the verse that speaks about the sanctity of the Land of Israel, we find that the sanctity of Rosh HaShannah is also mentioned, as it is written (*Devarim*, Ch. 11): "The eyes of Hashem your G-d are always upon it **'from the beginning of the**

3

year (*me'Reishis HaShannah*)' until year end", for the sanctity of the Land of Israel and the sanctity of Rosh HaShannah are in essence one thing. Happy is the one who merits to be counted among the gathering of the Tzaddik on Rosh HaShannah, for then the special illumination of the Land of Israel will shine on him.

The main way the Tzaddikim try to defend and justify each and every Jew, no matter where he is holding in life, is with the argument that as a whole the Jewish people are on a higher moral level than any other nation. It is for this reason that we recite a blessing every day "Who has not made me a heathen", for even if I am unable to find within myself any good point, I am thankful that "I am not a heathen." Therefore, Rebbe Nachman admonishes us (*Lekutei Mohoran*, Part I, Lesson 282 and Part II, Lesson 10) that one should always try to be happy and to push away the sadness and bitterness, and the main happiness is that one has merited to be of the seed of Israel and not a heathen. And this is the way of the Tzaddikim; they are always trying to justify the souls of Israel before the Throne of Glory and to plead before Hashem that no matter how the Jew appears he is still part of the people of Hashem and this people is still on a higher moral level than any other people in the world, for "Who is like Your people Israel, one nation in the Land?"

Reb Nosson explains that this was the secret of Amos the prophet when he said (*Amos*, Ch. 9): "Are you not like the Children of Kush to me, Oh Children of Israel, said Hashem." This is surprising, that Hashem would liken the souls of Israel to the Children of Kush, the least of all the nations. However, there was at that time a great accusation in Heaven against the souls of Israel (see Amos there), and no matter how much Amos the prophet wanted to justify the Jewish people before the Heavenly court, the accusers would overturn his words. Therefore, Hashem made him reverse his words and say that if it is true that the souls of Israel are so fallen and lowly, then, behold, they are like the "Children of Kush", the least of all the nations, because as soon as the prophet likened them to the Children of Kush, everyone, including the heavenly court, was able to perceive clearly that there is still a great difference between the level of the Children and the level of the Children of Kush and the other nations. And then it became impossible for the accusers to arouse judgment against the souls of Israel. Therefore, happy is the one who always seeks out the good points within himself and within the souls of Israel, for in this way, the balance of the entire world will tilt to the side of merit and this merit will be attributed to him. Happy is he and fortunate is his lot.

4

Mohorosh connected the above ideas to our parsha in the following way. It is written (*Devarim*, Ch. 9): "Do not say in your heart when Hashem your G-d drives them out from before you, saying, 'Because of my righteousness Hashem has brought me to posses this land and because of the wickedness of these nations Hashem drives them out from before you. Not for your righteousness and the uprightness of your heart do you go in to possess their Land; but because of the wickedness of these nations does Hashem your G-d drive them out from before you." Let us ask the following question: Why is the holy Torah telling us here not to imagine that our inheriting the Land of Israel is due to our merits and acts of righteousness, but rather that it is due only to the wickedness of these nations? Isn't it only proper for every one of us to find in ourselves merits and good points and to enliven and strengthen ourselves with our awareness of our good points? So why here when Israel was about to enter the Land does the Torah warn us that we should only think that our taking the land is due to the wickedness of the Canaanite nations? According to the teachings of Rebbe Nachman we can understand it very well. It was specifically when the Children of Israel were about to possess the Land – the Land where Hashem's pride in the souls of Israel is revealed in the most open way – that Hashem wanted to preempt any accusation that might have been brought against the souls of Israel. Therefore, if they would have said that their possessing the Land was due to their merits and righteousness, it would have been possible for the accusers to point out their shortcomings as well as the flaws and imperfections in their good deeds and this would have prevented the good from coming to them. But now that they know that Hashem is driving out these nations because of *nations'* wickedness, therefore, no accusation in the world could have any effect, for even the least of all Jews, because of his being a part of the people of Hashem, when we compare their level to even the best of any other nation, we will immediately see his advantage and how it is impossible to bring accusations against him at all. Therefore, it is specifically concerning the inheritance of the Land of Israel, whose entire sanctity is built upon "Israel, in you will I take pride", that the Torah reveals that the Jewish people should observe the wickedness of these nations, and then they will know their own level and why the sanctity of the Land of Israel if fitting for them. May Hashem help us draw down upon ourselves the sanctity of the Land of Israel; and our brothers, the Children of Israel, who dwell in the Land of Israel will be protected from the wickedness of the nations that want to swallow them, G-d forbid, and may we merit to soon see the redemption and salvation of Israel with the coming of our righteous Moshiach swiftly in our days. *Amen v'amen.*

5

Seuda Shlishis, Parshas Re'ay, 5766

At the third Shabbos meal, Mohorosh *Shlit"a* spoke inspiring words on the meaning of the verse (*Tehillim*, Ch. 95): "Today, if you would hearken to His voice", based on *Lekutei Mohoran*, Part I, Lesson 272.

Rebbe Nachman says: "It is written: 'Today, if you would hearken to His voice.' This is a great rule in the service of Hashem; that is, one should place before one's eyes only *this* day. Whether it is concerning a person's livelihood or other physical needs, he should not worry that he may lack what he needs tomorrow. The same thing applies to serving Hashem. He should place before his eyes only *this* day and *this* moment. For when he wishes to begin serving Hashem, it seems as though it is a huge burden which is impossible to carry. But, if he would think that all he has is *this* day alone, the heavy burden will disappear; and he won't put off till tomorrow what he can do today, saying, 'tomorrow I will pray with concentration and with the proper strength, etc'…For a person has in his world only *this* day and *this* moment in which he is currently living, for tomorrow is another world entirely. '*Today*, if you would hearken to His voice' – precisely '*today'*." (These are the words of Rebbe Nachman).

Mohorosh explained that this teaching of Rebbe Nachman's is one of the most important foundations of a person's life. If one places before his eyes only the day in which he presently lives, then he will be able to accept upon himself every kind of spiritual and physical work, since for just one day it is possible to do it all – to fill this one day with much Torah, prayer and good deeds. And this advice will undoubtedly lead to great success in life.

The main reason a person becomes lax in his service of Hashem and in any other type of work is because he worries about tomorrow and thinks, "Even if I will learn and pray a lot today, who can guarantee that I will be strong enough to do this again tomorrow?" And this is why he is neglectful in his service even today. In fact, this thinking will also prevent him from beginning anything good. Since there is no guarantee that he will be able to do it again tomorrow, it's not worth even starting. However, if he would place before his eyes only today, not worrying about what will be tomorrow, he will see how successful he can actually be.

This rule also applies to the material world. Even the poorest Jew usually has enough food and money for today. However, the main cause of one's distress and worry is thinking, "What will be tomorrow? What will I eat tomorrow? What will I eat the day after tomorrow?" And then there is a person who has enough provisions for this week, but he worries about what he will eat next week. There are those who have provisions for the entire month, but they worry about what they will have next month. And there are those who have provisions for many months and even for many years, but they still worry about what will be after that. So we find that the entire cause of a person's worrying is his thinking about tomorrow. But if he would focus on just today, he will lack nothing. Therefore, the more a person accustoms himself to thinking, "**Today**, if you would hearken to His voice", the more he will succeed and live a good and sweet life.

In truth, every single day that a person has is a wondrous gift from Hashem and he is able to fill this day with an abundance of true and eternal good. Each and every day, the Hidden Light reveals itself and through this light a person can get a taste of the pleasures of *Gan Eden*. But what holds a person back from this good? - The snakes and scorpions that encircle and surround the day, and that want to prevent a person from reaching the Hidden Light within it (*Lekutei Mohoran*, Part I, Lesson 84). These snakes and scorpions are the alien thoughts and confusions that besiege a person, not allowing him to focus on today. Instead, they overwhelm him with thoughts and worries about tomorrow and this tears him away from today's brilliant Hidden Light. All of this is the counsel of Amalek, about whom it is said (*Shemos*, Ch. 17): "Go out and fight against Amalek **tomorrow**." The entire basis of his impure advice is "tomorrow": "Tomorrow you will start learning." "Tomorrow you will start praying." His goal is to get a person to neglect today, and to completely despair from being able to do anything today. And so he comes to a person every day and pushes off his life till tomorrow. But we must fight against Amalek and say to him the exact opposite of what he says to us: "Tomorrow I will obey you!" "Tomorrow I will do as you say!" "But I am giving today to Hashem! And today I will do all I can, in Torah, prayer, mitzvos and good deeds!" And thus, we must push him off from one day to the next. And in this way, we will fill each and every day with true and eternal good, and live a truly good and sweet life.

On the mystical level, within the word "*HaYom* (today)" is hidden an amazing secret. The essence of our service of Hashem is to connect the

2

spiritual and the material together, in other words, to have a perception of the future world within the materialism of this world. It was for this purpose that the entire universe was created, as it is stated in the *Zohar* (*Parshas Bo*, 42a): "The entire creation was brought into being in order that we recognize Hashem", that is, so that we would merit to find Hashem within each and every detail of creation and to unify His blessed Name (i.e. His divine attributes) with all of our actions. The spiritual, i.e. perceptions of G-dliness, is hinted at in the four-letter name of Hashem – *Yud-Kay-Vav-Kay*. The explanation of this Name is "He was, is and will be". This is the spiritual – Hashem's G-dliness which brings into existence and constantly sustains the entire creation, from the first and highest of all worlds to the last and lowest of all worlds. The material world and the running of Nature are hinted at in the name *Elokim*, whose gematria (numerical value of the letters) is the same as that of the word *HaTeva* (Nature). For with the name *Elokim*, Hashem runs and directs Nature, and he clothes His G-dliness within the materiality of creation. Before the First Man sinned with the Tree of Knowledge of Good and Evil, G-dliness was revealed without any screens or coverings, as it is written (Bereishis, Ch. 2): "And they were both naked…and they were not ashamed." For they saw G-dliness revealed from each and every detail of creation, as our holy Sages have said (*Midrash Bereishis Rabbah*, 20:12): "In the 'Torah of Rabbi Meir' it was written: "And Hashem G-d made for Adam and for his wife garments of light - *aleph-vav-reish* [however, in the Torah it is actually written 'garments of skin - *ayain-vav-reish*, but Rabbi Meir changed the *ayin* to an *aleph*]", for every covering and garment was a piece of G-d's revealed light. However, after the sin of the Tree of Knowledge, the light was hidden, becoming "garments of skin" (skin represents a screen and a covering). Therefore, the essence of our service is to once again reveal the hidden light that exists in each detail of creation.

It is explained in the Zohar and in the writings of the Ariza"l that the essence of the sin of Adam was that he caused two separations: 1). A separation between the first two and the last two letters of the Tetregrammaton – that is, he separated *Yud-Hay* from *Vav-Hay*, and 2). A separation between the first three letters and the last two letters of the name *Elokim* – that is, he separated *Aleph-Lamed-Hay* from *Yud–Mem*. The letters *Yud-Hay* represent the holy intellectual faculties of *Chochma* and *Bina* which give us the ability to contemplate and perceive G-dliness from all of the details of creation. But when a person blemishes these holy intellectual faculties by following his own understanding, the letters *Yud-Hay* become separated from the letters *Vav-Hay*, leaving *Vav-Hay* by itself. All of our service is about returning the

3

Vav-Hay to the *Yud-Hay*. And this is the meaning of the *"Le'sheim Yichud"* prayer: "...to unite the name *Yud-Hay* with *Vav-Hay* in complete unity".

This also applies to the letters of the name *Elokim*. The goal is that the letters *Aleph-Lamed-Hay* be attached to the letters *Yud-Mem* in order to recognize "Who created these" – "Who (spelled *Mem-Yud*) created these (*Aleph-Lamed-Hay* – these)", as it is written (Isaiah, Ch. 40): "Raise your eyes on high, and see Who created these". The word "these (*Aleph-Lamed-Hay*)" represents the material world, those things which we can see and point to in the physical world. And *Mem-Yud* represents the Fifty Gates of Understanding (*Mem-Yud* has the *gematria* of 50). And through these Fifty Gates we can comprehend and come to the recognition of "Who created these". However, as a result of Adam's sin, the letters *Aleph-Lamed-Hay* became separated from the letters *Mem-Yud*. So, instead of seeing Hashem from within the material world, Adam and Chava blemished their *emunah* and fell into the destruction of *avoda zara* (idolatry) which is also referred to by the word "these (*Aleph-Lamed-Hay*)"*, as it is written (Shemos, Ch. 32): *"These (Aleph-Lamed-Hay) are your gods, O Israel."* Therefore, the essence of our service each and every day is to return these letters to their proper place, and to recognize Hashem from every detail of our "today". And "today (*HaYom*)" are the letters *Vav-Hay* and *Yud-Mem*; that is, we need to return the letters *Vav-Hay* to the letters *Yud-Hay* and the letters *Yud-Mem* to the letters *Aleph-Lamed-Hay*, which is the secret of the verse (*Bereishis*, Ch. 3): "And they heard the sound of Hashem (*Yud-Hay -Vav-Hay*) Elokim (*Aleph-Lamed-Hay-Yud–Mem*) moving in the garden towards the spirit of today (*HaYom*)", for Adam's sin caused the two names, Hashem and *Elokim*, to be separated from the "spirit of today (*HaYom*)", for now the letters of "today (*HaYom*)" - *Hay-Yud-Vav-Mem* - are separated from these two divine Names. And the essence of our service is to return them to their original places.

Mohorosh connected the above ideas to our parsha in the following way. In the opening verse of the parsha, Moshe Rebbeinu says to the Chldren of Israel (*Devarim*, Ch. 11): "See, I place before you today a blessing and a curse." What is the explanation of the word "today" in this verse? It appears to be unnecessary since the verse is speaking about the blessings and curses that would be said on Mt. Gerizim and Mt. Eival (as Rashi explains on this verse), and this ceremony would only be performed later after they had entered the Land of Israel under the leadership of Joshua. Let's try to answer this question according to the above teachings of Rebbe Nachman.

4

The word "today" in this verse alludes to the verse "Today, if you would hearken to His voice". Moshe Rebbeinu is teaching us the secret to a successful life, namely, if we would only focus on the day we are currently living in, not worrying about what will be tomorrow, we will be successful in every matter, spiritually and materially. And this is "See, I place before you **today** a blessing and a curse" – "I am giving over to you the power of 'today', which means to focus on each day unto itself and not to confuse yourselves with the next day at all." And this is an awesome secret for a successful life; for one who fulfills this with simplicity will have a "blessing". But one who disregards this will have a "curse", G-d forbid.

The wicked also utilize the advice of "today", but to their detriment, saying (Isaiah, Ch. 22): "Let us eat and drink [today], for tomorrow we shall die." Therefore, "The blessing: that you hearken to the mitzvos of Hashem, your G-d, that I command you '**today**'", for if you place Hashem before your eyes when you serve Him "**today**", you will succeed greatly and merit to learn much Torah and draw down upon yourselves all of the blessings, which is "The blessing: that you hearken", the finals letters of which spell the word 'Torah' (as brought in the Baal HaTurim). But the opposite, "And the curse: if you do not hearken to the mitzvos of Hashem, your G-d, and you turn away from the path that I command you - 'today' " – the main curse is the turning away from "today", which means to worry about what will be tomorrow, and this will not bring any blessings to a person's life, G-d forbid – "if you do not hearken to the mitzvos", the final letters of which spell "*el maves* (to death)", for without the advice of "Today, if you would hearken to His voice", a person is in danger of destroying his days and years, G-d forbid.

Most years, we read parshas Re'eh before *Rosh Chodesh Elul*, the month of *teshuva*, for the essence of *teshuva* is to return to filling each day with an abundance of true and eternal good. And even if all year long we did not treat each day with the proper care, now is the time to do *teshuva* for this and to fulfill "Today, if you would hearken to His voice" – to fill each day with much Torah, prayer, mitzvos and good deeds. May Hashem help us to properly watch over all of our days and years, and may we merit to elevate and connect them to Hashem, to be included in Him completely, for now and evermore. *Amen v'amen.*

5

Seuda Shlishis, Parshas Shoftim, 5760

At the third Shabbos meal, Mohorosh *Shlit"a* spoke inspiring words about the secret meaning of the month of *Elul*, based on *Lekutei Mohoran*, Part I, Lesson 6.

We have now entered the holy days of *Elul* – days of *teshuva*, forgiveness and mercy. Rebbe Nachman reveals to us in this lesson the secret of the meaning of *Elul*, which is the secret of *teshuva*. Rebbe Nachman says: "Every person needs to minimize his own honor and enhance the honor of Hashem. For he who runs after honor and glory will not merit the Glory of G-d, but only the glory of kings, as it says (*Mishlei*, Ch. 25): 'But the glory of kings is to investigate a matter', and everyone will investigate and scrutinize his deeds and ask: 'Who is he that people should show him so much honor; and they will argue with him, saying that he is not worthy of such honor. However, he who flees from honor, minimizing his own honor and enhancing the honor and Glory of Hashem, will merit the Glory of G-d, and people will not investigate whether or not he is deserving of such honor. About such a person it is said (ibid): 'It is the Glory of G-d to conceal a thing', for it is forbidden to investigate this type of glory. And it is only possible to merit this type of glory through *teshuva*. And the essence of *teshuva* is when a person hears his own disgrace and remains silent. And when a person wants to go in the ways of *teshuva*, he needs to be an expert at 'going' in two ways: 1). How to go forward and 2). How to go backward; as it is written (*Zohar, Vayakhel* 213b): 'Happy is the one who can go in [i.e. to ascend to lofty perceptions of G-dliness] and come out again', which is an aspect of (*Tehillim*, Ch. 139): 'If I ascend up into heaven, You are there' – the category of going in – of being an 'expert at going forward'; [and the continuation of this verse is] 'And if I make my bed in hell, behold, You are there' – the category of coming out – of being an 'expert in going backward'. And this is the meaning of the verse (*Shir HaShirim*, Ch. 6): 'I am my Beloved's, and my Beloved is mine' - 'I am my Beloved's' – this is an aspect of going in; and 'My Beloved is mine' is an aspect of coming out. And this is the secret meaning of *Elul*." (These are the words of Rebbe Nachman.)

Mohorosh explained that the goal of a person's striving for *shleimus* (wholeness) in this world is to come to an awareness of Hashem; specifically, to recognize His Glory and Honor from each and every detail of creation and to dedicate one's entire life to enhancing His Honor and Glory. Moreover, as a person comes to an awareness of Hashem, he also helps others to come to this awareness. And he merits all of this by considering his own honor null and void in relation to Hashem's honor. This means that he is not particular about his own honor at all, but only about the honor of Hashem. And he is concerned that whatever he does should only redound to Hashem's honor. And in this way, he will merit G-dly honor. About such a person it is said (*Mishlei*, Ch. 25): "It is the glory of G-d to conceal a thing", for this kind of glory is beyond the investigation of any human being. It is concealed and hidden from the eyes of all men. Moreover, it is something only between Hashem and the person who merits it, as it is said (Isaiah, Ch. 64): "No eye has seen it, G-d, except for You."

The meaning of "G-dly honor" is that a person merits to feel the Glory and Honor of Hashem hovering over him all day long; and from every aspect of creation all he sees is Hashem's Glory shining forth. This is something that is completely impossible to explain or relate in words. Furthermore, it is the very purpose of life and the reason a person was created and placed on this earth. And this purpose is to recognize Him and to see His Glory. However, to the degree that a person feels his own self-importance and "weight" in this world and desires to be "seen" by others, for example, he desires to be famous for his great wealth, or he desires to be a Rebbe or a leader, etc...he will not merit G-dly honor, but only the honor of kings, about which it is said (ibid): "But the glory of kings is to investigate a matter", which means that although it very well may be that people will show him honor and run after him, there will also be many critics who will scrutinize and investigate him, questioning whether he is truly worthy of all this honor. And many people will be envious and hateful of the person who has honor. Therefore, they will come to criticize and argue with him as they feel that he is not worthy of such honor. And he will have to suffer from numerous and bitter controversies and disputes from his "watchful foes (*Tehillim*, Ch. 27)". He will simply have no rest and peace from all his honor.

However, in truth, we find that even the greatest Tzaddikim throughout Jewish history have suffered from controversies and bitter disputes from coarse and unrefined people who quarreled with them for every possible reason and who harassed them in every possible way. So, there would seem to be a contradiction here in Rebbe Nachman's lesson: Why did these Tzaddikim have to suffer such persecutions when they have certainly merited

2

G-dly honor? But the truth is that from heaven they have compassion upon these holy Tzaddikim who serve and toil all the days of their lives and have reached very lofty levels in their perception of the *Ohr Ein Sof* (Endless Light), Blessed is He. These Tzaddikim are always fearful lest the smallest amount of self-importance and arrogance enters them. Since a person finds himself in a physical world, it is very likely that some thought of self-importance will enter his mind; for example, he might imagine that he has already reached a very lofty level in his perception and understanding of G-dliness. And this is exactly why from heaven they send to these Tzaddikim all kinds of opposition and controversy. And through these sufferings, their hearts become broken within them, completely shattering into tiny pieces, for they are in great pain over the fact that people are persecuting them for no good reason – even people that don't really known them. And these "watchful foes" open their mouths and speak against these Tzaddikim every evil thing, like dogs who bark at innocent passersby, as it is brought in the words of our Sages (*Talmud Yoma*, 83b): "A sign of a mad dog is that his jaw is always hanging open." And the Chafetz Chaim explains that one whose mouth is always open to speak about others is like a mad dog that barks for no reason at whoever passes by. Another sign of a mad dog given by the Talmud is that "its tail rests between its legs". This alludes to the blemish of the *Bris*, G-d forbid, for he who speaks against the Tzaddikim is surely very blemished in this area, which is an aspect of the verse (*Tehillim*, Ch. 55): "He [the opponent of the Tzaddikim] put forth his hands against them [the Tzaddikim] that were at peace with him; he has profaned his covenant." Therefore, when these wicked people speak evil about the Tzaddikim, this causes the Tzaddikim tremendous pain and it completely breaks their hearts and spirits until it is impossible for any thoughts of self-importance or arrogance to enter them. And this brokenness helps them merit a very high level of G-dly honor and it causes them to be included completely in the *Ohr Ein Sof*, Blessed is He.

So we find that the only way to merit G-dly honor is through *teshuva*. And the essence of *teshuva* is when a person hears his own disgrace and remains silent. For when a person hears himself being disgraced by others and yet he doesn't go out to quarrel with them and insult them back, but rather accepts it all with love, knowing that there is a divine purpose in his accepting the disgrace and embarrassment in silence, he thus becomes nullified and completely humbled in his own eyes and merits G-dly honor on a very high level.

3

The disgrace and embarrassment that we've been speaking about thus far are specifically those that a person receives from others. But, there is also a kind of embarrassment and disgrace that a person receives from himself. For example, when a person wants to be occupied in serving Hashem and he is constantly striving to grow and elevate himself higher and higher, but he notices that he keeps falling back into his negative character traits and base desires again and again. And because of this, he feels deeply embarrassed and disgraced in his own eyes. And when he does not accept the embarrassment and disgrace with love, his heart will fill with doubts and confusion and he asks himself, "Why must I always keep falling back into old negative traits and behaviors when Hashem knows that all I want is to be an upstanding Jew?" And from this thinking, he becomes very upset and discouraged. And now he is liable to throw in the towel and totally forsake serving Hashem, G-d forbid. However, as soon as he accepts everything he is going through with love and with the awareness that (*Tehillim*, Ch. 145) "Righteous is Hashem in all His ways, and loving in all His actions" and with the knowledge that it is indeed necessary for him to go through all of these falls and regressions before he can merit to enter the gates of holiness – if he has this attitude and concentrates on these thoughts, he will then be silent in the midst of all of the disgrace and embarrassment which he receives from himself. And in the end, he will merit to rise to the level of G-dly honor and to perceive Hashem's blessed light on the highest levels. Happy is he!

Everything we have spoken about so far is referred to as the "path" of *teshuva*. From the time one leaves his mother's womb until he returns to the earth from which he was taken, a person finds himself on a "path" - a "bridge" - on which Heaven is leading his soul from this world to the next, as Rebbe Nachman has said (*Lekutei Mohoran*, Part II, Lesson 48): "Know, that a person needs to pass over a very narrow bridge. And the main thing is not to be afraid at all." At the time a person is born, they place his soul into his physical body and say to him that he will now begin to walk upon this "path" which will bring him to his eternal goal in the World to Come. However, in order to go successfully upon this path he needs to have certain skills, for this path is a very narrow bridge and it is easy to fall off, G-d forbid, if he is not careful how he walks. Therefore, one needs to be a *baki* (one who is skilled) in "going forward and backward", which means one knows how to go upward and how to go downward. And these two skills (*bakios*) are themselves the actual "path", for two times the *gematria* of *baki* (112) equals the *gematria* of *derech* (path - 224).

4

On the one hand, a person needs to know how to go upward, which is referred to as being an expert in "going forward" – at constantly striving to raise oneself upward closer to Hashem, never thinking that one has finally reached the ceiling. When a person thinks that he has attained it all, this is a sign that he has still attained nothing, for the goal of knowledge is to know that we still don't know. And the goal of all of our service of Hashem is to know that we have attained nothing in relation to Hashem's Endless Light, for (*Tehillim*, Ch. 145) "His greatness is beyond investigation", and (*Tehillim*, Ch. 139) "If I ascend to heaven, You are there", which means that no matter how high I manage to go, You, Hashem, are found there, and I have still attained nothing in relation to Your Endless Light. All of this is called "being an expert in going forward".

Being an expert at "going backward" means that a person is highly skilled at going downward – that even if he falls and sinks to very low places, G-d forbid, and it seems to him that he is the lowest and most inferior Jew in the world, nevertheless, he will never let himself despair in any way whatsoever, for he knows that even in the enormity of his fall, Hashem is found there, which is an aspect of the verse (ibid): "If I make my bed in hell, You are there" – that even if I have already "made my bed" in the lowest level of hell, G-d forbid, even there You are found, as Rebbe Nachman cried out in a loud voice (*Lekutei Mohoran*, Part II, Lesson 78): "There is never – ever – such a thing as giving up!" For even in the lowest pit of hell, one can actually be very close to Hashem. But the main thing is to believe that no matter where a person is standing right now, Hashem is found there and so he should cry out to Hashem from that very place, which is an aspect of the verse (*Yona*, Ch. 2): "From the belly of hell, I cried out; You have heard my voice." When a person has these two skills – he knows how to go up and how to go down, he will go securely upon the path/*derech* of *teshuva* – and *derech* is *baki* (skilled) times 2 in *gematria*, and he will surely merit to draw close to Hashem from everything that he goes through in life.

This is the secret of the word *baki* (skilled), which is spelled out from the first letters of the words *Yichud Bracha Kedusha (from Bereishis 32:22: "And he[Yaakov]rose up that night, and took his two wives, and his two handmaids, and his eleven children, and passed over the Bridge of Yabok[yud-beis-kuf]; See Kisvei Ariz"l, Pri Etz Chaim, Shaar HaBrachos, perek 7)*. And the *gematria* of these three letters is the same as the gematria of the two divine names – *Yud-Kay-Vav-Kay* (26) and *Elokim* (86=112). *Yud-Kay-Vav-Kay* represents the divine attribute of *chesed;* and when the goodness and kindness

5

of Hashem is revealed to a person and he merits to climb from one level to the next in his perceptions and understanding of G-dliness, he will have the skill to know how to draw closer and closer to Hashem, never thinking that he already understands it all. The name *Elokim* represents the divine attributes of judgment and strength – when a person goes through difficult times and he sees himself slipping and falling time and again, he will have the skill to know how to stand his ground no matter what he goes through and his feelings of self-worth will not suffer at all. This is the matter mentioned above of "He hears his own disgrace and is silent" – which means that he will not become frustrated and discouraged at all. And in this way, he will merit to be included in the *Alufo shel Olam* (the Master of the World). The overall shape of the letter Aleph alludes to this path of *teshuva*. The *aleph* א has an upper point and a lower point and between them there is a line. This teaches us that a person always needs to ascend from the lowest point, even the lowest level of hell, towards the highest point, which is the Blessed *Ohr Ein Sof*. And the main way to do this is through the line which represents the letter *Vav* that is between them. This flat *Vav* alludes to the expanse of the sky that changes colors from sunrise to sunset; and these colors allude to the matter of shame and disgrace, like the face of one who is shamed that changes many colors. And through his enduring this shame and embarrassment in silence he merits to ascend from the lowest level to the highest and to be included in the Blessed Endless Light, and he will get a taste of the World to Come in his lifetime. Happy is he and fortunate is his lot.

Mohorosh connected the above ideas to our parsha in the following way. We find in our parsha the chapter dealing with the unintentional murderer, as it is written (*Devarim*, Ch. 19): "Prepare for yourself the path and divide into thirds the border of your land that Hashem, your G-d, causes you to inherit and it [the six cities of refuge] will be for every murderer to flee there." It is explained in the words of Reb Nosson (*Lekutei Halachos, Eiruvei Techumim, Halacha* 5) that the matter of the unintentional murderer alludes to one who kills his own soul unintentionally, tearing it away from its Supernal Root in Hashem. But the way it can save itself is to flee to one of the six cities of refuge, which are an aspect of the six words of the *Shema – Shema Yisrael Hashem Elokeinu Hashem Echad*. The *Shema* represents our overall holy *emunah* in Hashem. And through *emunah*, a person merits atonement for everything, as Rebbe Nachman says (*Sefer HaMiddos*, Ch. *Emunah* #33): "Through *emunah*, Hashem will forgive you for all your sins". Sins cause doubts and heretical thoughts to enter one's mind, G-d forbid, as also mentioned by Rebbe Nachman (ibid, #22): "One's willful sin causes heresy to

6

enter one's mind." Therefore, one's main rectification is through *emunah*. Perhaps we can say that the above teaching of Rebbe Nachman – that the essence of *teshuva* depends on two different but complimentary skills – is hinted at here in our verse: **"Prepare for yourself the path"** – you should prepare for yourself a "path" of *teshuva* - how to return in complete repentance, even the person who has already killed his own soul unintentionally, G-d forbid. This is accomplished through **"divide in thirds the border of your land"** – which refers to the three parts of the *Aleph*, mentioned before – an upper point, a lower point and the *Vav* in between.

It is explained in the words of Rebbe Nachman at the end of this lesson, that these three parts of the *Aleph* correspond to the three mitzvos that the Children of Israel were commanded to carry out when they entered the Land of Israel, and these are: 1) To cut off the seed of Amalek - the category of the lowest point of the *Aleph* which corresponds to being an expert in going backward which means to not fall into despair no matter what happens, even if one is being pursued by Amalek and his impure helpers, 2) To build for themselves the *Beis HaMikdosh* – the category of the uppermost point of the *Aleph* which corresponds to the attainment of wisdom and perceptions of G-dliness, 3) To appoint a king for themselves – the category of the *Vav* in the middle of the *Aleph*. And the *Vav* corresponds to the shame and disgrace that one must suffer before one merits G-dly honor (Note: How does the *Vav* correspond to the King/Tzaddik? The *Vav*, which means "and", is the letter which connects two words, and it also connects the highest point to the lowest point within the letter *Aleph*, so too the King/Tzaddik knows how to connect the highest worlds with the lowest worlds, i.e. he is able to bring the highest levels of G-dliness to *every* person and he can teach them how to raise themselves up from even the lowest levels). **"Divide in thirds the border of your land that Hashem *Elokecha* causes you to inherit"** – prepare for yourself a path of *teshuva* which is composed of all three categories of mitzvos that the Children of Israel were commanded to carry out when they entered the Land. **"...that Hashem (*Yud-Kay-Vav-Kay*), your G-d (*Elokecha*), causes you to inherit"** – the categories of the two divine names mentioned before – *Yud-Kay-Vav-Kay* and *Elokim* – which together equal the word *baki* (skilled) in *gematria* (112). Upon these two names rests the essence of the two necessary skills of *teshuva* – to recognize Hashem whether one is ascending (the attribute of *chesed*) or descending (the attribute of judgment). And through this **"it will be for every murderer to run there"** – for even the one who has already killed his own soul unintentionally, G-d forbid, through this skill in the path of *teshuva*, he is able to fix everything.

7

May Hashem help us to return in complete *teshuva* and to prepare ourselves to greet the holy days of *Rosh HaShannah*. And may we receive a good and blessed year, a year of redemption and salvation for all the souls of Israel, nationally and individually. *Amen v'amen*.

8

Friday Night, Parshas Ki Saytzay, 5766

Friday night, at the first Shabbos meal, Mohorosh *Shlit"a* spoke inspiring words on the topic of guarding oneself from the *klipa* (impurities) of Amalek, based on *Lekutei Mohoran*, Part II, Lesson 19.

Rebbe Nachman says: "There is a stumbling block in every type of wisdom, which is an aspect of Amalek. And this stumbling block can cause one to fall, G-d forbid. However, when the Tzaddik delves into these seven wisdoms [Note: Our Sages teach that there are seven general categories of wisdom in the world], he is able to fortify himself and remain standing on his level through *emunah*, which is an aspect of (*Habakkuk*, Ch. 2): 'But the righteous shall live by his faith'." (These are the words of Rebbe Nachman.)

Mohorosh explained that every type of wisdom in the world was created in order that we would be able to recognize Hashem through that wisdom. And it is certain that from everything in the world, one can come to an awareness of Hashem. Attaining this awareness was the main purpose of creation, as it is written in the Zohar (*Bo*, 42a): "The entire creation was brought into being in order that we recognize Hashem", that is, so that we would merit to find Hashem within each and every detail of creation. Therefore, everything that was created in this world exists only so that a person can reach this goal. And therefore, so long as a person's heart burns for Hashem with a holy fire, and his main desire being only to draw closer to Hashem, then he will undoubtedly be able to recognize the wisdom and the divine intelligence that exists in everything, and draw closer to Hashem through that very thing (*Lekutei Mohoran*, Part I, Lesson 1). For through his heart being on fire for Hashem, he will certainly come to recognize his own humility and the exaltedness of the Creator. And this awareness will arouse him to seek out and find the wisdom and divine intelligence in everything. And he will bring himself closer to Hashem by means of this very wisdom and intelligence.

However, the *klipa* of Amalek is the concept of "cooling off" and "heaviness" in serving Hashem, as it is written (*Devarim*, Ch. 25): "How he (the nation of Amalek) met you (*karcha*) on the way [*karcha* can also mean 'he cooled you off]..." for Amalek places within a person feelings of self-importance and arrogance; thus, the *gematria* of Amalek (240) is the same as that of the word *Ram* (high/lofty). And as soon as feelings of self-importance and arrogance enter a person, he begins to "cool down" in his service of Hashem; his mind starts getting confused and mixed up, and doubts in his *emunah* begin to creep in, G-d forbid, for the *gematria* of Amalek is also the same as that of the word *safeik* (doubt). Therefore, the essence of the stumbling block of Amalek is that within every type of wisdom it places the *klipa* of self-importance and arrogance. And then, instead of a person's heart igniting with the passion to find Hashem through that wisdom, the opposite occurs and that same wisdom only serves to cool down his heart and to confuse his emunah. And as a result, he begins moving farther and farther away from serving Hashem, G-d forbid.

Therefore, the main strategy to fight against Amalek is to draw close to the true Tzaddik who is an aspect of Moshe *Rabbeinu* who fought against Amalek and placed warmth and passion in the hearts of Israel so they should always burn with a holy fire for Hashem. For through drawing close to a true Tzaddik, humilty will begin to enter a person (*Lekutei Mohoran*, Part I, Lesson 10), and then he will have the strength to stand up against the *klipa* of Amalek and to come out from all of his doubts. Moreover, his heart will warm up in his service of Hashem. Not only will he himself begin to serve Hashem with more warmth and passion, but he will also have the power to transfer his warmth and passion to others. And the main thing is that he should be so inspired to serve Hashem until he is able to transfer his warmth to others (*Lekutei Mohoran*, Part I, Lesson 152). And by inspiring others, he simultaneously turns up his own heat and becomes inspired to an even greater degree than ever before, in the way of emanating light and reflected light, that is, as the light radiates to others it also reflects back to him (*Lekutei Mohoran*, Part I, Lesson 184). Therefore, happy is the one who merits to be close to a true Tzaddik, for through the Tzaddik, he will receive true inspiration and passion to serve Hashem and he will even merit to bestow of his goodness upon others and to inspire a multitude of souls in their service of Hashem. Happy is he and fortunate is his lot.

Mohorosh connected the above ideas to our parsha in the following way. It is written in our parsha (*Devarim*, Ch. 25): "Remember what Amalek did to you on the way when you were leaving Egypt; how he met you (cooled you down) on the way..." This is a positive commandment to always remember what Amalek did to Israel and how he sought to cool us down from serving Hashem. However, we need to understand why the matter of "on the way when you were leaving Egypt" is mentioned here in the context of recounting

2

the evil deed of Amalek. According to the words of Rebbe Nachman we can understand it very well.

Leaving Egypt was accomplished through Moshe *Rabbeinu* who placed within the Children of Israel holy passion so that their hearts would burn for Hashem. And this holy fire in their hearts would burn up all of the evil and impurity they witnessed in Egypt in the house of bondage and which left their mark on the souls of Israel. However, since Hashem created everything with its own corresponding counterforce – for the sake of free choice – the wicked Amalek tried to cool off the holy passion that Moshe Rabbeinu placed within them and to replace it with feelings of self-importance and arrogance, in order to fill their hearts with doubts and cynicism. Therefore, the holy Torah commanded us to always remember the evil deed of Amalek and to run to the Tzaddikim who will warm us up with holy passion and inspiration. For only through the true Tzaddikim do we have any hope of being able to stand our ground in everything we go through "on the way", that is, when we are running to leave all of our personal and collective boundaries and limitations. And through sincerely trying to come close to the Tzaddikim, we will merit to set our hearts ablaze with a holy fire, until we can inspire and ignite other Jewish souls to also serve Hashem with warmth and passion. And the merit of the community will be ascribed to us.

And this is what we find in our parsha with regard to the mitzvah *"hakeim takim* (helping your friend lift a fallen animal)", as it is written (Devarim, Ch. 22): "You shall not see your brother's donkey or his ox falling down on the way and hide yourself from them; you shall surely lift them up again with him." Aside from the physical mitzvah to help lift up the animal or the package that has fallen off the animal when you see he is unable to do it himself, there is also a corresponding mitzvah in the spiritual realm: when one sees his fellow "falling" on the way and the fire for Hashem in his heart is cooling down, one should help him in this difficulty and arouse his heart toward Hashem. And this is "You shall not see your brother's donkey or his ox falling down on the way" – "*chamor achicha* (your brother's donkey)" – *chamor* (donkey) is the *chomrius* (physicality) of your brother which causes him to fall and cool down from serving Hashem. "Or his ox (*shor*)" – *shor* has the connotation of "looking or seeing" (Lekutei Mohoran, Part I, Lesson 1), as it is written (Bamidbar, Ch. 24): "*Ashureinu v'lo karov* (I see it but not in the near future)." For a person's "seeing" can also be a major cause of the diminution of the holy fire for Hashem in his heart, as our holy Sages have said (see Rashi on *Bamidbar* 15:39): "The eye sees, the heart desires and the

3

body finishes the act." And when you see the powers of your fellow "falling down on the way", which is caused by the impurity of Amalek – the stumbling block which exists in every wisdom – which wants to trip a person up "on the way", you shall not "hide yourself from them". Even though your own *yetzer* will seduce you saying, "Why must I bother helping others, it is enough that I fulfill my own obligations." About this, the Torah says "you shall surely lift them up again **with him**" – if you involve yourself with lifting up your fellow, you yourself will also rise up with him. For, when you transfer your warmth, inspiration and passion for Hashem to others, your own warmth will gain energy and grow even warmer. May Hashem help that our hearts should always burn with passion for serving Him until we merit to ascend and be included in Him completely, for now and evermore. *Amen v'amen.*

Seudah Shlishis, Parshas Ki Saytzay, 5766

At the third Shabbos meal, Mohorosh *Shlit"a* spoke inspiring words about the power of thought, based on *Lekutei Mohoran*, Part I, Lesson 49.

Rebbe Nachman says: "There is an inclination for good and an inclination for bad, as our Sages say (*Talmud Brachos* 61): "'Then Hashem G-d formed (*Vayitzer*) the man [*Bereishis* Ch. 2]'. In this verse, the word *Vayitzer* – 'He formed' – is spelled with two *yuds* instead of the usual one *yud*, which alludes to the two inclinations – the good inclination and the evil inclination", that is, good thoughts are the good inclination, and evil thoughts are the evil inclination, for the essence of the inclinations are the thoughts and the wisdom in the heart, as it is written (*Breishis*, Ch. 6): '…and every inclination of the thoughts of his heart…' " (These are the words of Rebbe Nachman.)

Mohorosh explained that the essence of a person is his thoughts and that the thoughts are the abode of the *neshama*, as we say (in the prayer before putting on *tefillin*): "The *neshama* that is in my brain". And the *neshama*, which is thought, is Man's advantage over animals. Man has a *neshama* and the power of thought to steer him in whatever direction he desires. And where a person's thoughts are, that is where the whole person is (*Lekutei Mohoran*, Part I, Lesson 21). Therefore, a person's two inclinations – the *yetzer tov* and the *yetzer hara* – occupy the "space" in a person's thoughts. Good thoughts are the *yetzer tov*, and evil thoughts the *yetzer hara*. *Yetzer* is the language of

4

"forming" (*Vayitzer* – 'He formed') and it is also closely related to the words "to paint (*tziyer*)" and "artist (*tzayar*)". The good inclination paints in a person's mind all things positive, images full of light and goodness. And it gives birth within a person to good *middos* (character traits) and good deeds. On the other hand, the *yetzer hara* paints images of darkness and evil in a person's mind. And it gives birth to bad *middos* and evil deeds, G-d forbid.

Therefore, it is an essential part of one's divine service to sanctify and purify his thoughts to the extent that they are always painting pictures of light and life and the pleasantness of being attached to Hashem. And then these thoughts will actually bring him to an attachment to Hashem. They will also help to guard him from all sorts of alien and evil thoughts that can bring him to actual evil and impurity, G-d forbid, as Rebbe Nachman once said to Reb Nosson while they were taking a walk together (*Lekutei Mohoran*, Part II, Lesson 114): "It seems that a person needs to guard himself very much from evil thoughts, G-d forbid", for an evil thought gives birth to bad *middos* and evil deeds, and then it will be very difficult to separate himself from them, especially when he falls into sins that relate to blemishing the *Bris*, G-d forbid, for from these sins are born "plagues of human beings (*nigei bnei adam* – from Samuel II, Ch. 7; the Zohar and *Midrash Bereishis Rabbah* 20:11 explain that sins of the *Bris* bring into existence destructive spiritual beings which harm the person who brought them into being) and when the time comes for him to depart this world, these destructive beings follow after him, mourning and crying for him just as his other children would mourn for him, and they say to him, "Give us life! Give us food!" And this is a great disgrace and embarrassment for him after he passes away, may G-d save us (*Lekutei Mohoran, Part* I, Lesson 141).

Therefore, it is essential that a person sanctify and purify his thoughts with every sort of holy activity, and especially to increase his learning of the holy Torah, which is the main antidote for the *yetzer hara* as our holy Sages have said (*Talmud Kiddushin*, 30b): "Hashem said, 'I created the yetzer hara and I created the Torah as its antidote." For the more a person puts himself into learning Torah, the more the Torah will purify his thoughts until finally the love of the Torah will enter his heart. And then, he will not want to separate from the Torah at all, as Rebbe Nachman once said (*Sichos HaRan* #17): "When the Torah shows love to a person, then he has absolutely no desire for *Olam HaBah* (The World to Come), for he only wants the Torah itself." Therefore, happy is the one who merits to throw himself into the love of the Torah, thereby purifying his thoughts through his attachment to Hashem. He

5

will then get a taste of the World to Come in his lifetime, and live a good life in this world and the next, forever. Happy is he and fortunate is his lot.

Mohorosh connected the above ideas to our parsha in the following way. It is written (*Devarim*, Ch. 21): "If a man will have two wives, the one beloved and the other hated, and they have borne him sons, both the beloved one and the hated one. And the firstborn son will be hers that is hated." Perhaps we can say that the holy Torah is teaching us a great lesson concerning the sanctity and purity of thought. "If a man will have two wives" – "wife" alludes to the power of thought, for our thoughts give birth to deeds (as explained in the holy book "*Noam Elimelech*" on this verse). And therefore, "If a man will have two wives" – that is, two types of thoughts – good thoughts are called "the beloved wife", as it is the one who gives birth within a person to good *middos* and good deeds; and evil thoughts which are called the "hated wife" since it is the one who gives birth to bad *middos* and evil deeds [see Rashi, at the beginning of Parshas Noach which speaks about the offspring of Noach, where he says that "The main offspring of the righteous is their good deeds."]. And there will be a great war between them, which is the war that takes place within a person – the war between the *yetzer tov* and the *yetzer hara*. "And they have borne him sons, both the beloved one and the hated one" – for the good thoughts give birth to good children and good deeds. And the evil thoughts give birth to bad children and bad deeds, G-d forbid. Moreover, the verse continues "and the firstborn son will be hers that is hated" – meaning that the evil thoughts will overpower the person and give birth to his firstborn – his main "strength and initial vigor (Bereishis, Ch. 49)", and he will be unable to free himself from this son's claim to his rights as the firstborn.

The holy Torah is warning us so that we shall be aware of the enormity of the blemish of evil thoughts. "Then it shall be on the day that he causes his sons to inherit whatever he has" – when the time comes for a person to leave the world "he cannot give the right of the firstborn to the son of the beloved one ahead of the son of the hated one, the firstborn" – that is, he will not be able to free himself from his evil deeds which were born from his evil thoughts, for they have become *nigei bnei adam*, G-d forbid, and they demand life and an inheritance according to the rights of the firstborn. And this is a great shame and disgrace for the father, G-d forbid. And there is only one thing left for him to do in order to purify his mind and free himself from these punishments and that is to gather all of his strength and to put all of his thoughts into the Torah. And through his cleaving to the Torah, he can return

6

his inheritance to the son of the beloved wife – to the good thoughts – to illuminate his soul with the light of Hashem's G-dliness, for this is how the *Mishnah* decides the law (*Talmud Baba Basra* 126b): "In regards to one who divides his possessions and gives equal share to all his children. If he says that he is giving an equal **inheritance** to all of his children, he has said nothing, because the firstborn has the right to a double share of the father's inheritance; but if the father says he is giving equal portions of his possessions as a **gift** and not as an inheritance, then his words stand." Since it is being given as a gift, it is permitted for him to bypass the rights of the firstborn and to give his possessions to whatever son he wishes. If so, then he can free himself precisely through the holy Torah which is called a "gift", as our Sages have said (*Talmud Eiruvin* 54a) on the verse (*Bamidbar*, Ch. 21): "And from the wilderness (*Midbar*) a gift" – If a person makes himself like a desert (*midbar*) which everybody treads on, then the Torah is given to him as a gift." In this way, he can return the inheritance to the son of the beloved wife – the good thoughts – and he can hide himself from the son of the hated wife – the evil thoughts. As the verse continues (*ibid*): "And from *Matanah* (a gift) *Nachliel* (an inheritance)" – the inheritance of G-d (*Nachliel*) – the Torah – is given to him as a gift (*Talmud Eiruvin* ibid). For through *teshuva* and throwing himself into the Torah, he will merit to receive "*Matan Nachliel*" (The gift of the inheritance of G-d) – to behold the sweet radiance of the Torah and to enjoy the fruits of his good thoughts. And this is the allusion in the verse: "Then it shall be on the day that he causes his sons to inherit whatever he has" – the last letters of these words in Hebrew spell "Torah" (as is brought in the *Baal HaTurim*), for it is precisely through the holy Torah – which is given as a gift – that he will be able to cause his sons to inherit in the proper order and to give the greatness and the honor to the son of the beloved wife – the good thoughts – and return to being attached to Hashem. May Hashem help us sanctify and purify all of our thoughts through our attachment to the Creator, may His Name be blessed, so that we will always be attached and connected to the light of the holy Torah, for now and evermore. *Amen v'amen.*

7

Friday Night, Parshas Ki Savo, 5766

Friday night, at the first Shabbos meal, Mohorosh *Shlit"a* spoke inspiring words about the spiritual level of *mah* ("what") and the nullification of one's feelings of greatness, based on *Lekutei Mohoran*, Part II, Lesson 82.

Rebbe Nachman says: "When a person sees that things are not going as he had planned, he should know that he is suffering from feelings of greatness, that is [he thinks to himself], 'I shall reign'. He should do *teshuva* and humble himself, at which point he enters the category of *mah*, as Moshe Rebbeinu declared (*Shemos*, Ch. 16): '*v'nachnu mah* – 'for what are we [he and his brother Aharon]?' – and then things will start going according to plan for him. (These are the words of Rebbe Nachman.)

Mohorosh explained that the main purpose of *Adam* (Man) in this world is to merit the level of *mah*, which means that his ego will become more and more nullified before the *Ohr Ein Sof* (The Endless Light), Blessed is He, and he will gradually have less and less feelings of self-importance and greatness, as Moshe *Rebbeinu* said to the Children of Israel (*Shemos*, Ch. 16): "*v'nachnu mah?*" – by which he meant that he and Aaron *HaKohein* were completely nullified to Hashem and had no feelings of greatness and of independent existence at all.

When a person merits an aspect of *mah*, he has achieved an aspect of the category of "*Adam*", for "*Adam*" has the same *gematria* as "*mah*" (45), and then everything starts to go as planned and according to the person's will. But when do things go against a person's will and seem not to go as he had planned? This is when he feels that he has an independent existence separate from Hashem and when he is suffering from feelings of greatness. He wants such and such to be, but when it just doesn't go his way, then everything is "not according to plan" in his eyes and he becomes very broken. However, when he merits an aspect of being nullified to the *Ohr Ein Sof*, Blessed is He, and when his entire will is that everything should be only according to Hashem's will, then everything will start going "according to plan" for him, for he has given himself over entirely to Hashem with the knowledge that all Hashem does is the *best* possible plan.

So we find that when a person sees that things are not going his way – i.e. "not according to plan" – and he has many objections to the situation he finds himself in, he should know that he is suffering from feelings of greatness. He thinks to himself "I shall reign" – which means that he wants to be a king and rule over people. The attitude of "I shall reign" is the cause of things not going as planned for him. However, as soon as he does *teshuva* and lowers and humbles himself, he will merit the level of *mah*, and then everything will start to go according to plan for him.

How do we know that a person has truly merited the level of *mah*? The sign for this is when he is always acknowledging and praising Hashem for all the kindnesses He does with him at every moment. His mouth is filled with praise for Hashem for every detail of life. And he recognizes that the entire order of all the days of his life is dependent only on the hand of Hashem. And for all this, he expresses gratitude to Hashem with a full mouth and with his whole heart. Sadly, this is not the case when he is always complaining about the bitterness of his lot and is always crying about all the things he is lacking. This is a sign that he is suffering from feelings of greatness. And as a result of these feelings, nothing seems to go the way he had planned. He therefore feels no contentment and satisfaction in life. However, the main advice for such a person is to thoroughly remind himself how lowly and humble his former situation used to be, and how Hashem had compassion on him and raised him up from his poverty and anguish. Now, he will begin to contemplate the loving kindnesses of Hashem. And he will express gratitude to Him and begin to come out of his feelings of greatness until he merits true humility. And before his eyes, he will witness the "not according to plan" in his life transform into "according to plan". Therefore, happy is the one who always contemplates the loving kindnesses of Hashem and shows gratitude to Him for all of the kindness and compassion that He does with him at every moment, for then, all of life will go "according to plan", and he will get a taste of the World to Come in his lifetime. Happy is he and fortunate is his lot.

Mohorosh connected the above teachings of Rebbe Nachman to our parsha in the following way. We find in our parsha the mitzvah of bringing the First Fruits (*Bikurim*), as it is written (*Devarim*, Ch. 26): "And you shall take of the first of every fruit of the ground that you bring in from your Land… and go to the place that Hashem, your G-d, will choose to make His name rest there." There is also a mitzvah of "Declaration (*Kriah*)" that accompanies the bringing of the *Bikurim*, as it is written (ibid): "And you shall come to

2

whomever will be the Kohen in those days and you shall say to him, 'I declare today to Hashem, your G-d, that I have come to the Land that Hashem swore to our forefathers to give to us...then you shall call out and say before Hashem, your G-d, 'An Aramean tried to destroy my forefather...'" We need to understand why the mitzvah of the Declaration (*Kriah*) is added to the mitzvah of bringing the *Bikurim*, since *Kriah* is not found in connection with any of the other gifts that are given to the *Kohanim*. Also, why are the words "An Aramean tried to destroy my father", which refers to how Lavan the Aramean sought to destroy Yaakov and his entire family, mentioned in the course of the Declaration? Furthermore, why do we mention the Children of Israel's descent to *Mitzrayim* in the *Kriah*? Also, what is the meaning of that which our Sages learn from the verse (Bereishis, Ch. 1): "'In the beginning (B'reishis), G-d created', in the merit of the Torah which is called 'first (*reishis*)' and in the merit of Israel who are called '*reishis*' and in the merit of the *Bikurim* which are called '*reishis*' the world was created (*Midrash Aggados Bereishis*)." Why do the Sages so emphasize the importance of the mitzvah of *Bikurim* to the extent that the entire creation of the world was for its sake? Let's try to answer all of these questions according to the above teachings of Rebbe Nachman.

The main purpose of *Adam* in this world is to come to a true nullification before Hashem to the extent that he recognizes that all that he has is a free gift from the Creator, Blessed is His name. And he will not think for a moment "my strength and the power of my hand made for me this wealth (*Devarim*, Ch. 8)". These ideas are the foundation of the mitzvah of *Bikurim*. When one goes down to his field and sees the first ripe fig, he ties a string around it and declares, "Behold, this is *Bikurim*". As soon as he merits to see the first fruits of his field, he sets them aside for Hashem in order to show how grateful he is to Hashem for all of the kindness He has bestowed upon him. And this gratitude is the foundation of the mitzvah of the Declaration of *Bikurim* (*Krias Bikurim*), as Rashi explains (verse 3): "'You shall say to him [to the *Kohen*]' – that you are not ungrateful (see more on this in the commentary of the holy *Alshich*)." It is not enough to merely separate his first fruits and give them to the *Kohen*; but he also needs to bring them to the *Beis HaMikdosh* with much pomp and circumstance, and to recite the entire *Kriah* before Hashem, as in this way he reveals the purity of his heart, that he is truly grateful to Hashem and does not attribute his blessings to his own hands at all.

3

And this is the idea behind beginning the *Kriah* with the words "An Aramean tried to destroy my father" and with the entire matter of the Egyptian exile. Sometimes, feelings of self-importance and arrogance prevent a person from remembering the kindnesses of Hashem. And it may even seem to him that he was never lacking anything. So what must he thank Hashem for? Therefore, at the time of bringing the *Bikurim*, a person must remind himself of his entire past, from "An Aramean tried to destroy my father"…"He descended to Egypt"… "The Egyptians mistreated us and afflicted us and placed harsh labor upon us…" because this life cycle applies to each and every one of us in different forms, as our holy Sages have said (*Talmud Pesachim* 116b): "In every generation, one is obligated to see himself as though he had gone out of Egypt." For every one of us has at one time in his life been in a very lowly state, whether he was lacking financially, emotionally, intellectually or spiritually, until Hashem helped him leave that situation. Therefore, when we bring the *Bikurim*, which is when we are involved in nullifying our self-importance, we need to mention with a full mouth the enormity of the lowliness that had once been our lot until Hashem helped us out of it, and in this way, we fix solidly in our hearts that most precious and essential trait of gratitude.

And this is what we find in the *Mishnah* (*Bikurim*, Ch. 3, *Mishnah* 4): "They [those who brought their *Bikurim*] arrived at the Temple Mount; even King Aggripas placed the basket upon his shoulders and entered [the Temple]…" For when a Jew brought his *Bikurim* a nullification of his ego occurred in the light of Hashem's presence. Even the king had to completely submit and nullify himself and read the entire *Kriah*, for it is precisely through this mitzvah that we fix the trait of self-nullification in our hearts and merit to attach the "first fruits" of our minds and thoughts to Hashem. And as we said before, this was the main purpose for the creation of the world.

Therefore, the explanation of our holy Sages is understood very well (*Aggados Bereishis*): " 'In the beginning (*B'reishis*), G-d created' – for the sake of the Torah which is called '*reishis*' and for the sake of Israel who are called '*reishis*' and for the sake of the *Bikurim* which are called '*reishis*', the world was created." For it is precisely through the mitzvah of *Bikurim* that the true level of the souls of Israel is revealed - that they nullify themselves completely before Hashem. And this was the entire purpose of creation – to cancel our feelings of being independent entities separate from Hashem and to nullify our feelings of self-importance – i.e. to merit the level of *mah* - and to

4

connect the concept of "not according to plan" to "according to plan". Happy is the one who merits this in truth.

My father and master, author of *Sefer Minchas Ze'ev*, may his merit protect us, explained the above ideas in a very beautiful way. He writes that it is brought in the *Mishnah* (*Bikurim*, Ch. 3, *Mishnah* 5) that the wealthy people brought their *Bikurim* in baskets made of silver or gold and the poor people brought their *Bikurim* in baskets made of stripped willow. And it is explained in the *Talmud* (*Baba Kama* 92a) that the baskets of silver and gold were returned to the wealthy people after the *Kohanim* received the *Bikurim*, but the baskets made of stripped willow were left with the *Kohanim* along with the fruit. The noted commentator *Tosfos Yom Tov* wonders whether this difference in treatment between the wealthy and the poor wouldn't put the poor people to shame when the *Kohanim* confiscate their baskets while the baskets of the wealthy people are returned to them? My father and master answers that it is just the opposite, that there is no shame in this at all. It is rather a virtue and a great honor for the poor people that the *Kohanim* would keep their baskets of stripped willow, as our holy Sages explain (*Toras Kohanim Parshas Vayikra*) regarding the burnt offering of a bird brought by a poor person, that they would offer it on the Altar together with its feathers. We know that there is no odor as foul as that of burnt feathers. Despite the horrible smell, the bird was offered with its feathers in tact so that the Altar would be "satiated" with the poor person's offering, since if the feathers are removed a bird is embarrassingly puny and bony, but with their feathers covering them they look substantial. Likewise, the matter of giving the poor people's baskets of stripped willow together with the *Bikurim* to the *Kohanim* is an honor for Hashem. This is not so with regard to the wealthy people to whom the Kohanim returned their baskets of silver and gold, because Hashem has no desire for silver and gold. What is important to Hashem is a broken and humbled heart, as it is written (*Tehillim*, Ch. 51): "A broken and humbled heart, G-d, You will not despise". So too, our holy Sages have said (*Talmud Sotah* 5a): "I (Hashem) dwell with the humbled; he is with Me. Not so the arrogant man. Hashem says of him, 'I and he cannot dwell in the same world." Therefore, it is specifically the mitzvah of *Bikurim*, the essence of which is the Jew's self-nullification before Hashem, which demonstrates the great importance of the simple baskets of the poor people when their baskets are given to the *Kohanim* together with their first fruits. May Hashem help us reach the trait of self-nullification in truth, that all of our feelings of self-importance will be nullified before Hashem, until we merit to ascend and be included in Him completely, now and evermore. *Amen v'amen.*

5

Friday Night, Parshas Netzavim Vayelech, 5766

Friday night, at the first Shabbos meal, Mohorosh *Shlit"a* spoke inspiring words about the rectification of the *Bris* and the sanctity of thought, based on *Lekutei Mohoran*, Part I, Lesson 36.

Rebbe Nachman says: "The rectification of the *Bris* depends on the sanctity of thought, as it is brought in the Zohar (*Parshas Mishpatim* 110): 'The attribute of *Yesod* (the *Bris*) reaches up to the intellectual faculties, which are called *Abba* and *Imma*." (These are the words of Rebbe Nachman.)

Mohorosh explained that in many places in the books of Rebbe Nachman we find the teaching that the essence of the sanctity of the *Bris* depends on the sanctity of thought and that if a person purifies his mind to think only good thoughts, then his *Bris* will also be in a healthy and rectified state and he will be protected from blemishing the *Bris*. And these are the words of the Zohar mentioned above: "The attribute of *Yesod*" – which is the holy *Bris* – "reaches up to *Abba* and *Imma*" – the holy intellectual faculties of *Chochma* and *Bina*, which are called *Abba* and *Imma*, respectively. For through the sanctity of thought, the sanctity of *Yesod* is rectified.

However, when a person abandons his mind to thinking foreign and evil thoughts, G-d forbid, this is the opening which leads to the blemish of *Yesod*. And the blemish of *Yesod* leads a person to become literally mad, G-d forbid. This sin only comes from a spirit of folly, as our holy Sages have said (*Talmud Sota* 3a): "'*Ish ki sisteh* (Bamidbar, Ch. 5)' – a person does not sin unless a spirit of folly enters him." Moreover, all of the lusts that suddenly come to a person to do what should not be done stem from this blemish. Therefore, Rebbe Nachman mentions in this lesson that physicians say that a cure for madness is castration, since this lust literally makes a person mad, G-d forbid. Therefore, the main thing is to guard one's thoughts, as Rebbe Nachman once remarked to Reb Nosson (*Lekutei Mohoran*, Part II, Lesson 114): "It would seem that a person needs to guard himself very much from evil thoughts", for this is the opening to defilement and impurity.

On the other hand, when a person merits to sanctify his thoughts, then his mind and intellectual powers are opened up to perceptions of G-dliness, to the degree that he is able to ascend to the *Nukva d'Pardashka* ("the supernal opening of the nose", so to speak), which is the window to the upper worlds. And before his eyes will shine the combinations and unifications of the Holy Names of Hashem, which together add up to the same *gematria* as the word *Pardashka* (*Lekutei Mohoran*, Part I, Lesson 2), for everything depends on the degree to which a person sanctifies his thoughts. And where a person's mind is, that is where the entire person is (*Lekutei Mohoran*, Part I, Lesson, 21). Therefore, happy is the one who merits to sanctify his mind and thoughts at all times, for then the heavens will open up for him, and before his eyes will shine the name of Hashem (*Yud-Kay-Vav-Kay*) in all of it's letter combinations. And he will get a taste of the World to Come in his lifetime. Happy is he and fortunate is his lot.

Mohorosh connected the above ideas of Rebbe Nachman to our parsha in the following way. It is written (*Devarim*, Ch. 30): "It is not in heaven for you to say, 'Who can ascend to heaven for us and take it for us, so that we can listen to it and perform it?" And it is brought in the Baal HaTurim as well as in the *Tikkunei Zohar* (*Tikkun* 6): " '*Mi Ya'aleh Lanu Hashamaymah* (Who can ascend to heaven for us)', the first letters of these words spell '*Mila (Bris)'* and the final letters spell Hashem's four-letter name *Yud-Kay-Vav-Kay*." We need to understand why the hints to *Mila* and Hashem's name are found specifically in this verse which speaks about ascending to heaven. Perhaps we have an answer according to this lesson of Rebbe Nachman.

It is precisely through the sanctity of the *Bris* (the guarding of the holy Covenant), which comes about through the sanctity and guarding of thought, that a Jew merits to ascend heavenward even during his life in this world, to the extent that his entire mind will be bound to the upper worlds and to the various letter combinations of Hashem's divine names. In other words, the first letters of this verse which spell *Mila* and the final letters which spell *Yud-Kay-Vav-Kay* allude to the fact that one thing depends on the other. That is, to the degree that one has sanctified and purified the *Mila* – which is the sanctity and purity of thought – one will merit the revelation of the name *Yud-Kay-Vav-Kay*, blessed is He. And it is for this reason that we travel to Tzaddikim on *Rosh HaShanah* – in order to merit sanctity and purity of thought (*Lekutei Mohoran*, Part I, Lesson 211). May Hashem help us to be at Rebbe Nachman's *tzion* in Uman on Rosh HaShanah and we will drawn down upon ourselves sanctity and purity of thought until we merit to be attached and bound to Hashem in truth and to receive a good and sweet year, a year of redemption and salvation for all of Israel. *Amen v'amen.*

2

Seudah Shlishis, Parshas Netzavim Vayelech, 5766

At the third Shabbos meal, Mohorosh *Shlit"a* spoke inspiring words about the power of the Tzaddik to be above and below, based on *Lekutei Mohoran*, Part II, Lesson 68.

Rebbe Nachman says: "The essence of the wholeness of the Tzaddik is that he can be above and below at the same time. He can show the one who is above and who imagines that he is on a very lofty level that it is actually the opposite. On the other hand, he can show the one who is way down below at the lowest level, literally in the earth, that he is right next to Hashem. And this is one of the reasons a person needs to leave children and students behind in the world. This seems surprising, for isn't the main goal to break away completely from physicality? If so, then why is it an obligation to leave behind children and students in this physical world who will take his place? But in truth, the main perfection is to be above and below, in heaven and on earth, for being in only one world is no perfection. And when he has children and students in this world, it is considered as if he is both above and below." (These are the words of Rebbe Nachman.)

Mohorosh explained that Rebbe Nachman reveals to us in this lesson a very great innovation, namely, that a true Tzaddik is above and below at the same time. On the one hand, he is always cleaving to very loft perceptions of G-dliness. He knows what is going on in the upper worlds and his mind is completely attached to Hashem. On the other hand, he is below in this world, and he knows very well what is going on here. He is able to run a home and raise a family with a wife and children. He is also capable of bringing himself down to all types of people in order to help them with all of their myriad needs. All of this is a very great innovation, as the majority of people do not know how to connect these two things together and it seems to them that if a Tzaddik is cleaving to the upper worlds, then he must be unable to bring himself down below. And if he is below amid the physicality of this world, then he must be unable to be above cleaving to Hashem. However, Rebbe Nachman reveals to us that it is just not so, that there is no contradiction between these two things at all. Only the true Tzaddik is able to be above and below at the same time. In fact, the more he cleaves to the upper worlds, the

3

more he can bring himself down into this world, to reveal Hashem's compassion even to all those who are the most fallen.

And even after his departure to the life of the World to Come, he still remains below in this world. In fact, he is then found below to a greater degree than during his physical lifetime, as it is brought in the Holy Zohar (*Parshas Acharei* 71b): "A Tzaddik, even though he has passed from this world, is found in all worlds more than during his normal lifetime." For as long as he is still clothed in a physical garment, he is confined to only one place, but after he takes off his body and puts on a spiritual garment, he can literally be everywhere, as we have seen with respect to all of the true Tzaddikim, that after they passed from this world, they left behind holy books that reveal and publicize Hashem's G-dliness throughout the entire world. Through their books they were left behind in this world, for the face, intellect and *neshama* of the Tzaddik is found within his books (*Lekutei Mohoran*, Part I, Lesson 192).

So we find that although he has ascended from the world we are in, his passing is only with respect to the physicality of his body, but his face, intellect and *neshama* are still found below in this world, and especially if he has left behind children and students who continue to perpetuate his teachings after him. For then, it is considered as though he were literally alive, as our holy Sages have said (see Rashi at the end of parshas *Vayeilech*): "He who leaves behind a student...it's as if he were alive", and as we see with regard to Rebbe Nachman, that from the time of his passing almost 200 years ago, the number of those who have been drawing close to his teachings, and those who go to his holy *tzion* (gravesite) in Uman, are increasing from year to year. And may they continue to increase! For the teachings of Rebbe Nachman remain alive and enduring in this world through his books and through his holy students. Therefore, more and more people are coming close to his teachings all the time.

Reb Nosson *zal* – Rebbe Nachman's chief disciple – was the one who began to perpetuate Rebbe Nachman's books in the world. When Reb Nosson began to reveal and publicize Rebbe Nachman's teachings in the world after Rebbe Nachman's passing, he aroused tremendous excitement among Rebbe Nachman's followers to learn Rebbe Nachman's books and to travel all the time to Rebbe Nachman's *tzion* in Uman, particularly on Rosh HaShanah. This also provoked great opposition against Reb Nosson from other Chassidim, for if a person can attach himself to a Tzaddik even after the

4

Tzaddik's passing through learning his holy books and through going to his holy *tzion*, then all of the importance of traveling to "live" Tzaddikim, seems insignificant, for it is possible for one to attach himself to a Tzaddik who is in the World to Come. But Reb Nosson's goal was to perpetuate Rebbe Nachman's teachings and to show the world that they are very much alive until this very day. In the same spirit, it is brought in the holy *Sefer "Yismach Lev"* (on tractate Shabbos) by the holy Rav, Rabbi Nachum of Chernobyl, may his merit protect us, that one can accomplish the act of prostrating oneself on the graves of the Tzaddikim by prostrating oneself on their holy books. So we find that even though the Tzaddik has passed from this world, it is precisely then that he is found very much in this world and he is revealed to whoever will attach himself to him. Therefore, happy is the one who merits to be close to a true Tzaddik who is always found above and below, for then his attachment to the Tzaddik will be a constant attachment in this world and the next world forever. Happy is he and fortunate is his lot.

Mohorosh connected the above ideas of Rebbe Nachman to our parsha in the following way. It is written (*Devarim*, Ch. 31): "Moshe went and spoke these words to all of Israel." We need to understand the meaning of the words "Moshe went" as the verse does not say where he was going. Also, what is the connection of "Moshe went" to "And he spoke these words to all of Israel"? Let's try to answer these questions according to the words of Rebbe Nachman.

The words "And Moshe went" hint to the passing of Moshe *Rebbeinu* on that very day to the life of the World to Come, as it is written in the very next verse: "I am 120 years old today." Precisely on the day of his passing when he ascended higher and higher to the upper worlds he was also found below among the souls of Israel even more than during his normal lifetime. Therefore, it is written "And Moshe went", that is, he went to the life of the World to Come. But it was precisely then that "he spoke these words to **all** Israel", for his holy words were able to reach every soul of Israel for all generations. Because he went and ascended above, he had even more power to descend below and to cause all of the souls of Israel to inherit the teachings of the holy Torah to the end of all generations.

The most essential teachings of the Tzaddik are his teachings about *emunah* (faith) – the *emunah* that we have inherited from our holy forefathers, Avraham, Yitzchak and Yaakov, the first people to reveal and publicize *emunah* in the world. And our forefathers received the inheritance of the Land

5

of Israel, the place where *emunah* is manifest to the greatest degree, as it is written (*Tehillim*, Ch. 37): "Dwell in the Land and be nourished by *emunah* (*Lekutei Mohoran*, Part I, Lesson 7)." In the Land of Israel *emunah* is revealed to a greater degree than in any other place in the world, for in the Land there is a special revelation of Divine Providence, as it is written (*Devarim*, Ch. 11): "A Land which Hashem, your G-d, seeks out; the eyes of Hashem, your G-d, are always upon it from the beginning of the year until year's end." And there sparkles the light of the merit of our forefathers, the first ones to receive the inheritance of the Land of Israel (*Lekutei Mohoran*, Part I, Lesson 55).

Moshe *Rebbeinu* brought down the Torah for us and showed us how *emunah* is treasured away within each and every mitzvah of the holy Torah, as it is written (*Tehillim*, Ch. 119): "All of Your mitzvos are *emunah*". Through fulfilling the Torah, we attach ourselves to our holy forefathers who revealed *emunah* and who received the inheritance of the Land of Israel - the place of *emunah*. Therefore, the words of the *Baal HaTurim* at the beginning of our parsha (verse 1) concerning the juxtaposition of the two parshas *Nitzavim* and *Vayeilech* are understood very well. The words immediately preceding parshas *Vayeilech* are "...to Avraham, to Yitzchak and to Yaakov, to give them (these are the last words in parshas *Nitzavim*)." And immediately following these words are the first words of parshas *Vayeilech* – "And Moshe went" - he went out to the Children of Israel to tell them that Hashem is fulfilling his oath and He will now bring the people of Israel into the Land (*Baal HaTurim*). At first glance, it is not clear what the connection is between these two verses. But according to what we have explained before we can see the connection. Moshe *Rebbeinu* with his passing caused us to inherit the holy Torah which is the light of *emunah* and he also bequeathed to us the sparks of the merit of our forefathers which is most revealed in the Land of Israel. Therefore, on the day of his passing, when he was found in this world more than during his normal lifetime, he was very much connected to our forefathers, Avraham, Yitzchak and Yaakov, and he revealed to them that now their children have merited to receive the light of *emunah* to the highest degree.

And now in these days before the holy *Rosh HaShanah*, it is upon us to make an accounting of our souls, and to do *teshuva* on everything we have blemished during the past year. And the main thing is concerning sins between man and his fellow. When it comes to sins between man and Hashem, everyone begs for pardon, forgiveness and atonement and they

6

return in perfect repentance. However, when it comes to sins between man and his fellow, it is the way of people to treat them lightly and not to seek atonement for them. On this our holy Sages have said (*Talmud Yoma* 85b): "Sins between man and his fellow, *Yom Kippur* does not atone for them until the sinner has appeased his friend." And so we conclude the prayer of *Neila* – which is the deadline for pardon and forgiveness for all our sins – with the prayer "so that we can withdraw our hands from oppression and return to You", which means that we will return in repentance for having wronged and harmed our fellows. And if a person had caused any financial damage to his fellow, there is no forgiveness or atonement for this until he appeases his friend and reimburses him the damage. Therefore, it is upon us to judge ourselves as to whether we have inflicted any damage against our fellow's honor or against his property, and to return in complete repentance for this. May Hashem help us return in complete repentance and may we receive a good and sweet year, a year of redemption and salvation for all the souls of Israel. *Amen v'amen.*

7

Seuda Shlishis, Parshas Haazinu, 5767

At the third Shabbos meal, Mohorosh *Shlit"a* spoke inspiring words on the subject of *Tikun HaBris* (the Rectification of the holy Covenant), based on *Lekutei Mohoran*, Part I, Lesson 141.

Rebbe Nachman says: "A person will merit to truly feel the pain of his sins when he circumcises the foreskin of his heart, for as long as his heart is uncircumcised and stopped up, it is impossible for him to truly feel this. Only when he will circumcise the foreskin of his heart and make an empty space in his heart, will his heart truly feel the enormity of its pain. And then he will begin to sincerely grieve and regret; and the regret will grow stronger and all of the hearts of all of the drops that came from him will also feel it. Wherever they may have ended up, from that place they will feel it. Whether those drops that came from him became his human children, or whether they ended up in a different place, G-d forbid, also there they have a heart and other limbs.

And when he circumcises his heart, his heart will feel the enormity of its pain and he will begin to sincerely grieve and regret. Then, all of the hearts of the drops will begin to feel the pain no matter where there are, and the truth will become known to them how they are lying in a place of filth in the lowest level of hell, for at first they thought that things were good for them - because they are destructive spiritual beings that damage the world. It is only afterwards when their hearts are circumcised through the heart of their father being circumcised that they will feel where they are and they will begin to mourn and grieve, and a great tumult will erupt among them. And this is (*Devarim* Ch. 30): "And Hashem will circumcise your heart and the heart of your seed", that is, when Hashem will circumcise a person's heart, the heart of his seed will also be circumcised no matter where the seed has ended up - if as a human being, then his children are obligated to also feel a thought of *teshuva* through the heart of their father being circumcised; and if they ended up in a different place, G-d forbid, then from there their hearts will be circumcised and they will feel it, as mentioned before.

And the most auspicious time for this is the month of *Elul*, for the letters of the month of *Elul* (**אלול**) stand for "אֶת-לְבָבְךָ, וְאֶת-לְבַב" (Hashem, your G-d, will circumcise *your heart and the heart* of your seed)", which means that Hashem will circumcise his heart and the heart of anyone or anything that depends on him, namely, the hearts of his children and the hearts of the drops that have come from him, wherever they have ended up. Whether they became human children or whether they have ended up, G-d forbid, in another place - they are also his children and they depend on him. Therefore, at the time a man passes from the world, they follow after him at his funeral and mourn over him, exactly as his human children would mourn for him. However, the fact that they follow after him and mourn for him at his funeral is a tremendous embarrassment and disgrace for him, may G-d spare us from these punishments." (These are the words of Rebbe Nachman.)

Mohorosh explained that the rectification of the *Bris* is the foundation of the holiness of the Jew. When a Jew merits to rectify the *Bris*, which is also the rectification of thought and the purity of the heart, and his mind and heart are guarded from foreign and evil thoughts, then he has a vessel to receive and hold a supernal holiness, and he will merit to feel the truth of Hashem's existence surrounding him always and he will bind himself to Hashem in truth, for the verse will be fulfilled in him (*Devarim*, Ch. 30): "And Hashem, your G-d, will circumcise your heart". And as soon as the foreskin of his heart is removed, his heart will be open to feel Hashem's G-dliness as well as the pain of his sins, and this will arouse him to return in complete repentance for all of his sins and for whatever he had blemished in the past.

His heart will be circumcised together with the heart of his seed – whether it is the heart of his physical children or the heart of the drops that came from him – since they are both considered his children. And then they will begin to seek a remedy for themselves. However, when a man's heart is stopped up with foreign and evil thoughts – and this is the beginning of blemishing the *Bris*, G-d forbid – it is impossible for him to grasp any perceptions of G-dliness and he will not even feel the pain of his sins. As a result, the heart of his seed also becomes closed off from everything holy, and they all suffer from this, G-d forbid. Therefore, his main *teshuva* needs to be for the blemish of the *Bris*, to beseech Hashem with all of his heart to purify his thoughts and to circumcise the foreskin of his heart, and then the verse will be fulfilled in him "And Hashem, your G-d, will circumcise your heart and the heart of your seed", for the heart of his seed will also be circumcised with him, and he will merit to straighten everything that was twisted.

2

The most auspicious time for this is the month of *Elul*, as hinted to in the verse: "אֶת-לְבָבְךָ, וְאֶת-לְבַב (Hashem, your G-d, will circumcise *your heart and the heart* of your seed)", the first letters of which spell "*Elul*". From the beginning of the month of *Elul* a path of *teshuva* is opened up, which is an aspect of the verse (Isaiah, Ch. 43): "Who places a path in the sea", which means a path of *teshuva* (*Lekutei Mohoran*, Part I, Lesson 6). And the main *teshuva* is for the blemish of the *Bris*, to cleanse our minds and hearts from the lusts of this world, and to place within ourselves the light of Hashem's G-dliness, until the name of Hashem – *Yud-Kay-Vav-Kay* – shines before our eyes, as it is written (*Tehillim*, Ch. 16): "I have set Hashem (*Yud-Kay-Vav-Kay)* before me always." And this "path" continues until Yom Kippur, which is "a deadline for pardon, forgiveness and atonement for all our sins (from the *Yom Kippur Neila* service)". Therefore, immediately following the month of Elul begins the Ten Days of *Teshuva*, when we become deeply involved in the path of *teshuva*. And during these Ten Days we beseech Hashem in all of our prayers to give us a "good life", which means a true life, a life of being attached to Hashem, for only this can truly be called life, as it is written (*Devarim*, Ch. 4): "And you who cling to Hashem, your G-d, are all alive today." When you are bound to Hashem, you are all alive today.

We merit *teshuva* and attachment to Hashem through an abundance of *tefilla* and *hisbodedus*, as it is written in the *Haftarah* of *Shabbos Shuva* (*Hoshea*, Ch. 14): "Take with you words and return unto Hashem", on which our holy Sages comment (*Midrash Shemos Rabbah* 38:4): "I [Hashem] ask from you only words." By being very stubborn in praying to Hashem every day that He should save you from blemishing the *Bris* and that He should purify your mind and heart from all kinds of foreign and evil thoughts, in the end you will surely merit purity of heart and true attachment to Hashem. Therefore, happy is the one who makes haste during these holy days and earnestly does *teshuva*, beseeching Hashem profusely to rectify the *Bris*, which is the rectification of thought, for then, a supernal holiness will shine upon him and he will merit to rectify all of the days that have passed by in darkness and to illuminate his days with the Light of life. Happy is he and fortunate is his lot.

Mohorosh connected the above ideas to our parsha in the following way. It is written (*Devarim*, Ch. 32): "שִׁחֵת לוֹ לֹא, בָּנָיו מוּמָם: דּוֹר עִקֵּשׁ, וּפְתַלְתֹּל (Corruption is His? No!; the blemish is His children's, a perverse and twisted generated." Perhaps we can show how all of the words of Rebbe Nachman mentioned above are alluded to in this verse in a very wondrous way. "שִׁחֵת לוֹ" – if a man stumbles, G-d forbid, with respect to the *Bris*, which is called "שַׁחַת", as it is written (*Bereishis*, Ch. 6): "כִּי-הִשְׁחִית כָּל-בָּשָׂר אֶת-דַּרְכּוֹ, עַל-הָאָרֶץ (for all flesh had *corrupted* its way upon the earth)", then he may think that the blemish only affects him alone, which is an aspect of "שָׁחֵת לוֹ (the blemish is his)", however, in truth, it is just not so "שָׁחֵת לוֹ - לֹא! (the corruption is his – no!)", because it is also "בָּנָיו מוּמָם" (the blemish is His children's), for it causes his children and seed to become corrupted, G-d forbid and this leads to a " דּוֹר עִקֵּשׁ, וּפְתַלְתֹּל (a perverse and twisted generation)", for wherever they may have ended up, they still have a heart and other limbs, but they are lying in a place of filth in the lowest level of hell, and they think it is good for them there, for they are destructive spiritual beings that damage the world, which is " דּוֹר עִקֵּשׁ, וּפְתַלְתֹּל (a perverse and twisted generation)". And the most auspicious time to do *teshuva* for this is during the month of *Elul*, which is alluded to by the words in this verse "לוֹ לֹא", which are the letters of *Elul*. For if, G-d forbid, "שָׁחֵת לוֹ לֹא" - he also destroys the holy time of the month of *Elul*, then " בָּנָיו מוּמָם" - his children will remain scarred and blemished, G-d forbid and they will be a "דּוֹר עִקֵּשׁ, וּפְתַלְתֹּל (a perverse and twisted generation)", G-d forbid. But if he returns in complete *teshuva*, especially during the days of *Elul* and the Ten Days of *Teshuva* and is very stubborn in prayer and *hisbodedus* to beg Hashem to help him rectify all that he twisted, which is "דּוֹר עִקֵּשׁ, וּפְתַלְתֹּל" – he will be "עִקֵּשׁ (also means stubborn)" in "וּפְתַלְתֹּל (also has the connotation of *tefilla and hisbodedus*, as Rashi explains the name *"Naftali"*, which has the same root letters as וּפְתַלְתֹּל, in Bereishis 30:8 to mean to stubbornly pray many prayers)" - then he will repair his heart and the heart of his seed. And he will see upright and blessed generations attached to Hashem in truth. May Hashem help us return in complete repentance before Him until we merit to purify our hearts and the hearts of our seed, and to ascend and be included in Him completely, for now and evermore. *Amen v'amen.*

.

4

Parshas Zos HaBracha and the Yahrtzeit of Rebbe Nachman

At the meal commemorating the *Yahrtzeit* of Rebbe Nachman on the second intermediate day of *Sukkos*, Mohorosh *Shlit"a* spoke inspiring words on the verse from *Parshas Zos HaBracha* (*Devarim*, Ch. 33): "And this is the blessing with which Moshe, the man of G-d, blessed the Children of Israel before his death."

Mohorosh said: Perhaps we can say that hidden in this verse is a hint to the awesome nature of the passing of the true Tzaddikim - how even after their passing they remain with us in this world, as our holy Sages have said (*Talmud Berachos* 18b) on the verse (*Shmuel* II, Ch. 23): "'And Benayahu the son of Yehoyada the son of a living man...' – this teaches that the Tzaddikim in their death are called alive." In fact, on the day of their death they ascend to a level much higher than they had ever reached during their life in this world. And on this day, they also receive mighty powers to bring down wondrous lights to all the souls of Israel and to bestow upon them an abundance of spiritual and material gifts.

The day of their passing is referred to as "*Yom Hilula*", which is synonymous to a wedding day, for on the day of their passing they are busy unifying and binding themselves to the holy *Shechinah*, and they cause a great unification in all of the worlds. And on this day of their rejoicing they bestow gifts to all of the souls of Israel.

The passing of Tzaddikim is only from *our* worldly perception, i.e. the viewpoint of our eyes since we can no longer see the Tzaddik's body, but the *neshama* and the light it gives off increases in power and intensity on the day of his passing and great spiritual and material bounty is bestowed upon the souls of Israel. And this is the secret of "And this (*zos*) is the blessing with which Moshe, the man of G-d, blessed" – "*zos*" refers to the revelation of the *Shechinah* and the illumination of holy *emunah* as it is brought in the *Tikkunei Zohar* (*Tikkun* 6): "One who desires to reach the King only has permission to reach him through the *Shechinah*. This is what is written (Jeremiah, Ch. 9): 'Only with this (*b'zos*), shall he who glories take pride in understanding and knowing me.' Aharon HaKohein only went into the Holy of Holies on Yom Kippur with this (*b'zos*) as it is written (*Vayikra*, Ch. 16): 'With this (*b'zos*) shall Aharon come into the Holy.' And Moshe blessed the

Children of Israel with this, as it is written (Devarim, Ch. 33): 'And this (*v'zos*) is the blessing (*V'zos ha'bracha*).' " For the service of the Tzaddikim all the days of their lives is to completely bind themselves to holy *emunah* and to bring it down to all the souls of Israel, for everything depends on *emunah*, as Rebbe Nachman has said (*Sichos HaRan* #33): "By the world, *emunah* is a small thing, but by me the main thing is only *emunah*", for everything is included in *emunah*. And the essential level of a person is measured according to his *emunah*. Moreover, the true Tzaddikim, after all of the lofty perceptions of G-dliness they have achieved always return to simple *emunah* in Hashem, as the holy Baal Shem Tov once said that after all of his lofty perceptions he always returns to praying like a small child - with simple *emunah*. Therefore, "And this (*v'zos*)" – *emunah* - is the *main* "blessing (*ha'bracha*)" with which the Tzaddikim bless Israel.

The word "the blessing (*ha'bracha*)" in this verse is written with two *hays* – one at the beginning of the word and one at the end, and they both allude to the two *hays* in Hashem's four-letter name – Yud-Kay-Vav-Kay. The first *hay* of the Name corresponds to the *sefira* of *Bina* (the faculty of understanding) and the final *hay* to the *sefira* of *Malchus* (Kingship), as is known in Kabbalah (*Kisvay H'arizal - Shaar Eser Sefirot*). For the main blessing of *emunah* is when it brings a person to deep reflection and contemplation of the loving kindnesses of Hashem, to meditate upon all of the details of one's life and how Hashem does unearned kindnesses with a person at every moment. This is the first *hay* of Hashem's four-letter name, which alludes to the *sefira* of *Bina*.

After a person has attained this level of understanding, i.e. *Bina*, he then needs to bring the *Bina* down into *Malchus*, and *Malchus* is speech - the final *hay* of Hashem's four-letter name. Now he will praise and glorify His blessed name for all of the unearned kindnesses Hashem does with him at every moment, because it is not enough for *Bina* to remain only in the heart, but it must also be brought down into *Malchus* – into speech - to bring out of one's mouth words of praise and thanks to Hashem for all of His kindness and compassion. So we find that the blessing of *emunah* that is hinted to in the word "*zos*" is itself the complete blessing when it includes the two *hays* – *Bina* and *Malchus*. And when a person has combined these two *hays* in his life, this is the sign that the blessing of *emunah* is truly resting upon him.

It is brought in the *Midrash* (*Devarim Rabbah* 11:4) on the words "Moshe, the man of G-d" in the verse "With which *Moshe, the man of G-d*, blessed":

2

"Moshe, from his middle down, a man; and from his middle up, *Elokim*" This teaches us that the main completeness of the Tzaddik is that he can be above and below at the same time (*Lekutei Mohoran*, Part II, Lesson 68), to bind the upper worlds with the lower worlds – spirituality with physicality.

The Tzaddik is bound above through his lofty perceptions of the upper worlds, but he also brings himself down to all the simple people and he listens to their needs and helps them in every matter. And this is what is said about Moshe *Rebbeinu* (*Shemos*, Ch. 19): "And Moshe went down from the mountain unto the people" – which means he was able to bring himself from the highest perceptions of the upper worlds down to the simplest people. And in this way, he tied the upper worlds to the lower worlds, for he revealed how a person can find Hashem's G-dliness in everything in this world and within all physical activities because there is no absolute existence at all besides Hashem. And he revealed to them that Hashem created this world in order for us to serve Him from within the physicality of the world; that we should eat, drink and sleep and elevate all of the smallest levels to the service of Hashem. And in this way, the Tzaddik connects the upper worlds with the lower worlds and teaches us how we can do the same.

The service of the Tzaddik also entails revealing to those who are on very high spiritual levels and those who *think* they have already reached very lofty perceptions and understandings of G-dliness that they have still grasped nothing, for "His greatness is beyond investigation (*Tehillim*, Ch. 145)". On the other hand, those who inhabit much lower levels and those who think they are very far from Hashem, to them the Tzaddik reveals that Hashem is very close to them and that there is no absolute existence at all besides Hashem (*Lekutei Mohoran*, Part II, Lesson 7). Therefore, the true Tzaddik is called "A man of G-d (*Ish HaElokim*)", for he ties together the aspect of "*Ish* (man)" which encompasses all physical matters, to the aspect of "*Elokim* (G-d)" which includes all spiritual matters and he can teach those who are very high and those who are very low the knowledge of G-dliness that each one needs in order to reach his maximum potential.

And this is the verse "the Children of Israel before his death" – for the passing of Moshe *Rebbeinu* was only from *our* worldly perception, that is, from the point of view of physicality, but from the spiritual perspective he is alive and enduring forever and he stands and serves in the heights as he did during his lifetime in this world. And he brings Torah and comprehensions of G-dliness down to the souls of Israel and teaches them how to find Hashem's G-dliness

3

within all of the materiality of this world. Therefore, *now* as before his death, he is always standing and blessing - "And this is the blessing with which Moshe, the man of G-d, blessed the Children of Israel **before** his death", as though today was still before his death, as though the concept of death did not really apply to him, for each and every day the souls of Israel learn the Torah of Moshe and they say, "Hashem spoke to Moshe, saying" and "Hashem said to Moshe, saying", as though he were alive in this world today. And all of this is included in the blessing of "**And this is the bracha** (*V'zos ha'bracha*) with which Moshe blessed" - which is the blessing of *emunah* as mentioned before.

And an essential part of *emunah* is *emunas chochamim*, because without *emunas chochamim* it is impossible to attain complete *emunah* in Hashem, as it is brought in the *Midrash* (*Mechilta Parshas Beshalach*) on the verse (*Shemos*, Ch. 14): "'They believed in Hashem and in Moshe His servant' – Whoever believes in the Shepherd of Israel [Moshe], the Torah considers it as though he believes in the One Who spoke and the world came to be." Therefore, through learning and remembering the Torah of Moshe *Rebbeinu* always, as it is written (*Malachi*, Ch. 3): "Remember the Torah of Moshe, My servant", Moshe *Rebbeinu* lives and endures with us, which is an aspect of "before his death", i.e. before he left this world. And each time we learn the Torah of Moshe, we receive his blessing anew – the blessing of *emunah* - which includes within it all of the blessings, as it is written (*Mishlei*, Ch. 28): "A man of faith [shall have], abundant blessings."

And all of these blessings are revealed to an even greater extent on the Tzaddik's *yahrtzeit*, for on the day of his passing he ascends higher and higher, reaching new and loftier perceptions that he had never before attained. And he brings down from there new revelations to all the souls of Israel and he gives out precious blessings and gifts to them. This is the great importance of Rebbe Nachman's *yahrtzeit* that we are celebrating today on the fourth day of *Sukkos*. For anyone who learns the books of Rebbe Nachman and fulfills his advice, Rebbe Nachman is actually alive and enduring with him, and he receives new vitality and encouragement from Rebbe Nachman every time he learns his books, as when Rebbe Nachman was alive in this world, and how much more so on his *yahrtzeit* when he brings down to the souls of Israel *completely new* lights.

What is the inner connection between Rebbe Nachman's *yahrtzeit*, the festival of *Sukkos* and the fact that his *yahrtzeit* is on the day on which the *ushpizin* is

4

Moshe *Rebbeinu*? The main idea of the *sukkah* has to do with binding spirituality and physicality together. And this was the service of Moshe *Rebbeinu* all the days of his life, as mentioned before. For the essence of the mitzvah of *sukkah* is to eat, drink and sleep within the *sukkah*, to bring all of the physical acts of service beneath the shadow of the *sukkah* – which is also called the shadow of *emunah* (Zohar Emor 103a) – in order to reveal that there is G-dliness within all of these physical activities. Therefore, the word "*sukkah*" has the same *gematria* as the sum of the two divine names *Yud-Kay-Vav-Kay* and *Ado-ai*, and this shows the connection between spirituality and physicality as follows: *Yud-Kay-Vav-Kay* represents the spiritual revelations of Hashem's G-dliness on all of the higher levels and *Ado-ai* is the indwelling of the *Shechinah* in the lower worlds and in all things material. For through the *sukkah* we reveal that "His kingship rules over everything (*Tehillim*, Ch. 103)", and that there is no absolute existence at all other than Hashem. And this was the service of Moshe *Rebbeinu* all the days of his life as well as after his death. And this is the same thing that Rebbe Nachman wants to plant in us - and that is to recognize Hashem from each and every detail of all the days of our lives.

And how fortunate is the one who merits to bring himself close to Rebbe Nachman in truth and to follow all of his holy advice, for then he will get a glimpse of eternity in his lifetime and taste some of the hidden light that will be revealed in the time to come. May Hashem help us merit to be close to Rebbe Nachman in truth, to internalize all of his wondrous teachings until we merit to see the light of the Redemption and to sit within the *sukkah* of the skin of the *Livyasan* swiftly in our days. *Amen v'amen.*

5

Achron Shel Pesach 5766

On the last day of Pesach, at the last meal which is called "The Seudah of Moshiach" or "The Seudah of the Baal Shem Tov", Mohorosh Shlit"a spoke inspiring words on the uniqueness of the day based on Lekutei Mohoran, Part I, Lesson 2, which speaks about the revelation of Moshiach.

The last meal of Pesach is universally referred to by the Jewish people as "The Seudah of Moshiach" or "The Seudah of the Baal Shem Tov". It is called "The Seudah of Moshiach" after the Haftarah that is read on the last day of Pesach, which speaks about the coming of Moshiach, as it is written (*Isaiah* 10): "And a staff will emerge from the stump of Jesse and a shoot will sprout from his roots..." which refers to Moshiach. In the Land of Israel where they celebrate this meal on the seventh day of Pesach, they read for the Haftarah the song of King Dovid (*Shmuel* II, ch. 22) who is called the Moshiach of Hashem, and as the song concludes (verse 51): "He Who is a tower of salvations for His king and does kindness for His Moshiach, to Dovid and his descendants forever." The reason it is called "The Seudah of the Baal Shem Tov" is for the great miracle that happened to the holy Baal Shem Tov, may his merit protect us, on his journey to the Land of Israel where he planned to meet with the holy Ohr Hachaim (Rabbi Chaim ibn Attar) at which time both of them together would be able to bring our righteous Moshiach. For the Baal Shem Tov had the *nefesh of Atzilus* of Moshiach and the Ohr Hachaim had the *ruach of Atzilus* of Moshiach, and together they wanted to draw down the *neshama of Atzilus* of Moshiach and bring the redemption. But from Heaven the Baal Shem Tov was prevented from traveling on and he reached the point where his life was in danger when he fell into the hands of pirates and cannibals who wanted to kill him. But on the last day of Pesach he was saved from death to life. Therefore, we have a third meal on the last day of Pesach and call it "The Meal of the Baal Shem Tov". Perhaps we can say, that in truth, these two names are really one, for the revelation of Moshiach and the revelation of the Baal Shem Tov are intertwined, as it is brought in a letter written by the holy Baal Shem Tov to his brother-in-law, the noted Torah scholar, Rabbi Avraham Gershon of Kitov, who had immigrated to the Holy Land (This letter was first published in 1781 as an appendix to *Ben Poras Yosef* [p.128a] by Rabbi Yaakov Yosef of Polnoye, one of the first and most dedicated of the Baal Shem Tov's disciples). In this letter the Baal Shem Tov describes how he performed an elevation of his soul. When he reached the chamber of the Moshiach, he asked him, "When will the master come?" And he said to him, "When your wellsprings will spread to the outside, when all of the *klipos* (husks) will be annihilated and all Israel will be able to perform *yichudim* ["*Yichudim*" are a form of kabalistic meditation based on different permutations and combinations of the divine names and attributes of G-d] and soul elevations as you can, then the redemption will come." We find that the coming of Moshiach depends on the spreading of the light of the holy Baal Shem Tov in the world until all of the souls of Israel will be able to perform *yichudim* and soul elevations like the Baal Shem Tov. It is known to us that one of the primary ways this "spreading of the wellsprings outward" is accomplished is through the dissemination of the works of Rebbe Nachman in the world. A great-grandson of the Baal Shem Tov, Rebbe Nachman began to reveal the light of Moshiach in the world, to spread the wellsprings of wisdom outward and to be involved with destroying the *klipos* from the world until one day all people will be able to perform *yichudim* and soul elevations like the Baal Shem Tov. It is explained in *Lekutei Mohoran*, Part I, Lesson 2, that *klipos* are negative forces that cover a person's eyes. It is also explained in this lesson that they are created from people's sins, especially from immorality, the sin of blemishing the *Bris*, G-d forbid. These sins create husks that cover one's eyes and prevent one from seeing Hashem's G-dliness. And because of this, everyone finds himself in a very deep and bitter exile. But as soon as a person begins to truly engage in prayer, and he gives himself over to pray to Hashem from the depths of his heart and with attachment to the true Tzaddikim of the generation, then he banishes these *klipos* from his eyes and begins to contemplate Hashem's G-dliness until he sees shining before his eyes all of the holy Names and the yichudim of the upper worlds, which are the four names *ayin-beis* (72), *samach-gimmel* (63), *mem-hay* (45) and *nun-beis* (52), with their three crowns *kuf-samach-aleph* (161), *kuf-mem-gimmel* (143) and *kuf-nun-aleph* (151), which together add up to 686 (plus 1 extra for the *kollel*), which is an aspect of the verse (*Bereishis* 49): "A charming son is Yoseif, a charming son to the eye ("Ben poras Yosef, ben **poras alei aiyin**"). The letters of the word **poras** add up to 686, and the words **alei aiyin** mean 'on the eye')." That is to say, these holy names (686) will shine upon his eyes – "**poras alei aiyin**". It turns out that Rebbe Nachman is all about spreading the wellsprings of wisdom outward into the world as well as destroying all of the *klipos*, which are those things which cover up the eyes, until all people will be able to perform *yichudim* and soul elevations like the Baal Shem Tov could. Therefore we have the following episode in the life of the Baal Shem

2

Tov. When the Baal Shem Tov was on the boat on his way to the Land of Israel a powerful storm arose that almost capsized the boat. The ship was about to break apart. At that moment the Satan came to him and gave him a choice: to throw either his writings or his daughter Eidel into the sea. His daughter said to him, "Father, throw the writings into the sea, for one day I will have a grandson who will write books even more beautiful than these." It is known that the intention of Eidel was on her grandson Rebbe Nachman. We find that the revelation of Moshiach depends on the revelation of the teachings that come from the loins of the holy Baal Shem Tov and these are the books of Rebbe Nachman. If so, then the two names for today's meal – "The Meal of Moshiach" and "The Meal of the Baal Shem Tov" – are truly one.

In the Haftarah of the second day of Pesach (*Yom Tov Sheini*) outside the Land of Israel, we read about the Pesach of King Yoshiyahu (see *Orach Chaim* #490). Our holy Sages say (*Talmud Taanis* 22b) that the prophet Yirmiyahu said of King Yoshiyahu (*Eicha* 4): "The breath of our nostrils, Moshiach of Hashem", since King Yoshiyau had within him an aspect of Moshiach. And our Haftarah testifies about him (*Melachim* II, ch. 23): "Before him there had never been a king like him who returned to Hashem with all his heart, with all his soul, and with all his strength in accordance with the entire Torah of Moshe, and after him no one arose like him." King Yoshiyahu destroyed idolatry from the Land of Israel, and he helped the Jewish people return to the ways of Hashem, until the people purified the *Beis Hamikdosh* and brought the Pesach sacrifice according to all the laws of the Torah. And the prophet testifies that there was no king before Yoshiyahu who so returned to Hashem the way he did and that after him there will be no one like him. This testimony is similar to the way the Torah bears witness to Moshe Rebbeinu, (*Devarim* 34): "Never again has there arisen in Israel a prophet like Moshe." However, we find that Yoshiyahu suffered a very difficult death, because he waged war against Paraoh Necho King of Egypt rather than allow Paraoh Necho to pass through the Land of Israel on his way to make war with another country. Even though initially Paraoh Necho was a "sword of peace", i.e. Paraoh Necho had no intention of attacking Israel, in the end he killed Yoshiyahu, as it is written (*Divrei Hayamim 35*): "And the archers shot arrows into King Yoshiyahu..." And our holy Sages said (*Talmud Taanis* 22b): "This teaches us that they made his entire body like a sieve." And the Sages ask (ibid), "For what reason was Yoshiyahu punished? Wasn't he a great Tzaddik?" And they answered that, "it was because he should have consulted with the prophet Yirmiyahu and followed his advice

3

[to let Paraoh Necho pass through the Land of Israel], but he did not." So we see that Hashem is very particular about *Emunas Chochamim* (faith in the Sages), to the extent that a great king and a true *baal teshuva* like Yoshiyahu, about whom the Torah testifies, "No one arose like him", was also obligated to submit himself to the Tzaddik and prophet of the generation (Yirmiyahu) and not to wage war according to his own decision. For the main fulfillment of the entire Torah depends on *Emunas Chochamim* and submitting oneself to them, as Rebbe Nachman says (*Lekutei Mohoran*, Part I, Lesson 123) that the root and foundation upon which everything depends is getting close to Tzaddikim and attaching ourselves to them. Therefore, as soon as Yoshiyahu turned slightly away from *Emunas Chochamim*, he was punished harshly, until his entire body was made like a sieve, G-d save us. And when Yoshiyahu's soul was leaving him, Yirmiyahu noticed that Yoshiyahu's lips were moving and that he was whispering something to himself. He thought that perhaps Yoshiyahu's pain was causing him to speak against Heaven, G-d forbid. Yirmiyahu put his ear close to Yoshiyahu and he heard that Yoshiyahu was agreeing to the judgment that was decreed upon him, and our holy Sages say (*Talmud Taanis* 22b) that at this moment Yoshiyahu was saying (*Eichah* 1): "Righteous is Hashem for I have rebelled against His word." And then Yirmiyahu said in reference to Yoshiyahu, (ibid 4): "The breath of our nostrils, Moshiach of Hashem." There are tremendous practical lessons to be learned from this. We learn how King Yoshiyahu immediately repented for his lack of *Emunas Chochamim*, i.e. for not following Yirmiyahu's advice and for not submitting himself to him, and he said, "Righteous is Hashem for I have rebelled against His word (literally, 'I have rebelled against *His mouth*')." For within and through the Tzaddikim who cleave to Hashem, the "*mouth*" of Hashem is revealed. And through accepting their Torah guidance and obeying them, it is considered that one has literally accepted the words of Hashem. And as soon as Yoshiyahu accepted the judgment of Heaven upon himself and he justified the punishment, Yirmiyahu called him, "The breath of our nostrils, Moshiach of Hashem." This is the level of the Moshiach – the level of accepting all that happens to oneself with love – without criticizing the ways of Hashem. Only our righteous Moshiach will bring this realization to the world in its completeness. Since for the most part, when pain and suffering pass over a person, G-d forbid, and especially when they are terrifying afflictions like those of King Yoshiyahu, then questions and doubts enter a person's mind, G-d forbid, as to why he is going through this, and he is in great danger of criticizing Hashem's ways. But when he uses all of his strength to justify Hashem's judgment, and he finds Hashem's G-dliness even within all of his pain and suffering, then he has the quality of Moshiach, the

4

aspect of "*erech apayim* (slow to anger; literally 'length of the nostrils')" which is "The breath of our nostrils, Moshiach Hashem." Through the trait of "*erech apayim*" one merits to be Moshiach of Hashem, for within each and every Jew there is an aspect of Moshiach (*Lekutei Mohoran*, Part I, Lesson 78). And through coming close to the Tzaddik, each and every Jew merits to reveal his own aspect of Moshiach until he finds Hashem within all of his troubles, and he thanks and praises Him for the wide expanses that Hashem opens up for him within his troubles, which is an aspect of the verse (*Tehillim* 4): "In my distress You have made an expanse for me." For through the pain itself, Hashem makes an opening for me. And this was the level of King David, who was the Moshiach of Hashem and from whom will come our righteous redeemer. Pain and suffering passed over him all the days of his life from childhood through old age, and in all of his suffering he found the open expanses of Hashem, and he made from them the Psalms and songs and praises to Hashem. And even in the worst trouble when his son Avshalom tried to kill him, he said the verse mentioned before, "In my distress you have made an expanse for me." Our holy Sages ask how can this Psalm of Dovid, which is about Avshalom's trying to kill him, begin with the words, "A **Song** of Dovid"? Instead it should have begun, "A **Lamentation** of Dovid." And the Sages answer, that from the time that Nathan the prophet said to him in the name of Hashem (*Shmuel* II, ch. 12), "Behold, I will raise up evil against you from your own house," he was worried that it would be a slave or a bastard who would not have compassion on him. But when he heard it was his own son, his mind was put at rest. The question is asked what kind of consolation is this? Doesn't this double the pain since it is his own son who is pursuing him? But the main consolation of King David was that he saw in this the hand of Hashem in a very awesome and clear way. For it is not the way of the world that a son should so hotly pursue his father. If it had been a slave or a bastard, whose nature it is to be insolent and brazen, he could have attributed their trying to kill him to nature, to the ways of the world. However, when he saw something that was completely above nature, a beloved son transformed into a mortal enemy, he saw the revelation of the hand of Hashem. And then he knew that he had no other choice but to flee to Hashem and hide in the shadow of His wings.

And this is the main revelation of Moshiach: the strengthening of a person at the time of his pain and bitterness. And this is the Haftarah for the seventh day of Pesach, which is the song of Dovid, who sang songs and praises to Hashem after all the pain and suffering that passed over him in his life. And this is also the Haftarah of the last day of Pesach, which speaks about the

5

coming of Moshiach who will sprout from the trunk of Jesse, and this is King David, peace be upon him. For the main point of Moshiach is the strengthening of a person within all of his pain and suffering. And the teaching of Moshiach is the teaching of "*erech apayim* (slow to anger), i.e. to find the road that Hashem opens up for a person within all of the troubles. And our righteous Moshiach will bring these teachings to the world in their completeness. And these are exactly the teachings of the holy Baal Shem Tov and the teachings that are revealed in the books of Rebbe Nachman. They provide powerful encouragement for each and every Jew. And the more a person merits to internalize these teachings, the more he will leave his own personal exile and be redeemed from all of his troubles. And in this way, all of the souls of Israel will be redeemed from their exiles. And may Hashem make us worthy to greet our righteous Moshiach swiftly in our days. *Amen v'amen.*

6

Ethics of Rabbi Nachman

Amazing! There is absolutely no reason whatsoever for despair.
(Chai Moharon)

There is really no such thing as despair.
(Likutei Moharon II; 78)

It is a tremendous mitzvah to constantly be happy.
(Likutei Moharon II; 24)

Histboddus (talking with G'd), is the highest concept and greater than all else.
(Likutei Moharon II; 25)

If you believe you are capable of destruction, then believe you are

capable of repair.
(Likutei Moharon II; 112)

There is such a concept as changing around everything to good.
(Rabbi Nachman's Praises)

. . . and knows that a person must cross over an extremely narrow bridge, and it is most essential not to be frightened at all.
(Likutei Moharon II; 78)

Say these ten Psalms -- they are a wonderful remedy for every sort of problem, especially Tikun HaBris (gaining sexual purity).

16-32-41-42-59-77-90-105-137-150

Pray with a minyan of Breslover Chassidim every Rosh Hashanah.

Study at least one law from the Codes of Jewish Law each day.

Speak with G'd in your own personal way as often as you can.

Break your sleep at midnight [six hours after dark -- all year round] in order to mourn over the Holy Temple's destruction.

About the Breslover Yeshiva

Our holy Breslover Yeshivah situated In Brooklyn, whose branches are spread throughout the Holy land, In such places as Jerusalem, Bnei Brak, Zefat, and Ashdod, has now undertaken the construction of Yavnael's Breslov city.

A new Bais Hamedrash already stands, housing a Koliel, Talmud Torah and Mikvah. Many more subsequent buildings are in the midst of erection which will provide homes for many Koliel families, a Yeshiva Gedola, and a Girl's School. Likewise, the blueprint for the great synagogue is already complete, which in the terms of the architects, will be "the Light of the Galilee". It will be a magnificent structure, including a tremendous Shule and an ultra-modern catering hall which will be available free of charge to any needy family or chosson and kallah. Construction is underway and we hope, please G'd, to see it's completion soon.

Our Institution Is continuously spreading the teachings of Rabbi Nachman which offers advice on every sort of problem. We print all of the Breslover publications, and have amassed an annual average of over one million copies, which has been spread throughout the world. We offer assistance to every person who comes to us seeking help, and have helped many broken homes find peace again, and many orphans find proper homes. We have also helped many couples In dire financial situations, enabling them to get married, and set up warm and comfortable homes.

We have many translations of our books, in English, Spanish, etc., which await printing, but cannot be published as yet, because of our tight financial situation. If you would like to have a share In our holy work, your generous donation would be greatly appreciated.

At the same time we continue to publish and spread the holy teachings of Rabbi Nachman throughout the world in many languages, and if you would like to have a share in our holy work, your generous donation would be greatly appreciated

Please mail your tax deductible contributions to: *11220*

Mesifta Heichal Hakodesh Chasidei Breslov

1129-42 St.
Brooklyn, N.Y. 11220

Feel free to write if you have any questions or just want to share your thoughts or problems.

Most of all though, keep praying to G'd.

For More Information or To Get The Books From Mohorosh

Go To www.Mohorosh.org

Made in the USA
Middletown, DE
18 July 2021